The Flowering of the Soul

A Book of Prayers by Women

THE
FLOWERING
OF THE SOUL

A BOOK
OF PRAYERS
BY WOMEN

EDITED AND WITH INTRODUCTIONS BY
LUCINDA VARDEY

BALLANTINE WELLSPRING
THE BALLANTINE PUBLISHING GROUP • NEW YORK

A Ballantine Wellspring Book
Published by The Ballantine Publishing Group

Copyright © 1999 by Lucinda Vardey

All rights reserved under International and Pan-American Copyright
Conventions. Published in the United States by The Ballantine
Publishing Group, a division of Random House, Inc., New York.

Ballantine Wellspring and colophon are trademarks of Random House, Inc.

Permission acknowledgments can be found on pages 433–447, which
constitute an extension of this copyright page.

www.randomhouse.com/BB/

Library of Congress Cataloging-in-Publication Data
The flowering of the soul : a book of prayers by women / edited and
    with introductions by Lucinda Vardey. —1st ed.
        p.   cm.
    Includes bibliographical references and index.
    ISBN 0-345-42230-9 (hardcover : alk. paper)
    1. Prayers.   2. Women—Prayer-books and devotions—English.
 I. Vardey, Lucinda.
 BL625.7.F56   1999
 291.4'33—dc21   98-46107

Manufactured in the United States of America

First Edition: April 1999
10 9 8 7 6 5 4 3 2 1

Book design by H. Roberts Design

*In memory and gratitude for St. Catherine of Siena
and for all women who pray*

Contents

PERSONAL
ACKNOWLEDGMENTS

*W*hen I began searching for women's prayers, I received help from a number of people. Eve Roshevsky at Women of Reform Judaism in New York offered sources and resources; Pat Cairns, Robin Slater-Rook, Lois Harrison, Brother Gabe McHugh, C.F.C., and Diana Dalla Costa-Rich found and sent me invaluable books. Friends like Adrienne Corti, Oriah Mountain Dreamer, Patricia Joudry, and Marion Woodman took time to create a prayer or two and contribute their deep spirituality to this volume. And Frances W. Dvorchik offered help with Jewish prayers, Martha Brakas gave me a vital prayer, Dana Mullen sent me a prayer found in a diary of a Quaker woman, and Chris Ng gave me Empress Wu's. Mr. R. K. Bhatia, the consul general of India in Toronto, was a great help, and Professor Julia Ching translated and, with her husband, Professor Willard G. Oxtoby, generously read the manuscript for religious accuracy.

Along the way, Timothy Hatcher was an invaluable scriptural interpreter. My mother, Edwina Vardey, always reliable, helpful, and creative, greatly assisted me in my research in the U.K. I thank you all for your gifts.

I also wish to offer my deep gratitude to my friend and colleague, Carol Mark, my stalwart supporter and researcher for this book. She and I have grown in our commitment to promote women's spirituality over the last three years. My agents, Jane Gelfman, Linda McKnight, and Gaby Naher have been a wonderful support and sounding board for me throughout the compilation of the manuscript. And the women who have assisted in its birth: Judith Curr, with her optimism and belief from the start; Louise Dennys, for always being there for my work, and always being an invaluable friend; and Elizabeth Zack, whose intelligence and clarity in editorship have made this a better book. Margaret Gorenstein and Samantha Haywood made the usual struggle of gaining permissions clearance a joy and a breeze, and I'm touched by the heartfelt response of many of the women we've written to.

My precious husband, John Dalla Costa, who loves the feminine Divine and has supported the inclusion of women's spirituality in tradition, has not only written beautiful prayers himself, but encouraged me and made me feel the depth and importance of this collection.

For all of you who have helped—and will help—this book, I offer a prayer of thanksgiving.

—Lucinda Vardey

EDITOR'S PREFACE:
A GUIDE TO THIS BOOK

*T*he reason for this book arose out of a deep personal need. Like a number of other women who are committed to spiritual growth, I am exploring how to know, love, and serve God more in my life and work, in my home, in my family and my community, and with my friends and within my own religious practice. As I mature, I find I need to uncover and recognize the feminine Divine and discover how I can participate in feminine sanctity.

Although the emancipation of women in this century has contributed to a wider consciousness and understanding of the feminine in both men's and women's lives, it is clear that our traditional ways of worship, the language we use, and the ancient laws of enlightenment are still embedded in patriarchy. The more we move in our secular Western lives towards openness and equality, the more difficult, even impossible, it becomes to recite prayers, hymns, or mantras composed solely by men.

I create my own prayers occasionally, and I attempt

to change exclusive language when reciting older prayers. Yet I still need a context, a historical and spiritual link with women not only of my own time but also from times past. I need the words of women; I need women's teachings, their prayers, and examples of their devotion, their lives, their work. My research into women's lives and prayers uncovered extraordinary examples of faith, perseverance, courage, conviction, and trust in the central goodness and direction of the Divine. These women were saints, heroines, pioneers, and masters ("mistresses" hardly seems an appropriate term), as well as poets and educators from Christian, Judaic, Buddhist, Islamic, Hindu, and Taoist backgrounds.

For *The Flowering of the Soul* I have gathered together prayers by, and teachings of, women of many nationalities, ages, and religions. I've also structured this book as a way of prayer such as those handed down by prominent women teachers. The parts of the book are broken down as they relate to their teachings on personal prayer. The first part is about Devotion: dedication to the devotional aspect of prayer, the necessity of gaining intimacy with the Divine, and the stages we go through in seeking this divine relationship. The use of ritual is part of the process. We ritualize our prayer to offer praise and thanks for our life and its many gifts. So prayers of worship, praise, and thanksgiving are collected here, as well as a selection of blessings for ceremonies—traditional rituals that link us with our past or affirm our present and future. The last part of the devotional section is that of oblations, or offerings. By offering ourselves—our vulnerabilities, strengths, work, and struggles—we learn to share who we are in partnership with the Divine, and experience humility and trust, two of the most vital of spiritual virtues.

The second part of the book is devoted entirely to Supplication: prayers of request. These are arranged according to areas in which we commonly ask for help, such as patience, hope, understanding, strength, comfort, compassion, and healing. The third part is about Surrender, which is the only place to live if we wish to have divinity respond in our lives. Part of the power of petitionary prayers is to be able to give away the results of what it is we petition. Moreover, the response to these prayers is seldom exactly as we imagined, or expected. The last two parts of the book—four and five—are about Contemplation and Action. The states of contemplation and action provide the balanced energies we need in life; when they are in balance, our deeds, work, and responsibilities in action are enhanced by our conscious contemplation.

To me this structure summarizes prayer in its many forms as I have experienced it myself, and have learned through the study and reading of prayers by women of all ages and backgrounds. My wish is to provide women today who pray, or want to pray, with a collective feminine spiritual wisdom that can be drawn on and shared openly. In this way I hope to further our efforts for equality in language and emotional and spiritual understanding.

I have included prayers that were written in English or have already been translated into English. Most have been published before, although there are some gems that are appearing in print for the first time. I have, where possible and with full respect for the text, updated the language by changing "Thee" and "Thy" to "You" and "Your." I feel strongly that archaic English, except in poetry, impedes intimacy with the emotion of the prayer. And I have also omitted "Amen" at the end of prayers so that they will flow more easily.

Women's prayers are more than words. Yet without their written prayers, we would gain only a partial understanding of their faith and their relationship with the Divine. The art of writing a prayer is close to poetry as the ultimate form of written expression. Yet a prayer is not a poem. A written prayer is an expression of the innermost sharing of thoughts and desires with the One who already knows them. Prayer is a work of art because of the faith involved in its creation, and as a form it is unique.

The prayers collected in this book are those written *directly to* the Divine—not musings about the Divine, or poetry about spirituality or sacredness. As you read them, I trust you will be nourished and moved by the intimacy of these women's words, as I have been while preparing this book.

The Flowering of the Soul

A Book of Prayers by Women

INTRODUCTION

The Necessity of Prayer

Heaven is reached, the blessed say,
by prayer and by no other way.
One may kneel down and make a plea
with words from book or breviary,
or one may enter in and find
a home-made message in the mind.
But true prayer travels further still,
to seek God's presence and God's will.[1]

FROM "PRAYER," BY JESSICA POWERS

Mother Teresa, whose book of her teachings, *A Simple Path* I helped compile, said to me once, "Prayer feeds the soul. As blood is to the body, prayer is to the soul." In my time observing and assisting Mother Teresa's Sisters and Brothers—the members of her Missionaries of

Charity—in different countries, I could not fathom, until I saw them in prayer, how they cheerfully labored day after day in such hard conditions to serve the poor. It made me aware that prayer—and the soul's health—is not only a basic necessity in our lives but the essential fuel to aid us in our tasks.

The fourteenth-century English anchoress Julian of Norwich taught that prayer makes God behold us in love and makes us partners in God's good deeds. It is God who moves us to pray and who gives us the grace to do what we are called to do. Without this relationship, life seems a hard and troubled road. The great sixteenth-century Spanish mystic St. Teresa of Ávila wrote, "Souls without prayer are like bodies, palsied and lame, having hands and feet they cannot use."[2] She defined prayer as an intimate divine friendship.

I believe that divine relationship is central in a prayerful life, and needs as much time as we would give to developing and sustaining an intimate human relationship. Our souls are our real Selves, the core of us, the center of us, and so with prayer our souls are nourished and developed and are given the means to grow in grace.

Daily prayer and meditation is called a spiritual practice. And, as with any practice, it takes time to make it perfect. As we walk the path of wisdom and divine partnership that prayer offers, we are led to transformation.

WHAT IS PRAYER?

Prayer has been described by some women represented in this book as "absolute, unmixed attention" and focus on the Divine. It can be in the form of praise, yearning, pleading, seeking, supplication, or listening. It can be in thought, in words, in feelings, in emptiness, in surrender, in movement. It takes the form of action in our work and duties. Prayer is consciously and attentively giving and receiving love and grace. Prayer guides us to live actively by divine inspiration. Prayer is the anchor of connectedness with all that matters, and a means to eternal existence. Prayer reminds us how small we are. Prayer reminds us of how much help we need, and is our "primary weapon" (St. Teresa of Ávila). Prayer unites us and makes us messengers of the spirit. Prayer is a force that lifts our hearts and infuses them with purity and openness. Prayer is the interior "conversation that sustains us" (Oriah Mountain Dreamer). Prayer promotes the flowering of the soul.

HOW TO SUSTAIN A LIFE OF PRAYER

The powers of the soul are vital in sustaining a life of prayer. Hildegard of Bingen, the eleventh-century German mystic, writer, composer, teacher, and healer, wrote, "the body is like a sap in a tree, and the soul's powers are like the form of the tree. How? The intellect in the soul is like the greenery of the tree's branches and leaves, the will like its flowers, the mind like its bursting first fruits, the reason like the perfected mature fruit, and the senses like its size and shape. And so a person's body is strengthened and sustained by the soul."[3] In another passage she explained, "For the soul gives life to the body as fire gives light to darkness, with two principal powers like two arms, intellect and will; the soul has arms not so as to move itself, but so as to show itself in these powers as the sun shows itself by its brilliance."[4]

Hildegard identified "intellect and will" as essential to sustaining a life of prayer; the English writer, teacher, poet, and mystic Evelyn Underhill adds a third: "heart." She taught that beyond desire and petition, and intellectual seeking, we are called to a place of adoring love.

Identifying these three elements allows us to explore the deeper properties of prayer.

The Will

British writer Sheila Cassidy wrote that "prayer is not something that just happens to us if we are in the right mood, but a positive movement on our part towards the God we cannot see."[5] Just as partaking in any relationship may be seen as a conscious act of choice, so the need or the desire to partake in the intimate friendship that prayer provides requires one's will: the will to want it, the will to give time to it, the will to learn from it and about it, and the will to concentrate at the soul level. French philosopher Simone Weil wrote, "[prayer] is the orientation of all the attention of which the soul is capable towards God."[6] Meditation and other spiritual practices expounded by the Eastern religions actually provide exercises for establishing attention, for stilling our chattering minds and coming to a peaceful place of detachment and purity. Canadian Shamanic teacher Oriah Mountain Dreamer wrote that the "act of prayer itself becomes part of my process of sorting, distilling out what really matters to me, discovering the essence of what my soul is asking for beneath the human preoccupation of the moment."[7] And the will to put yourself in a position— to place yourself before the Divine, to sit, kneel, lie, dance in front of an altar or sacred place—is also an act of prayer.

"Prayer only looks like an act of language," wrote Patricia Hampl. "Fundamentally it is a position, a placement of oneself. Focus. Get there, and all that's left to say is the words."[8]

The Intellect

The second power of the soul is that of the intellect. It provides the knowledge that the soul needs to grow, and aids in the very necessary development of consciousness. The many gifts of the mind—predominantly reason, observation, and judgment—can be used to discern the imprint of the Divine and the needs and aspirations of the soul. Marianne Williamson, the American writer and spiritual teacher, wrote in her prayer book *Illuminata* (New York: Random House, 1994) that our spiritual life takes the form of a pilgrimage and that "the pilgrimage is a process by which we change what we think and transform who we are." "Prayer," she writes, "is the pilgrim's walking stick." Intellectual prayer is the way of cognizance; it involves acquiring the knowledge of God's world and purpose beyond our own. Learning about the systems that humans have contributed in finding that knowledge (through studying stories of their lives, ways, and means) helps enlighten our own experiences in gaining it.

Underhill wrote, "Spiritual reading is, or at least it can be, second only to prayer as a developer and support of the inner life. In it we have access to all the hoarded supernatural treasure of the race: all that it has found out about God."[9] We learn from studying the traditional scriptures of the different religions, from listening to lectures, from discourse with others, or from sitting alone in formal or informal meditation. I myself discovered that I did not have to go far to find what I needed when I needed it; God provided what it was—whether the right book or message, a word from a friend or stranger, or some deep inspiration, or great idea.

Intellectual prayer recognizes the distinction between facts and truth. We use human reason and logical discernment to situate our lives within creation and within history. Out of that understanding we appreciate that knowledge is more than facts and that wisdom is more than experience. Contemporary society is showered with many books expressing ways of the soul and providing advice on spiritual systems and teachings to live by. But often new insights in psychology and anthropology only update the vocabulary for understanding ancient truths. I believe our task today is to retreat into ourselves to reflect and think, so that the learning that has occurred in our minds can be incorporated into our deeper selves, within our spiritual core and then into our daily lives.

The Heart

The thirteenth-century German mystic Mechthild of Magdeburg wrote about the power of prayer and the heart that

It makes an embittered heart mellow,
A sad heart joyful,
A foolish heart wise,
A timid heart bold,
A weak heart strong,
A blind heart clear-seeing,
A cold heart ardent.
It draws God who is great into a heart which is small.
It drives the hungry soul up to the fullness of God.[10]

Praying from and with our hearts provides the central link with the love of God and the Divine in our lives. When we love God, when we pray and listen, we open ourselves to the experience of prayer. One part of heart-centered prayer is petitioning. We can ask from our hearts with clarity for the help we need. We can do this without bargaining—just plain asking—and from prayer we learn humility; we learn how inadequate we are without prayer. And from a place of trust and love of God, we learn patience—to wait for God's intervention.

The other part of praying from our hearts is listening to God. Mother Teresa wrote, "it is in the silence of the heart that God speaks."[11] "The voice of God is a gentle one," wrote Sheila Cassidy. "We shall never hear it unless we learn to listen. We have to listen in different ways and in different places: in silence and in noise. Perhaps it is because so many people have lost the art of listening that they have also lost the ability to pray. God speaks to us through the things he has created; through the sea, through mountains, sunsets, and, in a much gentler voice, almost a whisper; through things such as wild flowers and dried up leaves."[12]

We need to contemplate. We are, as human beings, by nature contemplative, but how much effort is required to find the time and place to listen in quiet, or in nature! So rare is it to be in our natural silence, in the quiet of our hearts, that many women feel an emptiness and longing inside.

Contemplative prayer or listening prayer—where we give away all expectations, all concerns for the past and future, and just practice being in the "here and now" with the Divine—provides an experience of infinity, a sweetness and a peace. As the divine connection is made through our hearts, we then can recognize "listening prayer," contemplation, as the highest form of love. Angela of Foligno (1248–1309) refers to this highest form of love as "supernatural." "In this type of prayer the soul understands more of God than would seem naturally possible,"[13] she wrote. It leads one to mystical experiences, which encompass a feeling of being beyond self, of being in union with all things.

Five Key Virtues Shared by Women Who Pray

The most common question that arises when defining women's prayers is, "What makes women's prayers different from men's?" Through my research I discerned five virtues that prayerful women have shared—virtues which, by their very nature, are uniquely feminine. These key virtues are relatedness, perceptiveness, unity, dedication, and care. I'll explore each individually below.

1. Relatedness

Women's spirituality is born primarily from their connections with their bodies and their souls, with nature, and with community.

Body and Soul

In the classic languages the soul is placed grammatically in the feminine gender—in Latin, for example, it is called *anima*. This convention may contribute to the notion that women are more sensitive to things of the spirit than men.

Edith Stein (St. Teresa Benedicta of the Cross)—a German philosopher, a Jewish convert to Catholicism, and a member of the Carmelite order who died at Auschwitz—believed that women, by their own bodies and souls, "are fashioned less to fight and to conquer than to cherish, guard, and preserve." She wrote, "Woman's soul is present and lives more intensely in all parts of the body, and it is inwardly affected by that which happens to the body; whereas, with men, the body has more pronouncedly the character of an instrument which serves them in their work and which is accompanied by a certain detachment."[14] The American Carmelite writer and lecturer Sister Vilma Seelaus said in one of her talks that our bodies are our best spiritual directors. And it is through our bodies that we are increasingly reminded of our own ability to create. Every month menstruating women are reminded of their ability to create life. We are made aware of the very essence of embodied life through pregnancy. We create out of motherhood and the images of motherhood, out of the flow of blood and water. Our creativity is also fueled by the relationship of grace between our souls and our bodies. Mechthild of Magdeburg, who has left us a wealth of feminine spiritual writing, wrote about this infused creativity, "Neither can I write nor do I wish to write unless I first see with the eyes of my soul and hear with the ears of my eternal spirit and sense in all the members of my body the power of the Holy Spirit."[15]

Yet in most traditional religions' teachings—particularly teachings in the Abramic heritage of Judeo-Christian and Islamic religions—human bodies are perceived as shameful and the senses are to be controlled or ignored. At times our bodies have been referred to as "evil," with their wants and needs reminding us of the forbidden senses—especially those of a sexual nature. The sins of the senses led to the practice of penance by many dedicated to deadening their desires which included defying their bodies through methods of mortification. However, the surge of sexual liberation over the last forty years and the more recent interest in goddess worship and the mind/body therapies have helped to make the human body much better understood and loved than ever before. Women now are more receptive to interpreting messages through their bodies, and they use movement meditation, dance, yoga, tai chi, and chi kung to bring a wealth of experiential knowledge to spiritual teachings. The relatedness to their bodies has bred a new form of spirituality, one that includes the physical, the sexual, the sensual, and joyful expression. Now, as before, women who have entered further into their spiritual lives are made more aware of the divine embodiment within them. Towards the end of her life, Simone Weil wrote in a letter, "I too have a growing inner certainty that there is within me a deposit of pure gold." Earlier writings also reflect this experience: Catherine of Genoa, the fifteenth-century Italian saint, said, "My Being *is* God, not by some simple participation but by a true transformation of my being." And through her divine motherhood, Mary, by offering her body as a receptacle for the incarnation of Christ, gave birth to light in the world.

However, physical transformations which participated in the transformation of the soul took place in differing ways, depending on the faith practiced. In the case of many of the Eastern religions, physical purification was perceived as necessary for spiritual truth. This led not to salvation from sin but to higher states of consciousness, transformation, and wisdom. The teachings of Taosim in the East and the laws of alchemy widely practiced by women there were linked with the attributes and work-ings of the human body. And in the Christian religion many penitential practices in mortification of the flesh (more popular in medieval times) were a way of advanc-ing the understanding of the human physical sufferings that Christ endured, and becoming closer to divine hu-manity. As editor, Fiona Bowie noted, "It was primarily through identification with the human, incarnate Christ, in his tormented suffering, that the medieval female as-cetic was empowered to assert her own humanity, believ-ing it capable of redemption and transformation."[16]

Through suffering, physical weakness, and sickness, many women also have revelations, and these contribute to our understanding of the soul's message being en-hanced by the messages in our bodies.

Nature

Women's eye for aesthetics and for beauty in natural surroundings is centermost in their expression of a spiri-tual life. Their being nourished by nature is reflected in their prayers. Weil wrote that we yearn for the beauty of the world, "Beauty captivates the flesh in order to obtain permission to pass right through to the soul."[17] For most women, the beauty of the natural world reflects their un-derstanding of the creative God, and because this is so real a connection, the inner and outer experience merge physically and emotionally in the feminine.

Evelyn Underhill wrote, "Nothing in all nature is so lovely and so vigorous, so perfectly at home in its environment, as a fish in the sea. Its surroundings give to it a beauty, quality, and power which is not its own. We take it out, and at once a poor, limp, dull thing, fit for nothing, is gasping away its life. So the soul sunk in God, living the life of prayer, is supported, filled, transformed in beauty, by a vitality and a power which are not its own."[18]

Community

Women's spirituality is revealed in relatedness in community. Whether this community is domestic, monastic, pastoral, congregational, cultural, or social, women have needed, and still need, communal relatedness and the structures of community to teach, preach, pioneer, and reform. This community relatedness becomes prayer in action when it is formed by a divine purpose, and it breeds solidarity.

Some of the most powerful and moving testaments to the power of women's spirit and the direction they received from the Divine come from the African American women preachers and evangelical writers of the nineteenth century. Speaking to women in their own communities, and to others while traveling, they empowered women to act as examples of living faith and courage. Maria W. Stewart was one preacher who addressed the members of the First African Baptist Church & Society in Boston, to encourage solidarity:

> I am of a strong opinion, that the day on which we unite, heart and soul, and turn our attention to knowledge and improvement, that [the] day of hissing and reproach among the

nations of the earth against us will cease. And even those who now point at us with the finger of scorn, will aid and befriend us. It is of no use for us to sit with our hands folded, hanging our heads like bulrushes, lamenting our wretched condition; but let us make a mighty effort, and arise; and if no one will promote or respect us, let us promote and respect ourselves.[19]

2. Perceptiveness

It is women's relatedness, particularly in regard to their bodies and senses, that brings them highly developed intuitive skills, sometimes prophetic insights, and the ability to use their feelings to educate and guide them. In women's prayers, this perceptiveness is omniscient, and extended from the mystic's highly attuned ecstatic states, the healer's instincts, and the sagaciousness and sensibility of mothers, to the working instincts of women, pioneers, and educators.

The perceptiveness of devout women is known to us in some cases through scribes, like those who wrote down the dictation of St. Catherine of Siena while she received divine guidance through discourse with her God. Julian of Norwich, Hildegard of Bingen, and St. Teresa of Ávila, too, received wisdom through visions and trances and ecstatic states. For women who were not in monastic life, divine guidance and messages came to them through their daily activities in the home, farms, offices, and in the community.

The way that divine messages were experienced depended on circumstances. St. Teresa of Ávila, for instance, who had chosen the religious life, expressed her joy of perceiving God "among the pots and pans," as did St. Thérèse of Lisieux in the little things she did with love every day in the Carmelite convent. In the kitchens and chapels of this world, women's perception was tried and practiced, and it was from these rooms that many transformed society. Most women of prayer answered their calls to action by taking their perception of what the Divine needed them to do, and manifesting it. These women were pioneers and educators, social activists and feminist theologians who championed the fight for religious as well as political freedom and equality. Many women, who felt called to greater and nobler things, were embittered by the drudgery of the domestic everyday. Yet women, however liberated today, are still not free from domestic duties, for caring for families and friends and parents and in-laws. Women's prayers often still take place at the kitchen sinks, or on the run, caring for others while making a living.

Most of our spiritual heroines, and the saints of all traditions, had to take a lonely road to their destiny; the female mystical poets and teachers of the East—in Hinduism, Sufism, and Buddhism, particularly—left husbands and families, discarding their socially acceptable roles and garb, to follow the Divine's direction. The courage they had was not so much of conviction but of intuitive recognition of their calling. The expectations imposed on them through restrictive patriarchal and societal attitudes did not support them, so they journeyed alone. Yet their partnership with Truth and with the Divine guided their steps—both their interior life and their exterior action.

3. Unity

Partnership with the Divine, partnership with another in life, partnership with our creativity, our bodies, ourselves, our work, is what Edith Stein, our newest saint, called "loving union." She wrote, "The deepest feminine yearning is to achieve a loving union . . . such yearning is an essential aspect of the eternal destiny of woman. It is not simply a human longing but is specifically feminine."[20] In the monastic life where most of the great women mystics experienced divine union, women had the opportunity to concentrate on, and be supported in, living a life of prayer and devotion. The challenge today is to find the ways and means to experience divine union in an unsupportive secular environment. Canadian Jungian writer Marion Woodman gave a talk once regarding women's essential need for this—that the aspect of loving union with God and the Divine is frequently forgotten in women's thrust for unity in other spheres of life.

Women's prayers *are* women's lives. And women's prayers *are* women's work. Edith Stein reminded us that the liberation of women's work without true intention and spiritual vocation disempowers us. She believed that whether a woman "is a mother in the home, or occupies a place in the limelight of public life, or lives behind quiet cloister walls," her first vocation and her primary calling above her duties, or work, is "to be in the image of God." I believe that this is vital teaching for women today, that we have the responsibility of embodying the feminine Divine, and all the virtues that accompany this.

It is becoming more evident each day that the economic and social lives we live, which are formed upon the masculine model, are causing women as well as men much pain. The resulting spiritual emptiness and lack of balance in secular daily lives is responsible for provoking feelings of alienation and hopelessness. Harmony in environment is vital for many women. But while women may work in environments that are predominantly hostile to the feminine, and that do not uphold or support the power of the feminine virtues, this used not to be the case. In the past, the smaller communities of the home and local workplaces supplied women with the opportunity for a more balanced interior and exterior partnership, although other hardships were present. For example, while traveling in France and visiting Chartres Cathedral, I discovered images in stone carvings of women solitarily sewing with their prayer beads beside them. I remember that my grandmother found her quiet time in a nearby convent with contemplative nuns, who embroidered vestments and altar cloths one afternoon a week, to which activity they invited women from the outside. And even today, Mother Teresa's Missionaries of Charity pray for those in daily action while they serve the poor, sick, and dying; the purpose behind the Missionaries of Charity's work is formed by a deeply spiritual vocation in partnership and love with God. The action and the service given by members of the order manifest this love.

So until the prayer of contemplation and action, involving the giving, receiving, and circulating parts of our nature, has a platform for expression through our homes, offices, and communities, we will feel incomplete, out of balance, and disconnected from the natural feminine divinity in ourselves.

The steps towards reconciliation among men and women, in faith, in relationships, in ecumenical movements in religion, in the East and the West, towards world peace, equality for all people, usually are begun one step at a time. But as most of the women in this book have proven, nothing is possible without our being first united with God and the Divine. The greatest weapons women have are their spiritual virtues and their ability to express them; it is only in unity with them that we can hope and help to renew the world.

4. Dedication

The foremost virtue that many women possess is simple and unflagging faith and the patience, perseverance, and persistence that accompany it. This sort of dedication is common even in lesser-known women. The writer, Marsha Norman found the prayer journals of her deceased mother, and looking through the daily entries, counted what she perceived as being about a billion prayers for herself, and about half a million for the works of missionaries. Dedication is also evident in the work of women reformers; their clarity of mission and dedication to their task surmounted all else. The late-nineteenth-century American feminist Elizabeth Cady Stanton said of her friend Susan B. Anthony, "Every energy of her soul is centered upon the needs of the world. To her work is worship. She has not stood aside shivering in the cold shadows of uncertainty; but has moved on with the whirling world, has done the good given her to do, and thus in the darkest hours has been sustained by an unfaltering faith in the final perfection of all things."[21]

Out of her deep concern for the poor and sick, St. Elizabeth Seton (1774–1821) founded the Society for the Relief of Poor Widows with Small Children. After converting from Protestantism to Catholicism, she founded a girls' school in Baltimore. Later, she lived a life of a religious: she founded the American Sisters of Charity, based on the rule of St. Vincent de Paul. Seton showed how to combine motherhood with the religious life, and as an educator she laid the foundations for the American parochial school system. Another reformer is the English Quaker Elizabeth Fry (1780–1845), a mother of eleven children, reformer of prisons, women's educator, and a founder of schools and a pioneer institution for nurses. Florence Nightingale took nurses from this institution with her to the Crimean War. The then Duke of Argyll wrote about Elizabeth Fry, "She was the only really very great human being I have ever met, with whom it is impossible to be disappointed. She was in the fullest sense of the word a majestic woman. It was impossible not to feel some awe before her as before some superior being . . . the words that came to my mind when I saw her were 'The peace of God that passes all understanding.' "[22]

These women, among so many we do not know or I could not include here, are heroines of dedication and faith. They dedicated their work in friendship with their God. They all carried the power of God's presence, as the Duke of Argyll had witnessed in Elizabeth Fry; it came from their ability to be humble in their reforming tasks. As they all offered their work to God, it became God's work. They were given the spiritual energy and zeal and purpose to carry it out, sometimes against all odds, and they lived their lives selflessly for the greater good and effected change beyond what they had set out to do.

Another form of dedication is that of devotion—the zeal given to worship and to spiritual practice. The Taoist women practitioners, perfecting the course of enlightenment and purity and spiritual liberation, were in a number of cases married and visible in society. Yet their path to humility was virtually invisible to the public eye. "A skilled artisan leaves no traces," and "The skilled appear to have no abilities, the wise appear to be ignorant."[23] Luckily we have some writings about the process from some of these Taoist "immortal sisters" left to teach us.

Examples of the dedication of bhakta poets and the Sufi saints are included in this book, but what we know of their lives is sketchy. One thirteenth-century Sufi named Bibi Fatimah Sam, whose shrine is still visited to this day in New Delhi, said, "Nothing will earn greater reward in this or in the next world than the piece of bread and the water given to the hungry and the thirsty. The blessings of god for this are greater than for hundreds of thousands of *namazes* and for many days spent in fasting."[24]

5. Care

The last of the virtues, care, is the one that encapsulates all the others. Women are moved to care for their families, those around them, those in need. Whether there is a belief in God, or in Truth, or no belief at all, caring compassion is recognized as the supreme human virtue, one that can move mountains. But it is women of faith, and women who pray, who carry the consciousness that mountains cannot be moved without divine intervention.

Two examples of feminine care have stayed with me for a long time. They have moved me to an awareness of the vast holiness present in the large and small acts of immense care for others. Both women were Carmelite nuns and both were facing imminent death. Edith Stein was captured and imprisoned by the Nazis because she was Jewish. During her time in a Dutch camp before her deportation, she spent her final days caring for the mothers and children around her. She did this right to the end— including being with them as they traveled by freight car to Poland. She was last seen walking through the gates of Auschwitz. Thérèse of Lisieux, of the Child Jesus and the Holy Face(commonly known as the Little Flower) was seriously ill with tuberculosis and had suffered for many months in the infirmary. She had the reputation of serving members of her cloistered community with a selfless and simple love. One night, another sister who sat with her had fallen asleep after she had passed Thérèse some water in a cup. Thérèse spent the whole night awake cradling the cup so as not to wake the sister.

Women also take care to uphold traditions. They prepare and maintain the little things and without this care the magic in the home, in places of worship, in the environment, and in the world, would vanish. They offer simple acts: laying a table, lighting candles, cleaning a church, arranging flowers on altars, placing devotional offerings in tiny shrines, creating a garden, decorating, designing in community, and providing details in artworks, crafts, lace, and cloth. They also offer the less tangible care of just plain giving to their children, of cooking in soup kitchens, of sitting with the old and sick. They contribute to the caring professions of nursing and doctoring, and of advising, counseling as therapists, spiritual teachers, healers. And they care for the environment, for refugees, for those who are homeless, and for missions in faraway places. Women have a heartfelt need to contribute to the heart of the world, and sometimes they do so at great cost.

Mother Teresa once said, "You may be exhausted with work, you may even kill yourself, but unless your work is interwoven with love, it is useless. To work without love is slavery." As the virtue of care is so much a part of women's makeup, giving to others without a conscious connection with the Divine does lead to fatigue and sometimes burnout. Fatigue is, I believe, a result of centuries of women's service to others accompanied not so much by self-sacrifice as by self-neglect. Caring for ourselves before we care for others is a necessity we have woken up to only in recent years. And we have a lot of catching up to do!

As we end this century, with the women of prayer who have gone before as our models, we have the obligation as women, I believe, to instill all of the above virtues of relatedness, perceptiveness, unity, dedication, and care into the consciousness of the human race. In doing so, we will contribute to the heritage of women's spirituality, and we will move the collective consciousness towards a more balanced and united place.

The Language of Women's Prayers

"... shall we keep silent, or shall we speak?
And if we speak, what shall we say?"

This question of Dorothy Day's (which formed a prayer after the United States declared war on Japan) has rung in the ears of women for centuries. Silence was usually the chosen answer, probably precipitated by doubts, fears, and isolation, as well as by the lack of an appropriate forum outside the home, convent, or monastery, in which women could express themselves verbally. As a result, silence has been the familiar, and therefore chosen, condition for women's thoughts, ideas, opinions, and teachings. In past times even actions could seemingly be a safer vehicle for communicating women's beliefs.

therefore, if there would have been more philosophers, ethics would have been developed sooner

Luckily, some women also chose the written word as the way to share and teach out of the silence. Many of these women are represented in this book, the most prominent being St. Teresa of Ávila, who wrote under the threat of persecution by the Inquisition. In some convents and monasteries, however, superiors sometimes would order the more expressive sisters to put pen to paper. This was the case with St. Thérèse of Lisieux.

Upholding her vow of obedience, St. Thérèse wrote her *Story of a Soul* in the latter years of her life behind cloister walls. This book brought her life and holiness to the world (otherwise we would have known very little about her and her teachings of the "little way" to God). Likewise, St. Teresa of Ávila's extraordinary spiritual teaching, *The Interior Castle,* was written under the order of one of her spiritual advisers. She wrote in the introduction, "Rarely has obedience laid upon me so difficult a task as this of writing about prayer." She added, "He who bids me write this, tells me that the nuns of these convents of our Lady of Carmel need someone to solve their difficulties about prayer: he thinks that women understand one another's language best and that my Sisters' affection for me would make them pay special attention to my words."[25]

The Beguine mystics of the thirteenth and fourteenth centuries developed a special language to express the ways they experienced God through visions and the sensations that arose from their spiritual marriage with their beloved bridegroom, Christ. These experiences may have been rooted in the sentiments evident in Solomon's

Song of Songs in the Old Testament, where divine love between masculine and feminine is portrayed in the language of betrothal.

Among the earlier mystical giants represented in this book are Mechthild of Magdeburg, Hadewijch of Brabant, and Beatrice of Nazareth. These women wrote inspired by the poetic tradition of human sexual love and courtly love, in which they were educated. The woman who stands out as leader of them all is Hildegard of Bingen (1098–1179), founder and first abbess of the Benedictine community at Bingen in Germany. She wrote almost uncannily modern works, including the book *Scivias,* which has been described by Professor Barbara J. Newman as a "prophetic proclamation, a book of allegorical visions, an exegetical study, a theological summa," and she wrote music and drew and painted images of her experiences.

From the nineteenth century onwards, as women's secular writing began to flourish, women had a choice of places to write down their prayers and teachings, spiritual reflections and guidance. In this century, many such writers—e.g., Simone Weil, Edith Stein, Evelyn Underhill, and Annie Besant—published in academic journals, and through their diaries, letters, and sermons, women preachers spoke about reform, redemption from patriarchy, and the feminine experience of God. The writings of our contemporary feminist theologians address urgently and intelligently our need for self-education on the patriarchal stronghold and its influences in our devotion. But there was one outstanding woman who paved the way. Elizabeth Cady Stanton (1815–1902), along with the group of women who were members of her Revising Committee, challenged the traditionally accepted translation of the Judeo-Christian scriptures by publishing a woman's interpretation of the Bible in 1898.

In her introduction to *The Woman's Bible,* Stanton wrote, "Bible historians claim special inspiration for the

Old and New Testaments containing most contradictory records of the same events, of miracles opposed to all known laws, of customs that degrade the female sex, of all human and animal life, stated in most questionable language that could not be read in a promiscuous assembly, and call all this, 'The Word of God.' " Of the Book of Genesis, she wrote, "It is evident from the language that there was consultation in the Godhead, and that the masculine and feminine elements were equally represented."[26]

Other women, like Frances Willard (1839–1898), president of the Woman's Christian Temperance Union, pleaded that women of linguistic talents should make a specialty of Hebrew and Greek study in order to contribute to the reform in linguistic interpretation "in the interest of their sex."[27]

In fact, learned women, especially those in monastic environments, had long known and studied the classical languages and were able to identify the use of the feminine gender in ancient Hebrew and its Greek translations. Attention to the term *hokmah*, meaning "spirit" in Hebrew (translated to *Sophia* in Greek), led to the study of feminine wisdom linked with the Holy Spirit in the later Christian teachings. And St. Gertrude of Helfta, the medieval German mystic, had written her *Spiritual Exercises* from a female perspective. Her editor and translator (Fiona Bowie and Oliver Davies, respectively) wrote that she expressed this "through the feminine grammatical endings in her Latin original. Such female prayer is, unfortunately, unusual for women in the Church even now, because for centuries women have been expected to pray under a male persona in absolutely all liturgical prayers. At the same time, Gertrude freely adapts well-known Bible passages so that she as a woman can identify with them. She sees herself, for instance, in the parable of the prodigal son as 'the prodigal daughter.' "[28]

Due to the pioneering work of these earlier women,

there came out of the women's movement of this century the requirement for the very necessary and apt exploration of the Truth, and with it, the introduction of inclusive language in scripture, liturgy, prayers, blessings, and meditations; the study and exposure of sexism in traditional texts; and gender change in ideas and descriptions of the Godhead. In the introduction to their 1986 book *Celebrating Women*, Janet Morley, Jennifer Wild, and Hannah Ward wrote, "Exclusive language . . . is both an accurate symptom of women's actual exclusion from many central forms of ministry and decision-making; and it is also a means of continually re-creating the attitudes which support such exclusion as 'normal', or within the purposes of God. Women can participate in this language, and speak the words that erase us, or we can choose to remain silent. Alternatively we can struggle to create a language that includes us."[29]

This struggle is evident sporadically in the prayers included in this book. Sadly, we have not had well-known prayers written by women that speak to a woman's experience. There has been an increasing study of women in scripture—predominantly made by Jewish women scholars, and recent writings being published on the biblical stories of Ruth and Naomi, Hannah and Judith. Kathleen M. O'Connor's interpretation of the female perspective in the Book of Lamentations is an example: "Besides offering women glimpses of the painful lives of their foremothers, Lamentations also provides women with a rare female voice in biblical liturgical prayer."[30]

Most women in their written prayers do predominantly refer to God as male, even though they may have experienced the Divine as female, as did Julian of Norwich, who introduced the idea of God as mother in her writings, yet still referred to "He" and "Him" and "His Motherhood." There are certainly exceptions, with God referred to as "She," but this has only appeared in writings of the last thirty years.

To gather together and include in this book innumerable women's prayers with God referred to in the male gender was difficult for me as an editor. I am of the opinion that publishing them only reinforces the already strong patriarchal grip on communicating with God. However, if I had disregarded them, this would be a very different book, one that would not link women's sentiments, needs, and words of prayer in historical, religious, and spiritual diversity, as was my intention. Therefore I believe it imperative to recognize the historical and religious roots in the formation of spiritual language, and to develop an understanding of the language of women's prayer in the past, its present status, and where it may be going in the future.

Towards a Feminine Image of God

In her essay "The Long Journey Home: Reconnecting with the Great Mother," Riane Esler wrote, "Slowly, I also began to understand how, as a woman, I was in a miserable situation if I only have a God who's a Father, a King, a Lord. It implies that the only relationship I can have with the male deity is indirect. If we as women are to access the divine in us, then a female deity, a divine Mother, is essential."[31]

As Edith Stein taught that women have a responsibility to live, work, and express ourselves above all as "the image of God," for many women this image remains unclear. The contemporary American theologian Rosemary Radford Reuther wrote that women have not had a direct relationship with God, due to the monotheistic religions' promotion of male hierarchy. As a result, women were made to feel inferior because of being "connected to God secondarily, through the male."[32] This image is still promoted and upheld particularly in the Catholic teachings, in that the representatives of God's covenant were males and "sons." Even though there are some women teachers who advocate replacing males with females—like replacing the word "son" with "daughter"—this is really only promoting the hierarchical single model of placing one sex over the other. The answer is in partnership between the two.

Naturally we have a way to go in seeking the feminine image of God beyond the established archetypes. As an example, the images of feminine holiness for Christian women have been confined to holy motherhood. Through the dogmatic teachings about Jesus' mother, Mary, being a perpetual virgin, girls were led to believe that feminine holiness meant being stainless of any sin of sexual desire or carnal experience. The other promoted image was of the repentant whore, which Christ's closest woman companion, Mary Magdalene, represented (even though we have no historical or scriptural fact to support this judgment). Mary Magdalene has become a vital symbol for Christian women as she was a woman who had an intimate and loving relationship with her Lord, and he loved her enough in return to seek her first after his resurrection. Mary Magdalene is a hopeful archetype for women who aspire to be "in the image of God," although the perception of her tainted past has made her seem lacking in holiness. Recent speculation, however, has suggested that she and Christ were married and that the marriage at Cana was theirs. Even if this is historically or scripturally inaccurate, the possibility of this idea of her being Christ's wife allows us to seek a place of equality and partnership as women with Christ.

Yet Christ also signifies, and taught, human partnership with God. For many women, Christ's humanity encompasses a pronounced femininity in balance with his masculinity; this brought hope and acceptance to those who were lost in a hierarchical heritage. His teachings and example, in fact, still instill hope, even though the rules of the institutional churches formed in His name tend to be lacking in balance and in feminine virtues.

In the spiritual realms of the Greco-Roman world, partnerships of all kinds were made between gods and goddesses. Just as it is necessary for masculine and feminine to join in human procreation, creation in the world at large requires male and female interaction. In the Eastern religions, the teachings themselves are based on the balance in partnership with Self (Buddhism), with Self and the Divine (Hinduism), and with the masculine and feminine energies inherent in the Way (Taoism). The feminine is symbolized by the moon, and the masculine, the sun. These energies have opposing qualities—like the contemplation and stillness of the feminine and the activity and outwardness of the masculine (although in Japan, the sun is a goddess).

In the East emphasis is placed on partnership in opposites. We can find examples of this everywhere. In Hinduism, which forms the basis for all subsequent devotional religions, the perfect manifestation of God is from opposition in partnership. This is evident through examples of Shiva (who is the personification of the masculine Divine), and Shakti (who is the personification of the creative, feminine Divine). The principle is that Shiva without Shakti is not able to create or even affect anything. It is taught that Shiva is a "possessor of power" and that Shakti (meaning "power") is like the bride whose "life is made complete by the bridegroom." Shakti is also referred to as the "agent of change and destruction." But because destruction is commonly associated with male superiority and power in Western thought, it is common for women to disassociate themselves from their place of spiritual power and disclaim the truth that is inherent in feminine spiritual strength.

Before we explore the places to find Her, it is imperative to see where Her manifestations have occurred in the collective consciousness of the past. Divine feminine spirit is recorded in ancient literature and scripture under a variety of names and manifestations. First, there are the agents for Her spirit, like those in the Greek and Roman myths (Aphrodite/Venus, who is the goddess of love; Artemis/Diana, the hunter; and Athena/Minerva, the goddess of many counsels). There are the mother of corn, Demeter/Ceres, and the goddess of the earth, Gaia. Second, there are the consorts of the gods in various religions—Lilith, and Hera, and the Hindu goddesses Sarasvati (the goddess of speech and learning), and Kali (the "black" goddess, who represents the destructive aspect of the Divine), and last, the Buddhist bodhisattva consorts—Kuan Yin (the goddess of compassion) and the playful Tara (the goddess who is in all nature and at the doors of life and death). Third, there are the humans—biblical women like Miriam and Sarah, and the Christian and Eastern saints, many of whose words are in this book and who by their actions, words, and work bring divine life into the concrete reality of matter and every day. Mary, the mother of Jesus, also has been an effective mediator between the realms of heaven and earth. It is believed that she, in her role as mother of divinity, has the mighty power to be heard and responded to by Christ, and so she is petitioned to intervene in the lives of Christian believers. She has been portrayed as Queen of Heaven, the Star of the Ocean, and the Sorrowful Mother (grieving for our world). In effect she has been placed in the role of Goddess, because of her supreme status and because she was God's chosen vessel as mother of Christ.

Finally, there is the feminine spirit of Wisdom. Wisdom in the Proverbs of the Old Testament is always referred to as "She," and in the Song of Songs is depicted in the wooing of the two lovers, like that of the divine bride and groom. Wisdom is available through the Holy Spirit or through the kundalini of yoga: she dwells in those who uphold its divine virtues. And Wisdom is devoted to the good of all; if we open ourselves to Her, there she is. Rosemary Radford Reuther wrote, "In the Wisdom tradition the female image appears as a secondary persona of God, mediating the work and will of God to creation." In explaining Wisdom's part in creation Reuther said, "Wisdom is the manifestation of God through whom God mediates the work of creation, providential guidance, and revelation. She is the subtle power of the presence of God, permeating and enspiriting all things."[33]

Even though it is safer to infer that the Holy Spirit is androgynous, it is still referred to in the masculine in many of the traditional Christian prayers. As mentioned earlier, the Hebrew word *Hokmah* translates into Greek as *Sophia*. And this is where the identification of the spirit of God as female has taken root. Through an understanding of her as present in all things, as the spirit of God, she can be identified with goddesses of all beliefs, and she unifies them all, us all, in nature. In her essay "Women and Culture in Goddess-Oriented Old Europe," Marija Gimbutas wrote, "There were, in my opinion, two primary aspects of the Goddess (not necessarily two Goddesses) presented by the effigies. The first is "She Who Is the Giver of All"—giver of life, of moisture, of food, of happiness—and "Taker of All," i.e., death. The second aspect of the Goddess is Her association with the periodic awakening of nature: She is springtime, the new moon, rebirth, regeneration, and metamorphosis."[34]

It has been believed and honored that many goddesses and agents for the feminine, like witches, work within the order of the natural world and understand the workings of nature and the use of her elements. Many women are now recognizing that the Goddess is not just a symbol for nature, but is represented *in* nature. To come to an understanding of the character of the feminine

God, women need to look at the natural world, and inside themselves and their bodies.

Women who increasingly live and work in urban environments are robbed of the natural ability to experience how the Goddess can reveal herself in the natural environment. Yet many are now realizing the very real necessity of their soul's calling to nature, and so are finding the time to be in natural surroundings. Like witches before them, many women today create their own rituals from their life experiences and their need for honoring life's passages, such as menstruation and puberty, conception, motherhood, menopause and croning, healing a broken heart, letting go of abusive relationships, making room for the new. And the revelations of the feminine God are not defined through the sacred and pure images that come to us from the East, or from the teachings about the virginal purity of Mary, but through the experiences and details of the messiness of motherhood. The spirit of the motherhood of God is held in our wombs—borne in us and our bodily functions. She is in places most spiritual teachers of the past, and even the present, are afraid to go—namely, into the feminine bodily fluids of procreation (blood, water, and milk). However, recent writings from the experience of women who are exploring the Mother God are giving her names like the following: "Source of My Life, One Who Wipes Away Tears, Womb of Compassion, Fertile Womb of All, A God with Breasts Like Mine, Midwife, Faithful Mother, Comforting Mother, Nurturer, Healer, Nursing Mother, the Divine Womb of Darkness, Laboring One, Ferocious Mother Bear, Soaring Mother Eagle, Gathering Mother Hen."[35]

American artist and writer Meinrad Craighead, who wrote of her experiential knowledge of her Mother God in *The Mother's Songs*, calls her by her ancient names: "Ma, Amma, Ana, Nu, Mena, Marni, Maran, Mammu."

Craighead found links with these names and the name of her own grandmother, Mernaw. She searched for and discovered bits of Mother God in herself and in the spirituality of her own mother and grandmother. "This is who God is," she wrote. "My mother is water and she is inside me and I am in the water. I am born connected. I am born remembering rivers flowing from my mother's body into my body. I pray at her Fountain of Life, saturated in her milk and blood, water and honey. She passes on to me the meaning of religion because she links me to our original in God the Mother."[36]

And so we come round full circle in knowing that God teaches us about wisdom and truth through knowledge of ourselves. In getting to know ourselves, we find Mother God in our own emotions as women, in our blood, our own sweat, our pains and torments, frustrations, realizations, the water of our tears, the comfort of our milk. In these ways, we contribute a small but vital piece to Her composite image. And as we awaken Her in ourselves, She lives and works Her grace through our lives and thus out into our world. As we speak Her, write Her, touch Her, we are contributing to the feminine's quest for unity in partnership and equality. By doing so we come closer to the image of Her in harmony with Him. By embodying Her in the deepest part of us, in the creative centers of our wombs, and in our masculine logical part, our heads and minds finally are able to meet in the middle place—like the middle way that the Buddha teaches: right in the center of us, the place of our hearts.

The women in this book have all contributed in their own way to the image of the feminine God. By reading their prayers, learning about their lives and their struggles, we pray our own in unity with them. I hope that doing so may bring us to a peaceful place, where a soft wind blows in the silence of our own hearts.

Notes to Introduction

1. Jessica Powers, "Prayer," in *Selected Poetry of Jessica Powers*, edited by Regina Siefried and Robert Morneau (Kansas City: Sheed & Ward, 1989), page 144.
2. Teresa of Ávila, *The Interior Castle* (London: Harper-Collins, Fount paperback ed., 1995), page 7.
3. Hildegard of Bingen, *Scivias*, book 1, vision 4, no. 26, translated by Mother Columba Hart and Jane Bishop (New York: Paulist Press, 1990), page 124.
4. Ibid., no. 18, page 120.
5. Sheila Cassidy, *Prayer for Pilgrims* (London: Harper-Collins, Fount paperback ed., 1980, 1994), page 11.
6. Simone Weil, "Reflections on the Right Use of School Studies with a View to the Love of God" in *Waiting on God*, translated by Emma Craufurd [1942] (London: HarperCollins, Fount paperback ed., 1959, 1977) page 53.
7. Unpublished essay on prayer by Oriah Mountain Dreamer.
8. Patricia Hampl, quoted in *Wise Women: Over Two Thousand Years of Spiritual Writing by Women*, edited by Susan Cahill (New York: W. W. Norton, 1996), page 272.
9. Evelyn Underhill, *Concerning the Inner Life* [1926] (Oxford: Oneworld Publications, 1995), page 54.
10. Mechthild of Magdeburg, *On the Tenfold Value of the Prayer of a Good Person*, 5:13, in *Beguine Spirituality: Mystical Writings of Mechthild of Magdeburg, Beatrice of Nazareth, and Hadewijch of Brabant*, edited and introduced by Fiona Bowie; translated by Oliver Davies (London: SPCK, 1989).
11. Mother Teresa, *A Simple Path*, compiled by Lucinda Vardey (New York: Ballantine Books, 1995), page 7.
12. Cassidy, pages 12–13, footnote 5.
13. Angela of Foligno, *The Book of Blessed Angela (Instructions)*, in *Complete Works*, translated and with an

introduction by Paul Lachance (New York: Paulist Press, 1993), page 287.

14. Edith Stein (St. Teresa Benedicta of the Cross, Discalced Carmelite) in *The Collected Works of Edith Stein, vol. 2, Essays on Woman,* edited by Dr. L. Gelber and Romaeus Leuven; translated by Freda Mary Oben (Washington, D.C.: ICS Publications, 1987), pages 73 and 95.

15. Mechthild of Magdeburg, op, cit., 4:13, in Bowie, *Beguine Spirituality,* page 52, footnote 10.

16. Bowie, *Beguine Spirituality,* introduction, page 9, footnote 10.

17. Simone Weil, *Gravity and Grace* (London: Routledge & Keegan Paul, 1963), page 135.

18. Evelyn Underhill, *The Golden Sequence* (New York: Harper Torchbooks, The Cloister Library, 1960 reprint), p. 173.

19. Maria W. Stewart, in *Spiritual Narratives,* Schomburg Library of Nineteenth Century Black Women Writers (New York: Oxford University Press, 1988), page 15.

20. Stein, *Essays on Woman,* page 93, footnote 14.

21. Elizabeth Cady Stanton in *Our Famous Women: Comprising the Lives and Deeds of American Women,* ed. by Harriet Beecher Stowe, et al. (1884) (Hartford, CT: A. D. Worthington), page 59, as quoted in *Protestant Women and Social Reform* by Joanne Carlson Brown, collected in *In Our Own Voices, Four Centuries of American Women's Religious Writing,* edited by Rosemary Skinner Keller and Rosemary Radford Reuther (San Francisco, HarperCollins, 1995), page 254.

22. Quoted in Georgina King Lewis, *Elizabeth Fry* (London: Headley Brothers, 1909).

23. Chan Buddhist quoted in the introduction to *Immortal Sisters: Secret Teachings of Taoist Women,* translated and edited by Thomas Cleary [1989] (Berkeley, California: North Atlantic Books, 1996).

24. Bibi Fatimah Sam, in *Women Bhakta Poets*, nos. 50–52, translation supplied by K. A.: Nizami (New Delhi, India: Manushi, 1989), page 8.

25. Teresa of Ávila, op. cit., pages 1–2, footnote 2.

26. *The Woman's Bible*, by Elizabeth Cady Stanton and her Revising Committee members [1895] (Salem, New Hampshire: Ayer, 1972, 1991), pages 12 and 14.

27. *The Women's Bible Commentary*, edited by Carol A. Newsom and Sharon H. Ringe (London: SPCK, 1992), page xiii.

28. Bowie, *Beguine Spirituality*, page 304, footnote 10.

29. *Celebrating Women*, edited by Hannah Ward, Jennifer Wild, and Janet Morley (London: SPCK, 1995), page 6.

30. Kathleen M. O'Connor, in *The Woman's Bible Commentary*, "Lamentations," pages 180–181, footnote 27.

31. Riane Esler, "The Long Journey Home: Reconnecting with the Great Mother," 1990, in *For the Love of God: New Writings by Spiritual and Psychological Leaders*, edited by Benjamin Shield and Richard Carlson (San Rafael, CA: New World Library, 1990), page 15.

32. Rosemary Radford Reuther, "Sexism and God-language," in *Weaving the Visions: New Patterns in Feminist Spirituality*, edited by Judith Plaskow and Carol P. Christ (San Francisco: Harper & Row, 1989), page 151.

33. Ibid.

34. Marija Gimbutas, "Women and Culture in Goddess-Oriented Old Europe," 1980, in *Weaving the Visions: New Patterns in Feminist Spirituality*, page 68, footnote 32.

35. Patricia Lynn Reilly, *A God Who Looks Like Me: Discovering a Woman-Affirming Spirituality* (New York: Ballantine Books, 1995), pages 90–91.

36. Meinrad Craighead, *The Mother's Songs: Images of God the Mother* (New York: Paulist Press, 1986), page 29.

PART ONE

DEVOTION

*F*rom ancient times devotional prayer has taken various forms—from building temples, sacred places, and altars to sacrificing animals, lighting candles, offering flowers and food, and even sharing a meal together—but to what purpose? The purpose of any act of devotion is to make a divine connection: to prepare a place where the meeting of divinity and humanity can occur. It requires preparation, a giving of oneself, a placing of oneself, a state of mind, a repose. The beginning of any course in prayer, to allow one to make this connection, also requires some aspects of regular devotion. This has frequently been perceived as attending a service or a ritual once a week, yet perfunctory attendance is only a minor part of devotion. The prayers and acts of devotion are in finding a personal relationship with the Divine, of conversing, of listening, of just being with, of feeling the presence, of beholding the glory, of praising the greatness. This not only enables us to enter a state of humility in the presence of divine greatness, but also to participate in divine grace—to be able to step over the line that divides the finite from the infinite and to gain knowledge and experience of the other realm.

In this first part of the book, I introduce the stages commonly traversed to gain divine awareness and relationship. The prayers here reflect the emotions of the soul's need for this very necessary nourishment and connection. Our natural longing and destiny is for infinite revelations; we thirst for a partnership and friendship with the Divine. So we begin with our looking within for answers and guidance. Worship, Praise, and Thanksgiving follow; they are necessities in devotional prayer. Nowadays, we don't sacrifice livestock to offer gifts to God, but what we substitute as oblations is just as necessary. What we offer contributes to the building and sustaining of divine relationship.

1

DIVINE RELATIONSHIP

*T*here can be no prayer without divine relationship, and no divine relationship without prayer. There are various stages that we go through while searching for relationship with the divine; the struggle to identify what it is we need; the need to find what it is we are searching for; the looking within ourselves for the answers. Aspirations, or aspiring prayers, follow this search, and the recitation of them is like uttering cries in quest of our desires. Next, there are revelations, which give us the opportunity to see and experience God's love and acceptance of us. This leads to prayers of friendship—the company our souls long for, the Divine in our daily lives, God loving us and we loving God in partnership.

THE SEARCH

About our search for divine relationship, Hildegard of Bingen wrote that "those who do not seek it will not find it, as a fountain does not flow for people who know of it but do not come to it. They have to approach it if they want to draw its water" (*Scivias*).

To begin one's search requires faith that there is something to find—what Taoist teacher Sun Bu-er described as the "living, active, unified original spirit." Denise Levertov's revelation that it is not God, but herself, who is absent, is an important insight. She refers to her Divine as "the sapphire," the one she knows is there.

The Hindu Mahādēviyakka described in her prayer how she struggled to find the clues to the hiding places of her Lord. The search becomes a struggle because we have our own expectations of the ways of the Divine; our demands are for revelations, answers, miracles—and all in record time! We want answers to "Who are you?" A Mother God, a Father God, the Holy Spirit—show us your face. Who are we to have a relationship with? Hildegard's advice is that "you cannot look on Divinity with your mortal eyes, you cannot grasp its secrets with your mortal minds, except insofar as God permits you" (*Scivias*). Julian of Norwich taught that the soul's continual seeking for God pleases God greatly. And The Mother (of Sri Aurobindo's Pondicherry Ashram in India) advised that "one is sure to find what one seeks—if one seeks it in all sincerity; for what one seeks is within oneself."

As we journey inward to look within ourselves for answers, we get in touch with our own wisdom, the sapphire, "what we lost in the beginning" (Hildegard). The Mother spoke of this as "Truth." "We are all divine," she said, "but we hardly know it. And in us, it is precisely that which does not know itself as divine which we call 'ourselves.' "

The images used by these women's prayers of their souls, their inner selves, are diverse in symbolism. The American Carmelite Jessica Powers found beauty within as "a slim young virgin in a dim shadowy place." A woman from the British St. Hilda community called her soul "grass where streams of living water flow." St. Catherine of Siena wrote of the Trinity as a "deep sea" which she enters inwardly to find—and then the more she finds, the more she seeks.

Why are we on earth?
To find the Divine who is in each of us and in all things.

THE MOTHER

Not seeing you in the hill, in the forest
from tree to tree I roamed,
searching, gasping:
Lord, my Lord, come show me your kindness!
till I met your men and found you.
You hide lest I seek and find.
Give me a clue,
O lord white as jasmine,
to your hiding places.

MAHĀDĒVIYAKKA

Lord, not you,
it is I who am absent.
At first
belief was a joy I kept in secret,
stealing alone
into sacred places:
a quick glance, and away—and back,
circling.
I have long since uttered your name
but now
I elude your presence.
I stop

to think about you, and my mind
at once
like a minnow darts away,
darts
into the shadows, into gleams that fret
unceasing over
the river's purling and passing.
Not for one second
will my self hold still, but wanders
anywhere,
everywhere it can turn. Not you,
it is I am absent.
You are the stream, the fish, the light,
the pulsing shadow,
you the unchanging presence, in whom all
moves and changes.
How can I focus my flickering, perceive
at the fountain's heart
the sapphire I know is there?

DENISE LEVERTOV

Ah blessed absence of God,
How lovingly I am bound to you!
You strengthen my will in its pain
And make dear to me the long, hard wait in my poor
    body.
The nearer I come to you,
The more wonderfully and abundantly God comes upon
    me.
In pride, alas, I can easily lose you,
But in the depths of pure humility, O Lord,
I cannot fall away from you.

For the deeper I fall,
The sweeter you taste.

MECHTHILD OF MAGDEBURG

Who Are You?

Womanly God, who are you?
The weaver of warm garments and magic tapestries;
The homemaker, welcoming and accepting;
The sister, second half—disturbingly other;
The listening, reassuring friend, silent consolation;
The delightful daughter, discovering and dancing;
The encouraging teacher, suggesting new worlds, new
    vision;
The backbreaking planter of fields, weeding, reaping; the
    treader of wine;
The nurse with full breasts and herbal remedies;
The virgin bride, the fulfilling wife, the desolate widow;
The free creative maiden; the long-living treasury of
    wisdom;
The wind that makes the heart sing.

MARY ANN EBERT

My God, You are a Spirit, neither male or female. You
have been my Father for so many years, today I ask to
know you as Mother. You are too vast to fit into only one
compartment. How foolish of us to confine you to one
image. It feels uncomfortable to call you Mother. They
have spoken of you as Father for centuries. Yet I have
always wondered how there could be a father without a
mother. How is it that the feminine face of God has been

obscured for so long? They tell me now that there is a
God who looks like me. It's hard to take it all in.

PATRICIA LYNN REILLY

Who are you, sweet light, that fills me
And illumines the darkness of my heart?
You lead me like a mother's hand,
And should you let go of me,
I would not know how to take another step.
You are the space
That embraces my being and buries it in yourself.
Away from you it sinks into the abyss
Of nothingness, from which you raised it to the light.
You, nearer to me than I to myself
And more interior than my most interior
And still impalpable and intangible
And beyond any name:
Holy Spirit—eternal love!

Are you not the sweet manna
That from the Son's heart
Overflows into my heart,
The food of angels and the blessed?
He who raised himself from death to life,
He has also awakened me to new life
From the sleep of death.
And he gives me new life from day to day,

And at some time his fullness is to stream through me,
Life of your life—indeed, you yourself:
Holy Spirit—eternal life!

Are you the ray
That flashes down from the eternal Judge's throne

And breaks into the night of the soul
That had never known itself?
Mercifully—relentlessly
It penetrates hidden folds.
Alarmed at seeing itself,
The self makes space for holy fear,
The beginning of that wisdom
That comes from on high
And anchors us firmly in the heights,
Your action
That creates us anew:
Holy Spirit—ray that penetrates everything!

Are you the spirit's fullness and the power
By which the Lamb releases the seal
Of God's eternal decree?
Driven by you
The messengers of judgment ride through the world
And separate with a sharp sword
The kingdom of light from the kingdom of night.
Then heaven becomes new and new the earth,
And all finds its proper place
Through your breath:
Holy Spirit—victorious power!

Are you the master who builds the eternal cathedral,
Which towers from the earth through the heavens?
Animated by you, the columns are raised high
And stand immovably firm.
Marked with the eternal name of God,
They stretch up to the light,
Bearing the dome
That crowns the holy cathedral,
Your work that encircles the world:
Holy Spirit—God's molding hand!

Are you the one who created the unclouded mirror
Next to the Almighty's throne,
Like a crystal sea,
In which Divinity lovingly looks at itself?
You bend over the fairest work of your creation,
And radiantly your own gaze
Is illumined in return.
And of all creatures the pure beauty
Is joined in one in the dear form
Of the Virgin, your immaculate bride:
Holy Spirit—Creator of all!

Are you the sweet song of love
And of holy awe
That eternally resounds around the triune throne,
That weds in itself the clear chimes of each and every
    being?
The harmony
That joins together the members to the Head,
In which each one
Finds the mysterious meaning of being blessed
And joyously surges forth,
Freely dissolved in your surging:
Holy Spirit—eternal jubilation!

EDITH STEIN (St. Teresa Benedicta of the Cross)

Looking Within

What one seeks is within oneself.

THE MOTHER

Not towards the stars, O beautiful naked runner,
not on the hills of the moon after a wild white deer,
seek not to discover afar the unspeakable wisdom,—
the quarry is here.

Beauty holds court within,—
a slim young virgin in a dim shadowy place.
Music is only the echo of her voice,
and earth is only a mirror for her face.

Not in the quiet arms, O sorrowful lover;
O fugitive, not in the dark on a pillow of breast;
hunt not under the lighted leaves for God,—
here is the sacred Guest.

There is a Tenant here.
Come home, roamer of earth, to this room and find
a timeless Heart under your own heart beating,
a Bird of beauty singing under your mind.

JESSICA POWERS (*The Kingdom of God*)

As one who travels in the heat
longs for cool waters,
so do I yearn for wisdom;
and as one who is weary with walking
so shall I sit at her well and drink.

For her words are like streams in the desert;
she is like rain on parched ground,
like a fountain whose waters fail not.
Whoever hears her voice
will be content with nothing less;
and whoever drinks of her will long for more.

But who can find wisdom's dwelling place,
and who has searched her out?

for many have said to me, lo, here is wisdom,
and there you shall find understanding;
here is true worship of God,
and thus shall your soul be satisfied.

But there was no delight in my soul;
all my senses were held in check.
My body became alien to me,
and my heart was shrivelled within me.

For I sought understanding without justice;
discernment without the fear of God.
I would have filled my belly with the husks of knowledge,
and quenched my thirst with what was already stagnant.

But you have blessed me with emptiness, O God;
you have spared me to remain unsatisfied.
And now I yearn for justice;
like an infant that cries for the breast,
and cannot be pacified,
I hunger and thirst for oppression to be removed,
and to see the right prevail.

So while I live I will seek your wisdom, O God;
while I have strength to search, I will follow her ways.
For her words are like rivers in the desert;
she is like rain on parched ground,
like a fountain whose waters fail not.

Then shall my soul spring up like grass,
and my heart recover her greenness;
and from the deepest places of my soul
shall flow streams of living water.

ST. HILDA COMMUNITY

You, O eternal Trinity, are a deep sea, into which the
more I enter the more I find, and the more I find
the more I seek. The soul cannot be satiated in your
abyss, for she continually hungers after you, the eternal
Trinity, desiring to see you with the light of your light. As
the heart desires the springs of living water, so my soul
desires to leave the prison of this dark body and see you
in truth. O abyss, O eternal Godhead, O sea profound,
what more could you give me than yourself? You are the
fire that ever burns without being consumed; you
consume in your heat all the soul's self-love; you are the
fire which takes away cold; with your light you illuminate
me so that I may know all your truth. Clothe me, clothe
me with yourself, eternal truth, so that I may run this
mortal life with true obedience, and with the light of
your most holy faith.

ST. CATHERINE OF SIENA

ASPIRATIONS

The cries and prayers of desire are examples of our
true longing for God; and it is through this longing that
Julian of Norwich claims "we are made worthy." Through
our cries and desires we are perfected ourselves, re-
arranged in order to be worthy to receive. This includes
the testing of our sincerity—what The Mother said was
vital so that "the Love answers spontaneously." This testing comes from the cries and pleading to be listened to—
here among prayers reflected not only to the Godhead,
but to women of scripture of the early Christian church,
to the Grandmothers of the shamanic traditions, and to
the Goddess.

All prayer seems to be our cry for access, our attempt in word or deed to touch God's hem.

MARSHA SINETAR

Come, man, come, you pearl of goodness, after having
   bathed in turmeric powder,
Having put on golden ornaments and dressed yourself in
   silk.
Your coming is the coming of my life, lord!
I am waiting longingly,
Thinking that he may come, the lord
who is as white as jasmine.

MAHĀDĒVIYAKKA

Cries

Out of the depths I cry to you, O God.
Hear my voice, O God, listen to my pleading.

My voice is weak. O God, my God,
Although it speaks for many.
It is the voice of Sarah, shamed before her servant,
Barren, and given no worth.
It is the voice of Hagar, abused by her mistress,
Driven out into the desert with her child.
It is the voice of Rachel, weeping for her children,
Weeping, for they are all dead.
It is the voice of Mary, robbed of her humanity,
Women, yet not woman.
It is the voice of Martha, taught to be a servant,
Challenged to choose for herself.

It is the voice of a nameless woman, bought and sold,
Then given back to herself.

It is the voice of women, groaning in labour,
Sweating in toil, abandoned in hardship,
Weeping in mourning, awakened in worry,
Enslaved in dependency, afraid of their weakness.

Do you hear my voice, O God, my God?
Can you answer me?
The words I hear all speak to me of men.
You said I am also in your image,
You are my father, are you also mother,
Comfort-bringing like the loving arms?

Do you hear my voice, O God, my God?
Can you answer me?
I can sing your song of praise no longer,
I am not at home in this world any more.
My heart is full of tears for my sisters,
They choke my words of joy.

Do you hear my voice, O God, my God?
Can you answer me?
You sent your son, a man, to love me,
But him they killed also.
What is the new life that you promise me?
I do not want more of the same.

KATHY GALLOWAY

Are you there? Can you hear?
Listen, try to understand,
O be still, become an ear,
For there is darkness on this land.
Stand and hearken, still as stone,
For I call to you alone.

Who can be what the weed was
In the empty afternoon?
Who can match me the wild grass,
Sighing its forgotten tune:
Who is equal to that shell,
Whose spiral is my parable?

No human eye reflects the weed
Burning beneath the lonely sun:
The wild hard grass spangled with seed
Is still unmatched by anyone;
The justice of the shell is still
Above the mind, above the will.

Since love and beauty, blown upon,
Are not desired, not spoken of,
Hear me, you solitary one,
Better than beauty or than love,
Seen in the weed, the shell, the grass,
But never in my kind, alas!

The ragged weed is truth to me,
The poor grass honour, and the shell
Eternal justice, till I see
The spirit rive the roof of hell
With light enough to let me read
More than the grass, the shell, the weed.

RUTH PITTER

Desires

*Watch with care, for everything passes quickly, even though
your desire make the certain doubtful and the short time long.
Behold the more you struggle the more you show the love you
have for your God and the more you will rejoice in your
Beloved with a joy and delight that cannot end.*

ST. TERESA OF ÁVILA

Dear God,

I am writing this letter because I often find it difficult to
communicate with You in other, more traditional ways.
You do not spring easily out of the pages of my
prayerbook, nor do You float ethereally among the
arched ceilings of my Temple. When I call Your name, I
hear no voice responding to my own.

Would our relationship be different if I knew You
on a daily basis? As it is, I seem to think of You only
in times of crisis or joy. Would I feel closer to You if
I turned to You at times other than when I am afraid
and pleading for Your help? I do praise You in my head
in rare moments of euphoria when I am especially
touched by the miracle of the world You have created.
Yet, this is not enough. I know there can be much more
between us.

At times I have felt a great intimacy with You. It is
clear, warm and all encompassing. But this sensation
dissipates like a dream that fades the longer I am awake.
I try to recapture that feeling but only a memory remains
and it too grows dim.

I am seeking renewal. Fill my soul with the breath of
Your magnificence. Surround me with Your goodness and
love. Rejuvenate me so that I may have the strength to

reach out to others and revitalize them. This is my
prayer, now and forevermore.

Sincerely yours,

RANDEE ROSENBERG FRIEDMAN

Grandmother of Our Ancestors,
in ancient times You lighted the paths of the matriarchs
and shone forth in their hearts and actions.
Nevertheless, there came a day when You turned your
   face from women
although they were created in the beauty of your image,
You allowed the intelligent and powerful to be pushed
   aside, their Wisdom overturned:
everything they had learned of You was reversed and
   repudiated.
The new religion was enforced at the point of death;
your chosen people ravaged in the lands and bodies and
hearts of the matriarchs and their daughters.

Yet when the hour was right, You sent us Jesus,
bronzed by the sun, his body wiry and nimble as a sheep;
impudent but able to charm, full of goodwill but single-
   minded in purpose.
Born of a woman, He knew the pain of poverty and
   oppression.
Your beloved Child sought out the marginalized and
   exploited ones.
He straightened the back of the bent-over woman,
and revived the daughter of Jairus.
He restored health to the woman with a hemorrhage
and brought sanity to the bruised psyche of Mary
   Magdalene.

Women followed Jesus in droves and became his
   disciples.
Your Spirit of Wisdom once more flowed through
their bodies and minds.
They preached and baptized;
they presided over the Eucharist and gave leadership in
   the early church.

Why then, did You permit their memory to be obscured?
The stories of their work to be lost?
The records of their teachings destroyed?
The apostolic succession of their gentle touch forgotten
   and left behind?
How could You allow your Church to become a fiefdom
   of men
who exerted power over others,
a club "for males only" in which women were seen as
   inferior and lacking?
In the power struggles of the early church, why did
You permit the names of Peter and Paul to dominate our
   tradition,
their gifts and their weaknesses giving masculine
shape to our community?
How we long for a woman's view!
How we mourn the loss of her ministrations!

Open the door to the women of our tradition!
Bring back the stories that have been lost to us!
Give us once more our connection to our beginnings;
allow us to feel the touch of the hand of Mary
   Magdalene, Apostle of the Apostles.

Give her her rightful place in our tradition, beside Sarah
   and Miriam, Esther and Ruth.
Restore Martha and Mary of Bethany, Joanna and Mary
   the mother of Jesus.

Return to us Priscilla, Lydia, Phoebe and the other
    women missionaries and leaders of house churches.

Open wide the hearts of your people, Mother of
    Creation!
For You are the Tree of the Knowledge of Good and Evil,
Wisdom emerging from the ancient past to flow in our
    present,
carrying us into your future to live with You in love
    forever.

MARY KATHLEEN SPEEGLE SCHMITT

Wwakwan, Great Grandmother
You who are the Void,
the first inhale,
The Sacred Emptiness
be with me.
Help me to simply be with what is
to feel the infinite spaciousness within me
to expand my capacity to hold in my heart
all of the world
all parts of myself
those I find acceptable
and those I want to change.
Hear the voice of this little one,
your great granddaughter,
you who are the Great Silence,
teach me to know of your living presence,
to find the strength of the dark womb
that can hold it all;
the grief and the sorrow
the joy and the celebration,
that I might truly learn to be with
myself

and the world.
Aho!

ORIAH MOUNTAIN DREAMER

Richly-throned goddess, O deathless Aphrodite,
Daughter of Zeus, subtle and sacred one,
Bear not my spirit down with too much suffering,
But rather come to me as sometimes you have come,
When my far prayer has reached your divine Presence,
And you have left for me your father's golden house,
Drawn in your chariot shimmering like the dawn;

Your fair fleet sparrows to herald you, whose wings,
Luminous still with the glory of heaven, have flashed
Radiance over earth. Then you have asked me,
How fared my eager heart and all its strong hopes:
"What would you do with love or have love do with you?
Sappho, who treats you cruelly? She who avoids you
Soon with desire shall burn, your gifts requiting
Many times, yours to be whether she will or not."
Goddess, come once again, free me from longing,
Crown me with victory. O be my own ally.

SAPPHO

I saw the swelling clouds
and Shyam,
my eyes began to rain.

Dark and yellow,
hugely massed,

they spilled, they poured
four hours.

Water lies
on every side. Green
the thirsty earth.

      Him,
he's far from home.
I stand in the dripping door.

      True one, far
one. Make true your word
and come.

MEERA

The Buddha's Law, supreme, profound, subtle and
   wonderful,
A rare encounter after tens of millions of aeons.
I see and hear, and now receive the teachings:
Desiring to understand
the Thus-Come One's true meaning.

EMPRESS WU

REVELATIONS

To receive inspiration, or divine disclosure, requires
an openness, a ready receptivity, an emptiness, a giving away of expectations. British poet, Elizabeth Barrett
Browning wrote of the revelation of being kissed through
the dark; Muslim Anne Marie Schimmel saw "the sun
at midnight." African American preacher Rebecca Cox
Jackson came to know the Mother of the New Creation
of God.

They say that God lives very high;
But if you look above the pines
You cannot see our God; and why?

And if you dig down in the mines
You never see Him in the gold;
Though from Him all that's glory shines.

God is so good, He wears a fold
Of heaven and earth across his face—
Like secrets kept, for love, untold.

But still I feel that his embrace
Slides down by thrills, through all things made,
Through sight and sound of every place:

As if my tender mother laid
On my shut lips her kisses' pressure
Half-waking me at night, and said
"Who kissed you through the dark, dear guesser?"

ELIZABETH BARRETT BROWNING

The soul that wanders, Spirit led,
becomes, in His transforming shade,
the secret that she was, in God,
before the world was made.

JESSICA POWERS (This Trackless Solitude)

"See, I tried everything, went everywhere,
But never found a friend as dear as you;
I drank from all the fountains, tried the grapes,
But never tasted wine as sweet as you."

I studied a hundred learned manuscripts:
In every letter I saw only you.
I washed away the letters with my tears:
A mirror was the shining page for you.

I heard your voice in every rustling breeze;
The snow, the grass were lovely veils for you;
I dived into the ocean without shore:
The lustrous pearls reflected only you.

Then came the storm.
The garden of my heart
Was shiv'ring in the cold, all leaves were shed.
There was the desert.
And the barren cloud.
And silence. And
    the sun at midnight—you.

ANNE MARIE SCHIMMEL

Good Lord, I see You, Who are Truth itself.

JULIAN OF NORWICH

". . . and let the questing mind be still. . . ."
In the ground of your being I have my home,
so do not seek me in the world apart.

Within your spirit true communion lies.
You are no homeless stranger in a land afar,
no alien on a foreign shore,
for I am with you.
Do but be still and know that I am God.
I look upon the world with your dark eyes;
I feel the flowing air on your cool cheek.
I hear the twittering in the moving trees,
for with your senses I perceive.
I am with you, I am within you.
So do not turn away but come to rest in me.
Within you is our meeting place.
Be but still, and I will speak in silence
to your loving, wayward heart.

PAULA FAIRLIE

Oh, how I love you, my Mother! I did not know that I
had a Mother. She was with me, though I knew it not,
but now I know Her and She said I should do a work in
this city, which is to make known the Mother of the New
Creation of God. Because you are the Mother of all the
children of Eve that ever can be saved, as Christ is the
Father of all the regenerated children of Adam. And
none can come to God in the new birth but through
Christ the Father, and through Christ the Mother. . . .
And I then understood the Mother I saw in the Deity, in
1834 or 1835, when the ministers shut their church
doors against me and gave orders to their members not
to suffer me to come in their doors, if they did they
should be turned out of church, and the drunken man
opened his house and said, "I don't belong to church. Let
the woman come and hold her meeting in my house."
And then it was that I had the first light on a Mother in

the Deity. And then I could also see how often I had
been led, comforted, and counseled in time of trial by a
tender Mother and knew it not.

REBECCA COX JACKSON

Mother God
Spirit of Life and Laughter
I hardly know you
And yet
Deep down
We have always been friends.
Your wind
Your sun
Your earth
Teeming with life
Have long been
Woven
As part of my prayer
Knowing they are all connected yet
Splitting into a thousand parts
And returning to you
The One.

I am a part
Of your pulsating rhythm.
When I close my eyes
And let your wind
Whip through me
I know I am
Born of You
And to You
I Shall return.

HELEN BATTLER

FRIENDSHIP

The needs of our souls are for divine company. Without divine company we can do nothing. The friendship and companionship of the Divine in our lives is the most familiar relationship when we find it. It is the feeling of coming home, and the *knowing* of that place in our deepest selves. St. Elizabeth Seton wrote that God is "more within us, than we are in ourselves." Catherine de Hueck Doherty, a Russian emigrant to North America who founded many homes for the poor, wrote, "By myself I can do nothing," and addressing Christ carrying the cross she prayed, "I have nothing to guide me but the imprints of your feet."

The prayers of daily partnership in this section are of the morning, day, and evening. The young Dutch woman Etty Hillesum, who died at Auschwitz, wrote of her daily prayer as "an uninterrupted dialogue with You." And through this conversation, this sustaining prayer, is developed the love that is unsurpassed. It is only through divine friendship that we find "all that we need" (The Mother).

Knowledge

Try to be wise enough to know that you do not know. Then the Divine can lead you forward into true knowledge, calmly, stage by stage.

MOTHER MEERA

Almighty God, I have found that to know you only as a philosopher; to have the most sublime and curious speculations concerning your essence, your attributes, your providence; to be able to demonstrate your being from all or any of the works of nature and to discourse with the greatest elegancy and propriety of words on your existence or operations, will avail me nothing, unless at the same time I know you experientially: unless my heart perceive and know you to be its supreme good, its only happiness; unless my soul feel and acknowledge that she can find no repose, no peace, no joy, but in loving and being beloved by you; and does accordingly rest in you as the center of her being, the fountain of her pleasure, the origin of all virtue and goodness, her light, her life, her strength, her all; everything she wants or wishes in this world and forever.

Thus let me ever know you, O God! I neither despise nor neglect the light of reason, nor that knowledge of you that may be collected from this goodly system of created things, but this speculative knowledge is not the knowledge that I want and wish for above all other. Teach me your way, O Lord!

SUSANNA WESLEY

Lord, you are my lover,
If you find it acceptable that I call you my lover,
If you don't seek to find in me the ideal woman which I
    am not,
If you don't demand everything while I give you so little,
If you see me as I am and not as you would like me to be,
If I make you happy despite my absences, my silences, my
    disappearing acts . . .
If you are never discouraged as you wait for me or seek
    me out,
If you love me enough to forgive me all my wrongdoings,
If you do not judge me on a solitary act of mine, but
    rather on my effort
which I am trying to make to become a little like you. . . .

If this is the case, I can tell you that your friendship
    makes me very happy.
I am more apt to be peaceful as I leave you,
reconciled with myself,
not nervous or lost
like I was before I encountered you.

But I don't dare believe that you will act toward me in
    exactly
this manner, and I am afraid that you may give up on me
and abandon me in my despair.

And yet if I can truly believe that this will happen,
I say it to you again, Lord, I would be utterly delighted by it
like a small child who is given a ride on his father's big
    shoulders,
and like a woman who dares to sit fearlessly next to her
    husband
and confides in him her most secret thoughts and
    feelings.
Tell me, Lord, can I truly believe
that the person you love is the real me?

> Anonymous woman (from Berthier,
> Puyo, and Trébossen's *Prayers for
> Everyday Life*)

And God said to the soul:
I desired you before the world began.
I desire you now
As you desire me.
And where the desires of two come together
There love is perfected.

> Mechthild of Magdeburg

67

Soul Company

Before God, I am ashamed that He sees me engaged
in ought besides Him.

LOBABAH MOTA'ABEDAH

For hunger,
    there is the town's rice in the begging bowl.
For thirst,
    there are tanks, streams, wells.
For sleep,
    there are the ruins of temples.
For soul's company
    I have you, O lord
white as jasmine.

MAHĀDĒVIYAKKA

I desire from You nothing else, O God, than that You
account me among the company of those who strive
forward unto You, that You exalt me to the degree of the
righteous near to You and let me join Your charitable
servants. Of all who pity, You are the most merciful. Of
all who love, You are the most loving, the Greatest of the
great, O Generous!

AJRADAH 'AMIYAH

O my joy, my longing,
O my sanctuary, my companion,
O provision of my way,

O my ultimate aim!
You are my spirit;
You are my hope;
You are my friend,
My yearning, my welfare.
Without You, O my life and love,
Never across these endless countries
Would I have wandered.
How much grace, how many gifts,
Favors and bounty have You shown me.
Your love I seek; in it I am blessed,
O radiant eye of my yearning heart!
You are my heart's captain!
As long as I live, never from You
Shall I be free. Be satisfied with me,
O my heart's desire, and I am fortunate, blessed.

RĀBE'AH OF BASRA

O You who vow good pleasure to Your friends,
Besides You I desire no one.

ḤAYYUNA

You are the life of my life,
O Krishna, the heart of my heart.
There is none in all the three worlds
Whom I call my own but you.

You are the peace of my mind;
You are the joy of my heart;
You are my beauty and my wealth.

You are my wisdom and my strength;
I call you my home, my friend, my kin.

My present and future are in your hands;
My scriptures and commands come from you.
Supreme teacher, fountain of wisdom,
You are the path and the goal,
Tender mother and stern father too.

You are the creator and protector,
And the pilot who takes me across
The stormy ocean of life.

MEERA

In the dark winter of affliction's hour
When summer friends and pleasures haste away,
And the wrecked heart perceives how frail each power,
It made a refuge and believed a stay;
When man all wild and weak is seen to be—
    There's none like thee, O Lord!, there's none like thee!

When the world's sorrows—working only death,
And the world's comfort—caustic to the wound,
Make the wrong spirit loathe life's daily breath,
As jarring music from a harp untuned;
While yet it dare not from the discord flee
    There's none like thee, O Lord!, there's none like thee!

When the tossed mind surveys its hidden world,
And feels in every faculty a foe,
United but in strife; waves urged and hurled
By passion and by conscience, winds of woe,
Till the whole being is a storm-swept sea—
    There's none like thee, O Lord! there's none like thee!

Thou, in adversity, can be a sun;
Thou has a healing balm, a sheltering tower,
The peace, the truth, the life, the love of One,
Nor wound, nor grief, nor storm, can overpower
Gifts of a king; gifts, infrequent and yet free—
     There's none like thee, O Lord!, there's none like thee!

                                        MARIA JANE JEWSBURY

No coward soul is mine
No trembler in the world's storm-troubled sphere
I see Heaven's glories shine
And Faith shines equal arming me from Fear

O God within my breast
Almighty ever-present Deity
Life, that in me hast rest
as I Undying Life, have power in Thee

Vain are the thousand creeds
That move men's hearts, unutterably vain,
Worthless as withered weeds
Or idlest froth amid the boundless main

To waken doubt in one
Holding so fast by thy infinity
So surely anchored on
The steadfast rock of Immortality

With wide-embracing love
Thy spirit animates eternal years
Pervades and broods above,
Changes, sustains, dissolves, creates and rears

Though Earth and moon were gone
And suns and universes ceased to be
And thou wert left alone
Every Existence would exist in thee

There is not room for Death
Nor atom that his might could render void
Since thou art Being and Breath
And what thou art may never be destroyed.

EMILY BRONTË

In Daily Partnership

*Every day is a god, each day is a god, and holiness holds forth
in time. I worship each god, I praise each day splintered
down, splintered down and wrapped in time like a husk, a
husk of many colors spreading, at dawn fast over the
mountains split.*

ANNIE DILLARD

Lord, you are the water of life.
As this day begins, I am an empty pitcher before you.
Fill me, O Lord.

You are the light of the world.
As this day begins, I am an unlit candle.
Your light can never shine through me to others unless
You shine in my heart.
You are the true light that lights every man
That comes into the world.
Light me, O Lord.

You are the true vine.
Unless I dwell in you this day,
I can bring forth no fruit.
My leaves turn brown, shrivel, blow away and I die.
Let your life always flow into me, your branch, O Lord.

ELAINE SOMMERS RICH

Loving Father, all this day
Bless me in my work and play:
Bless the good I mean to do,
Help me do it, Lord, for you.
Bless the people I shall meet,
Give me loving hands and feet,
Quick to help them, quick to do
All I can for love of you.

MARGARET KITSON

Divine Mother, who has created all manifestation out of
Yourself at the inspiration of the Father, awaken me to
Your presence at my table. There I take Your body into
my own. You are the food; it is made of Your divine
substance as I am myself. In my mouth two Divinities
meet, the Realized God and the unrealized God. Help me
to be conscious of this sacrament and not neglect You
with racing thoughts or empty speech or by reading,
working, worrying while I partake of Your grace. In our
union I offer the enjoyment of the food to You and
receive it back with increase. Preserve me from crowded
restaurants where still You hide deep within the noise
and make Yourself known in the silence of the listening
soul. If in crowds I must fight to reach You, let me
remember that You are reaching for me too and for all

who press around, unrealized Gods like myself, hungering for completion.

PATRICIA JOUDRY

Night is behind us, day again has arrived. O, how I long to know whether this night has been worthy in Your eyes, so that I may be felicitous and applaud myself, or whether You have rejected my devotion, so that I may console myself.

By Your Magnificence I swear, such is always my way of worship. I beg You inform me as long as I live, of my worthiness or Your disapprobation. If you cast me out, I swear I shall not leave Your doorstep, as nothing but Your grace and bounty can be contained in my heart.

ḤABIBA 'ADAWIYAH

You have made me so rich, oh God, please let me share out Your beauty with open hands. My life has become an uninterrupted dialogue with You, oh God, one great dialogue. Sometimes when I stand in some corner of the camp, my feet planted on Your earth, my eyes raised towards Your Heaven, tears sometimes run down my face, tears of deep emotion and gratitude. At night, too, when I lie in my bed and rest in You, oh God, tears of gratitude run down my face, and that is my prayer. I have been terribly tired for several days, but that, too, will pass; things come and go in a deeper rhythm and people must be taught to listen to it, it is the most important thing we have to learn in this life. I am not challenging You, oh God, my life is one great dialogue with You. I may never become the great artist I would really like to be, but I am already secure in You, God. Sometimes I try my hand at turning out small profundities and uncertain short stories, but I always end up with just one single word: God. And that says everything and there is no need for anything more. And all my creative powers are translated into inner dialogues with You; the beat of my heart has grown deeper, more active and yet more peaceful, and it is as if I were all the time storing up inner riches.

ETTY HILLESUM

O my God!
Imprint it on my soul with the strength of the Holy Spirit that by His grace, supported and defended, I may never more forget you are my All.

ST. ELIZABETH SETON

Through Love

O immeasurably tender love! Who would not be set afire with such love? What heart could keep from breaking? You, deep well of charity, it seems you are so madly in love with your creatures that you could not live without us! Yet you are our God, and have no need of us. Your greatness is no greater for our well-being, nor are you harmed by any harm that comes to us, for you are supreme eternal Goodness. What could move you to such mercy? Neither duty nor any need you have of us (we are sinful and wicked debtors!)—but only love!

ST. CATHERINE OF SIENA

I love you, God, with a penny match of love
that I strike when the big and bullying dark of need
chases my startled sunset over the hills
and in the walls of my house small terrors move.
It is the sight of this paltry love that fills
my deepest pits with seething purgatory,
and thus I love you, God—*God*—who would sow
my heights and depths with recklessness of glory,
who hold back light-oceans straining to spill on me, on *me*,
stifling here in the dungeon of my ill.
This puny spark I scorn, I who had dreamed
of fire that would race to land's end, shouting your
   worth,
of sun that would fall to earth with a mortal wound
and rise and run, streaming with light like blood,
splattering the sky,
soaking the ocean itself, and all the earth.

JESSICA POWERS (*This Paltry Love*)

O Lord,
Love me intensely,
Love me often and long!
For the more often you love me, the purer I become.
The more intensely you love me, the more beautiful I
   become.
The longer you love me, the holier I become.

MECHTHILD OF MAGDEBURG

O infinite goodness of my God! It is thus that I seem to
see both myself and You. O Joy of the angels, how I long,
when I think of this, to be wholly consumed in love for

You! How true it is that You bear with those who cannot bear You to be with them! Oh, how good a Friend you are, my Lord! How you comfort us and suffer us and wait until our nature becomes more like yours and meanwhile you bear with it as it is! You remember the times when we love you, my Lord, and when for a moment we repent, you forget how we have offended You. I have seen this clearly in my own life, and I cannot conceive, my Creator, why the whole world does not strive to draw near to you in this intimate friendship. Those of us who are wicked, and whose nature is not like Yours, ought to draw near to you so that You may make them good. They should allow you to be with them for at least two hours each day, even though they may not be with You, but are perplexed, as I was, with a thousand worldly cares and thoughts. In exchange for the effort which it costs them to desire to be in such good company (for You know, Lord, that at first this is as much as they can do and sometimes they can do no more at all), You prevent the devils from assaulting them so that each day they are able to do them less harm, and You give them strength to conquer. Yes, Life of all lives, You slay none of those that put their trust in you and desire you for their Friend; rather you sustain their bodily life with greater health and give life to their souls.

ST. TERESA OF ÁVILA

O Holy Spirit, O eternal God, O Christ, O Love,
come into my heart;
By your power draw it to you, my God, and give me
 charity with fear.
Protect me, O ineffable Love, from every evil thought;
 inflame me and permeate me with your exquisite love,

so that every pain may become a ray of light! My Holy Father and my sweet Lord, help me now in all of my ministries. Christ, Love, Amen!

ST. CATHERINE OF SIENA

2

WORSHIP, PRAISE, AND THANKSGIVING

*I*n beginning a practice of formal prayer, it is accepted and taught in the devotional traditions that our opening prayers are ones of honoring the Divine, giving praise and thanks for the gifts in our world and in our lives.

This practice enables us to learn about the sacredness of things in our every day, to give reverence to what we might otherwise have taken for granted. Also, we learn how to give thanks for life's trials, for the gifts that hide behind torment and turmoil.

The practice of giving praise teaches us the virtue of humility we need to employ to be in partnership with God. It also enables us to deepen our faith in learning the ways of the Divine.

Many women worship what has been revealed, and what they understand from their own religions. So Jessica Powers gives praise for beauty, Machig Lapdron gives homage to the Buddha as "bright as gold," and Christ is known as "the Lamb of God" and also as the "holy, living stream." Angela of Foligno advised her followers that in true worship we deepen our faith by bowing before the mystery of God's ways, by honoring "what you do not understand."

Julian of Norwich suggested that "we ought to rejoice greatly that God dwells in our soul, and much more greatly that our soul dwells in God." And through rejoicing in and giving praise to this spiritual partnership—in whatever form it takes—bestows on us "the blessed impulse of grace" (St. Elizabeth Seton). And grace enables us to participate in the divine life.

The French Carmelite nun Elizabeth of the Trinity wrote of "a praise of glory" as being a prayer. She explained it in four parts: 1) that we praise for all gifts even if we receive nothing; 2) that we praise in silence "like a lyre under the mysterious touch of the Holy Spirit," so we can hear the "divine harmonies" even in our sufferings; 3) that we praise as a soul who "gazes on God in faith and simplicity"; and 4) that we praise "always giving thanks" so that a soul in "each of her acts, her movements, her thoughts, her aspirations" is rooted more deeply in the eternal love. It is in glimpsing the divine love that German mystic St. Gertrude of Helfta echoes what many women discover: that she is unable to form "a single word that could, even distantly, come close to express adequately such extraordinary excellence."

The prayers here include feminine variations on the words of the "Our Father" (the Lord's Prayer), as well as a homage to Sophia, written in the eleventh century by Hildegard of Bingen, and one to Shekhinah, the kabalistic concept of the female aspect of God, by E. M. Broner. Jesus' mother, Mary, is hailed as—among other metaphors—"O greenest branch" (Hildegard), "bearer of the fire," "seedbed of the fruit," and "peaceful sea" (St. Catherine of Siena). There are prayers of gratitude for food and for protection, and a prayer of thanks from an orphaned aboriginal woman in Australia, Connie Nungulla McDonald, on reconciling with her natural father.

WORSHIP

When I think of the love of God, I become aware of my own emptiness of heart; when I think of the goodness of God, I recall my innumerable needs; when I think of the mercy of God, I remember my own failures; but when I think of the beauty of God, I cease to exist at all, I become a living adoration.

JESSICA POWERS

God be glorified!

O my Lord,
if I worship you from fear of hell, burn me in hell.

If I worship you
from hope of Paradise, bar me from its gates.

But if I worship you
for yourself alone, grant me then the beauty of your Face.

RĀBE'AH OF BASRA

My period had come for Prayer—
No other Art—would do—
My Tactics missed a rudiment—
Creator—Was it you?

🏵 81

God grows above—so those who pray
Horizons—must ascend—
And so I stepped upon the North
To see this Curious Friend—

His House was not—no sign had He—
By Chimney—nor by Door
Could I infer his Residence—
Vast Prairies of Air

Unbroken by a Settler—
Were all that I could see—
Infinitude—Had'st Thou no Face
That I might look on Thee?

The Silence condescended—
Creation stopped—for Me—
But awed beyond my errand—
I worshipped—did not "pray"—

EMILY DICKINSON

Lord, you are great and glorious,
wonderful in strength, invincible.
Let all your creatures serve you,
for you spoke, and they were made.
You sent forth your spirit, and it formed them;
there is none that can resist your voice.
For the mountains shall be shaken to their foundations
    with the waters;
before your glance the rocks shall melt like wax.
But to those who fear you you show mercy.
For every sacrifice as a fragrant offering is a small thing,

and the fat of all whole burnt offerings to you is a very
   little thing;
but whoever fears the Lord is great forever.

JUDITH 16: 13–16

O God, our Father and our Mother
The God who is and was and will be
before and beyond our little lives.
Who made all that is.
And who is known to us in our own hearts
And in the lives of others.

We come once more to trace the pattern
of death and resurrection
that is written throughout our world.

With the saints and ancestors
we behold that mystery
and beholding it adore you.

ST. HILDA COMMUNITY

The body of the Buddha is as bright as gold.
The leader, all knowing, I bow to you.
Manjushri, you are youthful with all the signs of
   accomplishment.
I bow to you.
Vajrapani, you who destroy great and powerful demons,
I bow to you.

MACHIG LAPDRON

Homage to you Buddha,
best of all creatures,
who set me and many others
free from pain.

All pain is understood,
the cause, the craving is dried up,
the Noble Eightfold Way unfolds,
I have reached the state where everything stops.

I have been
mother, son, father, brother, grandmother;
knowing nothing of the truth
I journeyed on.

But I have seen the Blessed One;
this is my last body,
and I will not go
from birth to birth
again.

Look at the disciples all together,
their energy,
their sincere effort.
This is homage to the buddhas.

Maya gave birth to Gautama
for the sake of us all.
She has driven back the pain
of the sick and the dying.

MAHAPAJAPATI GOTAM

Mixture of joy and sorrow
I daily do pass through;
Sometimes I'm in the valley,
Then sinking down with woe.

> *Chorus*—Holy, holy, holy is the Lamb
> Holy is the Lamb of God,
> Whose blood doth make me clean.

Sometimes I am exalted,
On eagle's wings I fly;
Rising above Mount Pisgah,
I almost reach the sky.—*Chorus.*

Sometimes I am in doubting,
And think I have no grace;
Sometimes I am a-shouting,
And camp-meeting is the place.—*Chorus.*

Sometimes, when I am praying,
It almost seems a task;
Sometimes I get a blessing
Wherever I do look.—*Chorus.*

Oh, why am I thus tossed—
Thus tossed to and fro?
Because the blood of Jesus
Hasn't washed me white as snow.—*Chorus.*

Oh, come to Jesus now, and drink
Of that holy, living stream;
Your thirst he'll quench, your soul revive,
And cleanse you from all sin.—*Chorus.*

JULIA A. J. FOOTE

GIVING GENERAL PRAISE

My heart is bubbling over with joy;
with God it is good to be woman.

PHOEBE WILLETTS

Keep my moments and my days;
Let them flow in ceaseless praise.

FRANCES RIDLEY HAVERGAL

O, let our souls praise You and our all be devoted to Your
service; then at the last we shall praise you "day without
night" rejoicing in Your eternal courts. By the light of
Your celestial glories all our darkness, pains and sorrows
will be forever dispersed. These clouds and griefs which
now oppress and weigh down the souls of Your poor
erring creatures will be gone and remembered no more.
These storms which now obstruct our path, these shades
which obscure the light of Your heavenly truth—all shall
be done away and give place to Your cheering presence,
to the eternal unchanging joys which You have in store
for the souls of Your faithful servants.

ST. ELIZABETH SETON

Lord! You who remains the God of my life, above all
things, in this our sorrow and perplexity cast us not out
of your presence, and take not your Holy Spirit from us;
keep us from evil and from the appearance of it; that
through the help of Your Spirit our conduct may be kept

upright, circumspect and clean in Your sight, and
amongst men! that in all things, at all times, and under
all circumstances, we may show forth Your praise.

ELIZABETH FRY

Praise God, from whom all blessings flow.

ZILPHA ELAW

Like a magnificent boulder left by a glacier,
You are ours to lean upon, O Eternal One of Israel.
May You ever stand firm to help us renew our own
    strength.
In Your infinite power and holiness,
You guide us in restoring the world to wholeness.
For this redemptive work, we praise You.

DENA A. FEINGOLD

Praised are You, Holy One, who sculpts the moon and
    sprinkles
the stars above, who shapes the world, and life, and time.
Who plants wonder in the world each day.
Who wipes our brow when we are weary, and
gives us drink when we are dry.
Who lights our soul with dance and hope.
Who blows upon the flame within us.
And delights in our glow.

VICKI HOLLANDER

O my Mother God, my God and Mother.

JESSICA POWERS

Our Mother, who art within us,
we celebrate your many names.
Your wisdom come.
Your will be done, unfolding from the depths within us.
Each day you give us all that we need.
You remind us of our limits and we let go.
You support us in our power and we act with courage.
For thou art the dwelling place within us,
the empowerment around us,
and the celebration among us.
Now and forever more.

PATRICIA LYNN REILLY

Our Mother,
who creates and sustains us,
Wisdom is your name.
Your blessings come
Your will be done on earth, as it is in heaven.
Give us this day our sense of One,
And forgive those of us who trespass against You,
And lead us to honor your gifts of the Earth,
And bestow on us your protection and peace.

LUCINDA VARDEY

Sophia!
you of the whirling wings,

circling encompassing
energy of God:

you quicken the world in your clasp.
One wing soars in heaven
one wing sweeps the earth
and the third flies all around us.

Praise to Sophia!
Let all the earth praise her!

HILDEGARD OF BINGEN

Shekhinah,
we sing a new song unto Thee
with soaring melody,
in Miriam's memory,
we sing a new song unto Thee.

Hallel for the Deity,
Hallel for the singer,
with honey on the tongue,
with gift of song,
and beads of words,
we ornament the air for Thee,
we sing a new song unto Thee.

E. M. BRONER

GIVING PERSONAL PRAISE

Listen, and tell your grief: But God is singing!
God sings through all creation with His will.
Save the negation of sin, all is His music,
even the notes that set their roots in ill
to flower in pity, pardon or sweet humbling.
Evil finds harshness of the rack and rod
in tunes where good finds tenderness and glory.

The saints who loved have died of this pure music,
and no one enters heaven till he learns,
deep in his soul at least, to sing with God.

JESSICA POWERS (*The Will of God*)

O eternal solstice, secure abode, place of total delight,
paradise of perennial pleasures, flooded over the rivers of
inestimable voluptuousness! One is attracted by the
spring-like greening of a manifold beauty, charmed by a
sweet sound, all the sweeter by melodies of the
musicians; one is refreshed by the fragrance of vital
spices, inebriated by the free flowing sweetness of inner
savour, and changed by the miraculous tenderness of
secret embraces! O three times happy, four times blessed,
and—if one may say so—a hundred times saintly are
those who let themselves be moved by the guidance of
your grace and deign to approach with innocent hands,
pure hearts, and clean lips. O what sight, what sound,
what fragrance, what taste, what feeling! But how little
of this can my embarrassed tongue stammer! Although—
favoured by divine grace in spite of my faults and
negligence—I was able to enter there, [but] I am as if
surrounded by a thick shell and probably cannot
understand anything. For even if all the capabilities of

angels and human beings were united in one worthy science, it still would not suffice to form a single word that could, even distantly, come close to express adequately such extraordinary excellence.

ST. GERTRUDE THE GREAT

May you be blessed, Lord, who have made me so unable and unprofitable! But I praise You very much because You awaken so many to awaken us. Our prayer for those who give us light should be unceasing. In the midst of tempests as fierce as those the Church now endures, what would we be without them? If some have gone bad, the good ones shine more brilliantly. May it please the Lord to keep them in His hands and help them so that they might help us.

ST. TERESA OF ÁVILA

Praise to God for making me,
Praise to God for giving me
    Hands to use and feet to run.
Thank you, God, for making me,
Thank you, God, for giving me
    Eyes to see and ears to hear.
Praise to God for making me,
Praise to God for giving me
    Mouth to speak and voice to sing
    My praise and thanks for everything.

MARGARET KITSON

I praise You, O God, for illuminating my mind and for enabling me to prove demonstratively that Your wisdom is as infinite as Your power. Help me to use these discoveries to praise and love and obey, and may I be exceedingly careful that my affections keep pace with my knowledge. Show me that if I study the divine perfections as matter of mere speculation, my acquests of knowledge will but enhance my guilt. Help me to know, that I may adore and love. As I am now more rationally persuaded that You are infinitely wise, so may I learn by this knowledge to practice a more hearty and universal subjection to You: more cheerfully to bow before the order of Your providence: to submit my reason so far to my faith as not to doubt or hesitate at those points of faith that are mysterious to me through the weakness of my understanding. May I adore the mystery I cannot comprehend. Help me not to be too curious in prying into those secret things that are known only to You, O God, nor too rash in censuring what I do not understand. May I not perplex myself about those methods of providence that seem to me involved and intricate, but resolve them into Your infinite wisdom, who knows the spirits of all flesh and best understands how to govern those souls You have created. We are of yesterday and know nothing. But Your boundless mind comprehends, at one view, all things, past, present, and future, and as You see all things, You best understand what is good and proper for each individual and for me, with relation to both worlds. So deal with me, O my God.

SUSANNA WESLEY

Hail, O greenest branch,
who in the blowing gust
of the saints' quest have come forth.

When the time came
that you were in bloom along your boughs,
hail, hail to you!
for the sun's heat sweated in you
like the fragrance of balsam.

For a fair flower was flowering in you,
which gave its scent
to all the herbs
that were dry.

And these then all appeared,
full in greenness.

Then the heavens sent down dew over the grass,
and the whole earth was made happy,
for its womb brought forth grain,
and the birds of heaven
set their nests in it.

So food was made for men and women,
and great was the joy of those who ate.
From this time forth, O sweet virgin,
no joy is lacking in you.

All these things Eve scorned.

But now praise be to the highest.

HILDEGARD OF BINGEN

O Mary!
Mary!
Temple of the Trinity!
O Mary, bearer of the fire!

Mary, minister of mercy!
Mary, seedbed of the fruit!
Mary, redemptress of the human race.

ST. CATHERINE OF SIENA

GIVING THANKS

*There is no better way to show one's gratefulness to the
Divine than to be quietly happy.*

THE MOTHER

O Lord, fill us, we beseech You, with adoring gratitude to
You for all You are for us, to us, and in us; fill us with
love, joy, peace, and all the fruits of the Spirit.

CHRISTINA ROSSETTI

We were enclosed,
O eternal Father,
within the garden of your bosom.
You drew us out of your holy mind
like a flower
petalled with our soul's three powers, . . .
You gave us memory
so that we might be able to hold your blessings
and so bring forth the flower of glory to your name
and the fruit of profit to ourselves.
You gave us understanding
to understand your truth
and your will—

your will that wants only that we be made holy—
so that we might bear first the flower of glory
and then the fruit of virtue.
And you gave us your will
so that we might be able to love
what our understanding has seen
and what our memory has held.

For this, we praise and thank you.

ST. CATHERINE OF SIENA

We are thankful that we are all imperfectly perfect—that
we can learn and improve—but are perfect as we are. We
are thankful—because we know we didn't do it by
ourselves.

TEMPLE ISRAEL SISTERHOOD

Lord, you have said, I am the Way—not that we shall
   never be confused.
You have said, I am the Truth—not that we shall have all
   the answers.
And, I am the Life—not that we shall never die.
Teach me to know you here on earth—
      in its tangled maze of pathways, to know you as the
      Way; in its unanswerable mysteries,
to know you as the Truth; in the face of suffering and
   death, to know you as the Life.
Thank you, Lord, for not offering us a method, saying,
      This is the Way.
Thank you for not granting us a set of invariable
   propositions, saying,
      This is the Truth.

Thank you for not delivering us from being human,
   saying,
     This is the Life.
Thank you, Lord, for saying instead, *I am*, and for thus
   giving us yourself.

ELISABETH ELLIOT

O most holy Will of God, I give You infinite thanks for
the mercy with which You have surrounded me; with all
my strength and love, I adore You from the depths of my
soul and unite my will to Yours now and forever,
especially in all that I shall do and all that You will be
pleased to send me this day, consecrating to Your glory
my soul, my mind, my body, all my thoughts, words and
actions, my whole being, I beg You, with all the humility
of my heart, accomplish in me Your eternal designs, and
do not allow me to present any obstacle to this. Your
eyes, which can see the most intimate recesses of my
heart, know the intensity of my desire to live out Your
holy will, but they can see my weakness and limitations.
That is why, prostrate before Your infinite mercy, I
implore You, my Savior, through the gentleness and
justice of this same will of Yours, to grant me the grace of
accomplishing it perfectly, so that, consumed in the fire
of Your love, I may be an acceptable holocaust which,
with the glorious Virgin and all the saints, will praise and
bless You forever.

ST. JANE FRANCES DE CHANTAL

For Food

We give You thanks, O Lord, for these Your gifts, and for all our tribulations from Your bounty, through Christ our Lord.

DOROTHY DAY

God, we are grateful for this food to nourish our bodies.
May we who enjoy an abundant share never forget those
  who are hungry,
That while we enjoy homes that are warm and secure,
many lie down without shelter against the cold night.
As we thank You for what we have, may we resolve to
  share our blessings with others.
May we be counted among those who give rather than
  those who need.

REINE KAPLAN

For Protection

All-gracious, All-merciful God! Your paternal goodness has permitted me to awaken after a refreshing sleep, and has sent the gladdening rays of morning to revive me anew.

O heavenly Father! how great is the mercy which You have shown unto me. My first emotion is, therefore, to thank You, from the innermost depth of my heart, for Your providential watchfulness over my life, and for having protected me whilst the darkness of night surrounded me.

How many of my fellow-creatures but yesternight ascended the couch in good health and hopes, and yet cannot leave it this day, from being bound to it by pains and suffering! how many may have yesternight sunk to sleep amidst riches and affluence, but who are brought to poverty this morning by sudden disaster. Alas! how many others are languishing, perhaps, in the dark gloom of a prison, into which no friendly ray of joy penetrates. And how large may be the number of those who fell asleep last night, never to awaken any more in this world.

How thankful ought I therefore to be, Heavenly Creator! for Your goodness, wherewith You have warded off every danger from me, have preserved my health, and restored me to the arms of my relations and friends. Oh! let me ever cherish this feeling of gratitude within my heart, so that I may faithfully discharge my religious and domestic duties; so that I may meet my fellow-creatures with loving kindness, such as You have shown unto me; and that I may ever extol You, who causes the sleeper to be awake, and who will cause those that sleep the sleep of death to awake to eternal life.

FANNY NEUDA

Almighty and everlasting God who rules over all the world with love, we thank You for Your presence among us in this strange country, where with Your help we have found refuge and friends. We ask You to take away all hate and whatever else may hinder love, unison and peace, and show us the way to everlasting friendship with our neighbours. We thank You, Lord, for helping us to find Your house of worship which we share with our loving neighbours. We thank You for sheltering us from poverty and starvation. Blessed be the Lord, for with Him we came and found love, hope and a new life in a strange country.

HANNA KHOURI

Thank you, God the Creator, for creating me.

Thank you, Father of all mankind, for being my father.

Thank you, my Divine Master, for taking over my life when I became bereft of my mother.

Thank you, dear Lord, for providing me all my wants and needs.

Thank you, dear Saviour, for the wonderful missionaries and people of Forrest River Mission (now Oombulgurri) for taking good care of me.

Thank you, Holy Father, for sending missionaries to teach us your Holy Word.

Thank you for easing the pain of broken bones, insecurity and loneliness.

Thank you, dear Lord, for your guidance, forgiveness, patience, care, love and all the good things you have given me all my life, family, relatives, friends and loved ones, happiness in adversity, joy in loving and serving you.

Thank you, Divine Lord, for bringing my parents and myself together in that spiritual vision and experience I had on the first time I met my father after thirty-five years. To forgive is divine.

Thank you, loving Father, for showing me what and how to love.

Thank you, loving Father, for reconciliation which took place between my father and me, and, on behalf of my father and myself, we thank you dear Lord.

Thank you, dear Lord, for my life which I re-dedicate to you every day.

CONNIE NUNGULLA McDONALD

O Beloved One, ever ancient, ever fresh, as I breathe in you today I sense a multitude of breaths flowing through me. I am sitting in a garden among the ruins of an old Abbey and sensing a connection with all who have lived before me and all who will come after me. The old stones come to life as I become aware of the layers of civilization that shaped them, gave them their colour, their sparkle—shades of grey, pink, rose, each one an irregular shape, resting on the other. Through the cracks are the most miraculous, tiny, perfect flowers in small bouquets, offering themselves as gift in total freedom. All is peace around me. Through the glassless window I behold the terraced hill with sheep and goats gracefully grazing, contented. The birds add their music as they find rest now and again on a tree branch or perch on what was once a bell tower that called people to prayer.

The calm within me matches the calm without. In this place there is no other place, no other time—only a being with you, my God, who are with all. My heart pulsates with gratitude for the gift of life which has become, once again, so precious. Though there is pain and suffering in this world, you, O unnameable One, continue to give joy, to give serenity, and I in turn continue to render you praise.

ADRIENNE CORTI

GIVING PRAISE AND THANKSGIVING IN NATURE

This section supplies us with extraordinary, very feminine prayers to the Divine in the natural world. Here the Goddess is revealed to us through our senses in the sights, colors, activities, and sounds of nature. She is discovered too in the resources of the Earth, and our connectedness with it. Earth is our Mother and we her mothers in partnership. Hildegard wrote:

> ... the power of God is to be honored through the earth, since she preserves humankind in all its bodily needs, who ought to praise and magnify God all the time, and since she even sustains the rest which are provided for human use, when she makes herself accessible to them for their nourishment.... And this also happens since the earth is fertile in diverse forms of generation, that is to say that all things formed among terrestrial creatures are produced from the earth because it is like the mother of diverse offspring, both those born from the flesh and those rising up of themselves from seeds. So all things having the form and life of terrestrial creatures shall have arisen from her, since even mankind, who is animated by reason and the spirit of understanding, is made from earth.*

> ... *heaven and earth both testify,*
> *that God is a meadow in some high way,*
> *a meadow moreover revealed in ours*
> *where only the children find the flowers.*

JESSICA POWERS (*A Meadow Moreover*)

*From Hildegard of Bingen, "The Book of Life's Merits LVM (4.20–21)," as quoted in *Secrets of God: Writings of Hildegard of Bingen*, selected and translated from the Latin by Sabina Flanagan (Boston and London: Shambhala Publications Inc., 1996), pages 52 and 53.

Heaven is my father and Earth is my mother, and I am a little child placed between them.

JULIA CHING

God, our Creator and Creator of the world, we sing Your
  praises in every season.
Your presence is known to us in autumn, when
  shimmering golden leaves catch our eye; we stand in
  the hushed forest and are filled with awe.
You cover us with a blanket of soft white snow, as a
  mother her child.
The fresh awakening of spring stirs in us a gladness.
Each spring You give us rebirth; we are cleansed as the
  earth in a spring rain.
And summer's full blossoming and gentle breezes is an
  overflowing of joy and beauty.

Life is a journey, like a meandering stream that skips over
  rocks and branches on the way to a mountain lake.
Sometimes we, too, encounter obstacles on our path, but
  we reach pools of contentment.
Nature gives to us beauty, joy and peace.
Let not the worldliness of the times diminish nature's
  simple joys.
Let us pause in our hurried lives to contemplate Your
  infinite wonders, and to know ourselves.
God, grant us the wisdom to preserve that which has
  been entrusted to us so that our children, and our
  children's children, will be free to find nature's solace.

LINDA GILMORE

Morning has broken like the first morning,
Black bird has spoken like the first bird.
Praise for the singing! Praise for the morning!
Praise for them, springing fresh from the Word!

Sweet the rain's new fall sunlit from heaven,
Like the first dewfall on the first grass.
Praise for the sweetness of the wet garden,
Sprung in completeness where his feet pass.

Mine is the sunlight! Mine is the morning
Born of the one light Eden saw play!
Praise with elation, praise every morning,
God's recreation of the new day!

ELEANOR FARJEON

O world, I cannot hold thee close enough!
    Thy winds, thy wide grey skies!
    Thy mists that roll and rise!
Thy woods, this autumn day, that ache and sag
And all but cry with colour! That gaunt crag
To crush! To life the lean of that black bluff!
World, WORLD, I cannot get you close enough!

Long have I known a glory in it all,
    But never knew I this;
    Here such a passion is
As stretcheth me apart. Lord I do fear
Thou'st made the world too beautiful this year.
My soul is all but out of me,—let fall
No burning leaf; prithee, let no bird call.

EDNA ST. VINCENT MILLAY

103

"O Earth,
I count the praises thou art worth,
By thy waves that move aloud,
By thy hills against the cloud,
By thy valleys warm and green,
By the copses' elms between,
By their birds which, like a sprite
Scattered by a strong delight
Into fragments musical,
Stir and sing in every bush;
By thy silver founts that fall,
As if to entice the stars at night
To thine heart; by grass and rush,
And little weeds the children pull,
Mistook for flowers!

    —Oh, beautiful,
Art thou, Earth, albeit worse
Than in heaven is called good!
Good to us, that we may know
Meekly from thy good to go;
While the holy, crying Blood
Puts its music kind and low
'Twixt such ears as are not dull,
And thine ancient curse!

"Praisèd be the mosses soft
In thy forest pathways oft,
And the thorns, which make us think
Of the thornless river-brink
Where the ransomed tread:
Praisèd be thy sunny gleams,
And the storm, that worketh dreams
Of calm unfinishèd:
Praisèd be thine active days,
And thy night-time's solemn need,

When in God's dear book we read
    No night shall be therein:
Praisèd be thy dwellings warm
By household fagot's cheerful blaze,
Where, to hear of pardoned sin,
Pauseth oft the merry din,
Save the babe's upon the arm
Who croweth to the crackling wood:
Yea, and better understood,
Praisèd be thy dwellings cold,
Hid beneath the churchyard mould,
Where the bodies of the saints
Separate from earthly taints
Lie asleep, in blessing bound,
Waiting for the trumpet's sound
To free them into blessing;—none
Weeping more beneath the sun,
Though dangerous words of human love
Be graven very near, above.

"Earth, we Christians praise thee thus,
Even for the change that comes
With a grief from thee to us:
For thy cradles and thy tombs,
For the pleasant corn and wine
And summer-heat; and also for
The frost upon the sycamore
    And hail upon the vine!"

ELIZABETH BARRETT BROWNING

The small ears prick on the bushes,
furry buds, shoots tender and pale.
The swamp maples blow scarlet.
Color teases the corner of the eye,

105

delicate gold, chartreuse, crimson,
mauve speckled, just dashed on.

The soil stretches naked. All winter
hidden under the down comforter of snow,
delicious now, rich in the hand
as chocolate cake: the fragrant busy
soil the worm passes through her gut
and the beetle swims in like a lake.

As I kneel to put the seeds in
careful as stitching, I am in love.
You are the bed we all sleep on.
You are the food we eat, the food
we ate, the food we will become.
We are walking trees rooted in you.

You can live thousands of years
undressing in the spring your black
body, your red body, your brown body
penetrated by the rain. Here
is the goddess unveiled,
the earth opening her strong thighs.

Yet you grow exhausted with bearing
too much, too soon, too often, just
as a woman wears through like an old rug.
We have contempt for what we spring
from. Dirt, we say, you're dirt
as if we were not all your children.

We have lost the simplest gratitude.
We lack the knowledge we showed ten
thousand years past, that you live
a goddess but mortal, that what we take

must be returned; that the poison we drop
in you will stunt our children's growth.

Tending a plot of your flesh binds
me as nothing ever could, to the season,
to the will of the plants, clamorous
in their green tenderness. What
calls louder than the cry of a field
of corn ready, or trees of ripe peaches?

I worship on my knees, laying
the seeds in you, that worship rooted
in need, in hunger, in kindship,
flesh of the planet with my own flesh,
a ritual of compost, a litany of manure.
My garden's a chapel, but a meadow

gone wild in grass and flower
is a cathedral. How you seethe
with little quick ones, vole, field
mouse, shrew and mole in their thousands,
rabbit and woodchuck. In you rest
the jewels of the genes wrapped in seed.

Power warps because it involves joy
in domination; also because it means
forgetting how we too starve, break
like a corn stalk in the wind, how we
die like the spinach of drought,
how what slays the vole slays us.

Because you can die of overwork, because
you can die of the fire that melts
rock, because you can die of the poison
that kills the beetle and the slug,

we must come again to worship you
on our knees, the common living dirt.

MARGE PIERCY

Let me live this jewel that is my garden—
    sunlight on tulip, incandescent red
    chickadees kissing in apple blossoms
    ancient pear apparelled in wedding dress
    pungence of thyme and basil—
Spirit made manifest in matter
Marriage of Heaven & Earth right here
    in my back garden.

MARION WOODMAN

Wind, weather, water and fire
have written the lines in the lips
of the aged Stone
written the song I sing to you now
In the freezing times gather the heat
from the Winter Sun and share warmth with each other
In the hot burning times
Be the cool breeze that blows in the desert
In the time when memory seems lost
And the people have forgotten who they are
Place your hands on my storied surface, touch my lips
Hear the sound of my voice humming in your chest
And awaken the seed sounds in the chests of your people
And they will remember Who We All Are.

CAROL PROUDFOOT-EDGAR

This long, green valley sloping to the sun,
With dimpling, silver waters loitering through;
The sky that bends above me, mild and blue;
The wide, still wheat-fields, yellowing one by one,
And all the peaceful sounds when day is done—
    I cannot bear their calm monotony!
    Great God! I want the thunder of the sea!
I want to feel the wild red lightnings run
Around, about me; hear the bellowing surf,
    And breathe the tempest's sibilant, sobbing breath;
    To front the elements, defying death,
And fling myself prone on the spray-beat turf,
    And hear the strong waves trampling wind and rain,
    Like herds of beasts upon the mighty plain.

ELLA HIGGINSON

The great sea
frees me, moves me,
as a strong river carries a weed.
Earth and her strong winds
move me, take me away,
and my soul is swept up in joy.

UVAVNUK

3

BLESSINGS FOR CEREMONIES AND RITUALS

*B*lessings are an extension of prayers of worship and thanksgiving. They promote a coming together of the material and spiritual worlds. Blessings, therefore, hold the power of the Divine for a number of occasions—they are the ways that a celebration can be sanctified, or that an offering of gifts, of food or water or wine, or the lighting of candles, can be consecrated and purified and placed in sacred hands. A blessing is a recognition of a gathering, of a community in one place at one time for a shared purpose. A blessing can bestow grace upon a dedicated act. Blessings give a sacred anointing to our intentions, our ceremonies, our rituals; they are for special occasions or for everyday acts. And blessings can be the crown of glory on preparatory work, like that for holidays, weddings, anniversaries.

A woman's blessing (or women's blessings) was common in early times, when women were priestesses in many of our traditions. Because of this, I find any feminine blessing profound, particularly when I am among women, or have a laying on of a woman's hands upon my head for my work, or for a path I am about to take.

St. Clare of Assisi's blessing (quoted in part in this section) on her sister nuns—the first women Franciscans, who lived in a small cloistered community for up to forty years—is important because of the right that Clare gave herself to bless other women when, in thirteenth-century Italy, this would have been frowned upon by church authorities. Following her example, we, as women in partnership with the Divine, and in full consciousness, can and should bestow blessings on others, as we should also receive them in our own rituals and ceremonies. And most of all in our daily acts we should remind ourselves of the sacredness—and God's presence—in all things. "Saying grace," not only for food but for everything in our daily lives, is a blessing that bestows grace upon everything we give, receive, or partake in.

O Lord, whom all Your good creatures bless and praise according to Your gift unto each of them, grant, we pray, that we on whom You have bestowed reason and speech may ever bless You with heart and lips, and may of Your infinite mercy inherit a blessing, even the eternal blessedness of heaven.

CHRISTINA ROSSETTI

The blessing of the God of Sarah and Hagar,
as of Abraham,
the blessing of the Son, born of the woman Mary,
the blessing of the Holy Spirit,
who broods over us
as a mother, her children,
be with you all.

LOIS WILSON

❀ 111

I should like a great lake of ale
For the King of Kings.
I should like the angels of Heaven
To be drinking it through time eternal.
I should like excellent meats of belief and pure piety.
I should like flails of penance at my house.
I should like the men of Heaven at my house;
I should like barrels of peace at their disposal;
I should like vessels of charity for distribution;
I should like for them cellars of mercy.
I should like cheerfulness to be in their drinking.
I should like Jesus to be there among them.
I should like the three Marys of illustrious renown to be
    with us.
I should like the people of Heaven, the poor, to be
    gathered around us from all parts.
I should like to be a rent-payer to the Lord.
So that should I suffer distress
He would bestow a good blessing upon me.

ST. BRIGIT OF KILDARE

Blessings on the Shekhinah,
the maker of fire.
Let us be aware
of the division
of light and darkness,
of work and rest,
of self and others,
of holiday and daily.

Let us, as daily women,
as well as women of holy days,
know that there is no holiday
without the preparing for it,

nor is there an ordinary day
unless we make the bed for it.
We are both slaves
and free women.

E. M. BRONER

Blessed Be the New Year

O Great Spirit of Hope, blessed be your holy seasons,
Blessed be this season when we move to a new year.
Blessed be this magical time for new beginnings and fond
    farewells.
Blessed be this "crack between the worlds" that we
    encounter at the New Year.
Blessed be this threshold place of transition between
    inside and outside.
Blessed be this transformation when spirits of hope and
    change gather.
Blessed be this passage from past securities to uncharted
    uncertainties.
Blessed be this shifting of emotions.
Blessed be this letting go of old hurts and pains.
Blessed be this reliable balancing act of nature.
Blessed be this rededication of values and meaning
    in life.
Blessed be . . . *(add others)*
O Great Spirit of Hope, blessed be your holy seasons.

DIANN L. NEU

We give you thanks
for this food which is our life,
for the fruits of the earth,
conceived in darkness,
rooted in the secret soil.
We offer you our part in the mess of creativity,
We wash, prepare, cook, present;
we eat, and taste, and enjoy with our bodies;
we clear away the mess.
We embrace with you the chaos that fulfils,
the secret labour that maintains life.

JANET MORLEY

We bless one another
We wash each other's hands.
We dip greens in salt water
And wash pain with tears.

We divide matzot
And hide our past.
We tell Haggadah
And each her own tale.

We bless matzot
And paths in the sand.
We eat maror,
Of the bitter past.

We set the table
For the women's supper.
We find the halved matza
That dropped from our lives.

We end with grace,
With blessing and song.
We greet the night
And the following dawn
In the bosom of friends,
The seder of our own.

E. M. BRONER

Blessing over the Sabbath Candles

May it be Your will, Lord my God and of my fathers, to
be gracious to me (and to my husband and children) and
to all my family, crowning our home with the feeling of
Your divine presence dwelling among us. Make me
worthy to raise learned children and grandchildren who
will dazzle the world with Torah and goodness, and
ensure that the flow of our lives will never be dimmed.
Show us the glow of Your face and we will be saved.

ANONYMOUS

Let us together bless the source of Life which wells up
through the ground and into the grain, into which we
connect as we turn it into bread, through which we live
and find our meaning in the acts of our lives.

ARIEL STONE-HALPERN

On Putting the Sabbath Loaf into the Oven

Lord of all the world, in your hand is all blessing. I come
now to revere your holiness, and I pray you to bestow

your blessing on the baked goods. Send an angel to guard the baking, so that all will be well baked, will rise nicely, and will not burn, to honor the holy Sabbath (which you have chosen so that Israel your children may rest thereon) and over which one recites the holy blessing— as you blessed the dough of Sarah and Rebecca our mothers. My Lord God, listen to my voice; you are the God who hears the voices of those who call to you with the whole heart. May you be praised to eternity.

REBECCA RACHEL LEAH

Let us bless the source of life
that nurtures fruit on the vine
as we weave the branches of our lives
into the tradition.

MARCIA FALK

Blessing of the Fruit of the Vine

Blessed are you, Holy One of the Harvest, for you invite us to come and drink deeply.

Blessed are you, Holy One of the Harvest, for you beg us to drink this fruit of the vine in memory of all who have died for peace.

Blessed are you, Holy One of the Harvest, for you help us to remember women's lives, women's blood, women who have been killed, martyred, raped and wounded at the time of war.

Blessed are you, Holy One of the Harvest, for even though we drink you keep us thirsty for peace.

Blessed are you, Holy One of the Harvest, refresh us with a firm and daring spirit.

Blessed are you, Holy One of the Harvest, for you create
the fruit of the vine and show us the way to liberation.
Let us extend our hands, palms up, and bless this fruit of
the vine.
Blessed are you, Holy One of the Harvest, bless this wine
and juice with your gifts of peace.

DIANN L. NEU

Daily Labour

I bless the daily labour of my hands,
I bless the sleep that nightly is my own.
The mercy of the Lord, the Lord's commands,
The law of blessings and the law of stone.

My dusty purple, with its ragged seams . . .
My dusty staff, where all light's rays are shed.
And also, Lord, I bless the peace
In others' houses—others' ovens' bread.

MARINA TSVETAEVA

For the Household

Lord, we beseech You to bless and prosper this Your
household. Grant us sweet reasonableness in all our
dealings with one another; make us large-hearted in
helping and generous in criticising, keep us from unkind
words and unkind silences. Make us quick to understand
the needs and feelings of others; and grant that living in
the brightness of Your presence we may bring sunshine
into cloudy places.

LUCY H. M. SOULSBY

For a Pregnant Woman

May our Mother God keep you safe until the time of your
　　deliverance.
May you, and those eagerly awaiting your "hour," be
　　enfolded in peace.
May our God of patient waiting be your strength during
　　these days of anticipation.
May our Midwife God protect and comfort you during
　　your labour.
May our God of love and life transform your labour pains
　　into joy, in the gift of a healthy child.
May our Nurturing Mother God provide you with an
　　abundance of milk, to nourish your newborn infant.
And may the blessing of the God who conceived us with joy,
　　birthed us in pain, and transforms us in love, to fullness of
　　life and fruitfulness; may this God bless you, and keep you
　　in her womanly tenderness today and always.

MARIA KERSTEN

Mother's Day

May God richly bless and keep you every day,
On your head His cup of joy o'erflow,
The angels guard and guide you on your way,
Heavenly hosts surround the way you go,
Enabling you to find contentment and peace,
Refreshing your heart with love that never cease,
Sending this day a message filled with love.

Dearest, you are a very special gift from above,
And wher'er we go, and what ever good we do,
You, dear mother, we owe it all to you.

LYN MARTIN

Bless, O God, all who dedicate their powers today to the
making of peace in the world;
Bless all who give their training and experience to feed
and clothe and house the destitute;
Bless all who lend their energies and skills to teach
impoverished people to till their land, to water it, and
to harvest it.
And give us all a lively concern for the underprivileged,
and show us practical ways of helping. For Christ's
sake.

RITA SNOWDEN

May the Lord bless you and keep you. May he show his
face to you and be merciful to you. May he turn his
countenance to you and give you peace. . . . May the
Lord be with you always and, wherever you are, may you
be with Him always.

ST. CLARE OF ASSISI

May Wisdom be in our minds, and in our thinking;
May Wisdom be in our hearts, and in our perceiving;
May Wisdom be in our mouths, and in our speaking;
May Wisdom be in our hands, and in our working;
May Wisdom be in our feet, and in our walking;
May Wisdom be in our bodies, and in our loving;
May Wisdom be with us all the days of our lives.

DIANN L. NEU

I add my thoughts of Good Intent to your thoughts
That your Life may be peaceful and content;
I add my breath to your breath
That your road may be healthy and long;
I ask our Grandmothers
To watch over you
And lovingly guide you
As you walk through your days.

CAROL LEE SANCHEZ

Our brother Jesus, you set our feet upon the way
    and sometimes where you lead we do not like or
    understand.
Bless us with courage where the way is fraught with
    dread or danger;
Bless us with graceful meetings where the way is lonely;
Bless us with good companions where the way demands a
    common cause;
Bless us with night vision where we travel in the dark,
    keen hearing where we have not sight, to hear the
    reassuring sounds of
    fellow travellers;
Bless us with humour—we cannot travel lightly
    weighed down with gravity;
Bless us with humility to learn from those around us;
Bless us with decisiveness where we must move with
    speed;
Bless us with lazy moments, to stretch and rest and
    savour;
Bless us with love, given and received;
And bless us with your presence, even when we know it
    in your absence.
Lead us into exile,
until we find that on the road

is where you are,
and where you are is going home.
Bless us, lead us, love us, bring us home
bearing the gospel of life.

KATHY GALLOWAY

May He be blessed by all, for I have seen clearly that He
does not fail to repay, even in this life, every good desire.

ST. TERESA OF ÁVILA

The blessing of God,
The eternal goodwill of God,
The shalom of God,
The wildness and the warmth of God
be among us and between us
Now and always.

ST. HILDA COMMUNITY

4

OBLATIONS

*T*he offering of self, of our actions, our service, and of ourselves and others in hardship, is one of the highest forms of devotion. Sharing in divine friendship is about sharing everything—the good and the not so good—equally. It is offering one's state of mind, emotions, thoughts, attitudes, and experiences as a sacrifice.

Here women offer their will, heart, love, souls, body, and mind. And as they offer they dig deep into their shadowy parts and offer the "dust and weed" of self (Mary Coleridge). St. Thérèse of Lisieux always perceived herself in relation to God as small (she likened herself once to a ball in God's hands). In her prayer here she strives to become "smaller still" in her effort to become childlike, and therefore helpless without her parent God. Written in her early twenties (she died at twenty-four), this prayer with its simplicity of faith illustrates her vast spiritual wisdom at so young an age. Jessica Powers offers her "emptiness"—one of the more advanced gifts, because through the feelings offered we are led to expectant emptiness, that which is ready for filling. Catherine de Hueck Doherty called this state "a chalice of my heart." The need to have the Divine dwell in a person has led to many archetypical and symbolic gestures; we offer ourselves as temples, as tabernacles, for the spirit, and eucharistic rituals thrive on this belief. By embodying the Divine, we have the opportunity to be in harmony with God as "one full responsive vibrant chord" (Christina Rossetti).

Queen Elizabeth I of England offered her duty on the occasion of her coronation in 1558, addressing her God as "O my King." Both St. Thérèse of Lisieux and St. Teresa of Ávila were responsible for the souls of others as teachers of novices and nuns, and they repeatedly prayed oblationary prayers to be guided by God in their duties.

In offering pain, suffering, and hardship, we are led even deeper into God's realms. Many people lose their faith over mortal tragedy. "Why would God allow this?" they repeatedly ask. There are so many questions that don't have logical and immediate answers; God's ways are not ours. Etty Hillesum shares her spiritual wisdom by turning the tables: instead of God helping her, she offers, "we can help you." "It seems, Lord, You try with rigor the person who loves You," she once wrote, understanding that the trials we experience are gifts of divine love. We are given these trials to test our faith, to see how we handle our difficulties. This is the true spiritual test.

If we offer our trials without complaint, questioning, or blame; if we lay our fears, anxieties, sickness, frustration into the lap of our God, we make them worth something. To suffer alone makes suffering worthless. Suffering shared and offered reaps enormous rewards and lessons. The gift of suffering is mostly given to teach us to let go of things that are inappropriate in our lives and that have to be shed to be transformed. This is always a painful process, yet no spiritual growth happens without pain. Through suffering we learn to help others; we are able to be truly compassionate from our experience. Love is always present throughout hard times, if we open ourselves to this love.

OFFERINGS OF SELF

Offering everything, pure and impure, is the best and quickest way to develop spiritually. If you offer everything to the Divine, the Divine will accept and change it, even the worst things. It is not what you offer but THAT you offer which is important. Offer everything, and you will acquire the habit of thinking always about God. THAT will change you.

MOTHER MEERA

The gesture of a gift is adequate.
If you have nothing: laurel leaf or bay,
no flower, no seed, no apple gathered late,
do not in desperation lay
the beauty of your tears upon the clay.

No gift is proper to a Deity;
no fruit is worthy for such power to bless.
If you have nothing, gather back your sigh,
and with your hands held high, your heart held high,
lift up your emptiness.

JESSICA POWERS (*If You Have Nothing*)

I found emptiness. I give you emptiness, The emptiness that stands to be filled by God. Emptiness that once seemed death but now is life. It died somewhere along

the way of my own life. I thought I died with it—but no.
The emptiness of things, of attachments, that were all
hollow anyhow. These died to be replaced with an
emptiness that was alive, expectant, ready to be filled
with love, with God. Yes, I give you emptiness, a chalice
of my heart.

CATHERINE DE HUECK DOHERTY

Oh, then my *adored Refuge*, let not frail nature
shrink at Your command; let not the spirit which You
vouchsafe to fill, reluctantly obey You. Rather, let me say,
"Lord, here am I, the creature of Your will, rejoicing that
You will lead; thankful that You will choose from me.
Only continue to me Your soul cheering presence and in
life or in death, let me be Your own."

ST. ELIZABETH SETON

All I have is Yours, do what seems best according to Your
divine will. Let not the cares or duties of this life press on
me too heavily; but lighten my burden, that I may follow
Your way in quietness, filled with thankfulness for Your
mercy, and rendering acceptable service unto You.

MARIA HARE

Take my life, and let it be
Consecrated, Lord, to Thee;
Take my moments and my days,
Let them flow in ceaseless praise.
Take my hands, and let them move
At the impulse of Thy love.

Take my feet, and let them be
Swift and beautiful for Thee.

Take my voice, and let me sing
Always, only, for my King;
Take my lips, and let them be
Filled with messages from Thee.
Take my silver and my gold;
Not a mite would I withhold.
Take my intellect, and use
Every power as Thou shalt choose.

Take my will, and make it Thine;
It shall be no longer mine.
Take my heart: it is Thine own:
It shall be Thy royal throne.
Take my love; my Lord, I pour
At Thy feet its treasure-store.
Take myself, and I will be
Ever, only, all for Thee.

FRANCES RIDLEY HAVERGAL

I am giving You worship with my whole life,
I am giving You assent with my whole power,
I am giving You praise with my whole tongue,
I am giving You honour with my whole utterance.
I am giving You love with my whole devotion,
I am giving You love kneeling with my whole desire,
I am giving You love with my whole heart,
I am giving You affection with my whole sense,
I am giving You my existence with my whole mind,
I am giving You my soul, O God of all gods.

ESTHER DE WAAL

Let me offer a sacrifice—myself—
    beloved,
      to your beautiful face.
Come, here in the courtyard, dark Lord,
The women are singing auspicious wedding songs;
My eyes have fashioned an altar of pearl tears,
And here is my sacrifice:
    the body and mind
Of Meera,
    the servant who clings to your feet,
    through life after life,
    a virginal harvest for you to reap.

MEERA

Lord of the Winds, I cry to Thee,
I that am dust;
And blown about with every gust
I fly to Thee.

Lord of the Waters, unto Thee I call
I that am weed upon the waters borne
And by the waters torn,
Tossed by the waters at Thy feet I fall.

MARY COLERIDGE

    O Lord, You would not inspire me with unattainable desires, therefore, in spite of my smallness, I shall aspire to sanctity. It is impossible, O Jesus, to make me great! Therefore I must bear with myself as I am, with all my imperfections. Yet, I shall look for a means of going to Heaven by a little path that is very very straight and very very short, a path that is entirely new.

We are in a century of inventions: it is no longer
necessary to climb the steps of a stairway, for in the
houses of the rich an elevator has replaced them
comfortably! And I want to find an elevator that will lift
me up to You, Jesus, for I am too little a creature to climb
the bitter stairway of perfection. . . . The elevator that
must raise me to Heaven is your arms, O my Jesus!
Therefore I do not need to grow in size, in fact I must
remain little and strive to become smaller still!

ST. THÉRÈSE OF LISIEUX

Lord, I make you a present of myself
I do not know what to do with myself.
Let me, then, Lord, make this exchange:
I will place this evil being into your hands.
You are the only one who can hide it in your goodness
and can so rule over me
that nothing will be seen of my own proper self.
On your part, you will grant your pure love,
which will extinguish all other loves in me
and will annihilate me and busy me so much with you
that I will have no time or place for anything or any-
    one else.

ST. CATHERINE OF GENOA

Earth cure me.
Earth receive my woe.
Rock strengthen my weakness.
Rain wash my sadness away.
Rain receive my doubt.

Sun make sweet my song.
Sun receive the anger from my heart.

NANCY WOOD

O Heart of love, I place my trust in you.
Although I fear all things from my weakness, I hope all
    things from your goodness.

ST. MARGARET-MARY ALACOQUE

Though my will is not yet free from self-interest, I give it
    to you freely.

ST. TERESA OF ÁVILA

I am your reed, sweet shepherd, glad to be.
Now, if you will, breathe out your joy in me
And make bright song.
Or fill me with the soft moan of your love
When your delight has failed to call or move
The flock from wrong.

Make children's songs, or any songs to fill
Your reed with breath of life; but at your will
Lay down the flute,
And take repose, while music infinite
Is silence in your heart; and laid on it
Your reed is mute.

CARYLL HOUSELANDER

Tune me, O Lord, into one harmony
With You, one full responsive vibrant chord;
Unto Your praise, all love and melody,
Tune me, O Lord.

CHRISTINA ROSSETTI

I look at gold and world and see
children's trinkets and sand.
Heaven-joy carries me
far beyond my self.

If only my breath
were a wind
through-sweetened with praise,
to carry Love's flames
starwards, toward You.

If only I,
out of Love,
could be the phoenix kindled,
could perish entirely out of bliss,
into my one desire.

Let me in thankfulness
be Your mirror, God—
Then Your own rays
might be returned to You,
in grace-words, in equal light.

CATHARINA REGINA VON GREIFFENBERG

My God, I wish to attend to nothing more in life than to
becoming a perfect imitation of You, and since Your life

130

was only a hidden life of humiliation, of love and of
sacrifice, henceforth this shall be my life also.

TERESA MARGHERITA

OFFERINGS OF LIFE AND SERVICE

*Whatever you do, give it to God with a grateful and humble
heart.*

MOTHER MEERA

O God, we bring you our failure.
We hold up our smallness to your greatness.

MONICA FURLONG

Gladly do I give my life to Thee,
Not solemnly, not grudgingly,
But I would take my life and fling
It at Thy feet—and sing and sing—
Happy to bring Thee this small thing.

MARY DIXON THAYER

God, lover of us all, most holy one,
help us to respond to you,
to create what you want for us here on earth.
Give us today enough for our needs,
forgive our weak and deliberate offences,
just as we must forgive others

when they hurt us.
Help us to resist evil
and to do what is good,
for we are yours,
endowed with your power
to make our world whole.

LALA WINKLEY

O Lord God everlasting,
Which reigns over the kingdoms of men. . . .
so teach me, I humbly beseech You,
Your word,
and so strengthen me with Your grace that I may feed
  Your people
with a faithful and a true heart,
and rule them prudently with power.
O Lord, You have set me on high.
My flesh is frail and weak.
If I therefore at any time forget You,
touch my heart, O Lord, that I may again remember You.
If I swell against You, pluck me down in my own
  conceit. . . .
I acknowledge, O my King, without You my throne is
  unstable,
my seat unsure, my kingdom tottering, my life uncertain.
I see all things in this life subject to mutability, nothing
  to continue still at one stay. . . .
Create therefore in me, O Lord, a new heart, and so
  renew my spirit that
Your law may be my study, Your truth my delight, Your
  church my care,
Your people my crown, Your righteousness my pleasure,
Your service my government;

so shall this my kingdom through You be established with
  peace.

QUEEN ELIZABETH I

I want to begin this day with thankfulness, and continue
  it with eagerness.
I shall be busy; let me set about things in the spirit of
  service
      to you and to my fellows, that Jesus knew in the
      carpenter's shop in Nazareth.
I am glad that he drew no line between work sacred and
  secular.

Take the skill that resides in my hands, and use it today;
Take the experience that life has given me, and use it;
Keep my eyes open, and my imagination alert, that I
  may see
how things look to others, especially the unwell, the
worried, the overworked. For your love's sake.

RITA SNOWDEN

My God, I offer You all the actions of this day in union
with the intentions and glory of the Sacred Heart of
Jesus. I wish to sanctify each and every heartbeat, every
thought, every simple little action by joining them to
His infinite merits; and I desire to make reparation for
my sins by casting them into the furnace of His merciful love.

O my God! For myself and for all my dear ones, I
implore the grace to perfectly fulfill Your holy will and to
accept for love of You all the joys and sorrows of this

passing life, so that one day we may be united in Heaven for all eternity.

ST. THÉRÈSE OF LISIEUX

Dear God, I am willing to relinquish my life of limitation and despair. I invite your spirit to renew my life.

MARIANNE WILLIAMSON

OFFERINGS OF SELF AND OTHERS IN HARDSHIP

"They may suffer at the hands of others, or from illness or poverty or the instability of the world. They may lose their children or other loved ones. All such things are thorns the earth produced because of sin. They endure them all, considering by the light of reason and holy faith that I am goodness itself and cannot will anything but good. And I send these things out of love, not hatred."

THE DIVINE'S VOICE IN ST. CATHERINE OF SIENA'S
THE DIALOGUE

For if we suffer tribulations, it is a sign that we are loved by the beloved God.

ANGELA OF FOLIGNO

Having no butter and milk to offer to You,
I will offer You a little of my pain.

O Kanna, at Your Feet I will offer the pearl drops of my
tears.

MATA AMRITANANDAMAYI

O my Lord, how certain it is that anyone who renders
You some service soon pays with a great trial! And what
a precious reward a trial is for those who truly love you if
we could at once understand its value!

ST. TERESA OF ÁVILA

God, there doesn't seem to be much you yourself can do
about our circumstances, about our lives. Neither do I
hold you responsible. You cannot help us, but we can
help you and defend your dwelling place inside us to
the end.

. . . I shall always labour for you and remain faithful
to you, and I shall never drive you from my presence.

ETTY HILLESUM

O my Lord, how You are the true friend; and how
powerful! When You desire You can love, and You never
stop loving those who love You! All things praise You,
Lord of the world! Oh, who will cry out for You, to tell
everyone how faithful You are to Your friends! All things
fail; You, Lord of all, never fail! Little it is, that which
You allow the one who loves You to suffer! O my Lord!
How delicately and smoothly and delightfully You treat
them! Would that no one ever pause to love anyone but
You! It seems, Lord, You try with rigor the person who
loves You so that in extreme trial he might understand

the greatest extreme of Your love, O my God, who has
the understanding, the learning, and the new words with
which to extol Your works as my soul understands them?
All fails me, my Lord; but if You do not abandon me, I
will not fail You. Let all learned men rise up against me,
let all created things persecute me, let the devils torment
me; do not You fail me, Lord, for I already have
experience of the gain that comes from the way You
rescue the one who trusts in You alone.

ST. TERESA OF ÁVILA

Penetrate these murky corners where we hide memories,
and tendencies on which we do not care to look, but
which we will not yield freely up to you, that you may
purify and transmute them. The persistent buried grudge,
the half-acknowledged enmity which is still smouldering;
the bitterness of that loss we have not turned into
sacrifice, the private comfort we cling to, the secret fear
of failure which saps our initiative and is really inverted
pride; the pessimism which is an insult to your joy. Lord,
we bring all these to you, and we review them with
shame and penitence in your steadfast light.

EVELYN UNDERHILL

I, Catherine, a useless servant and your unworthy
daughter, commend myself to you in the precious blood
of God's Son. How I long to see you slaughtered on the
tree of the sweet beloved cross—but not without me! I
see no other refreshment for us, dearest father, but to
agonize up there in blazing love. There will be no
demons, seen or unseen, who can take from us the life of
grace, because once we are lifted up, earth will not be

able to get in our way. As the mouth of Truth said, "If I am lifted up I will draw everything to myself"—for he draws heart and soul and will with all his strength. So, dearest father, let's make the cross our bed—for I am jubilantly happy with your message. To think the world is opposing us! I don't deserve much mercy from them, that they should give me the cloak our sweet eternal Father wore.

ST. CATHERINE OF SIENA

O most holy mother of Jesus, you who witnessed and felt the utter desolation of Your divine Son, help me in my hour of need. O Mother, I come to bury my anguish in your heart; and in your heart to seek courage and strength. O Mother, offer me to Jesus.

ST. BERNADETTE

Lord, when my heart was whole
I kept it back
And grudged to give it to You.
Now then that it is broken,
Must I lack Your kind word "Give it me"?
Silence would be but just, and You are just.
Yet since I lie here shattered in the dust,
With still an eye to lift to You,
A broken heart to give,
I think that You will bid me live,
And answer "Give it Me."

CHRISTINA ROSSETTI

What are you, my soul, you lean and bloodless thing
Like a withered fig that has survived the winter?
In youth it was so different: then the blood
Sang along the veins and it was easy both to love and
   welcome love.
But when you are old grace conquers only by hard
   victories;
You are stiffened, crusted by the salt spray
After the long sea voyage.

The lanes of memory may be as green
As in the year's paradise of spring.
It is the immediate present that slips unremembered,
Yet in love's presence there is only this one moment—
A question not of time but of understanding,
As when beauty seeps through the crevices of the soul
Burning the dead wood and illuming the self's verities—
This, only after a long journey.

So limping, my soul, we will together go
Into the city of the shining ones,
Of those whose crutches have been cast into the sea,
Whose love is garlanded across the festal stars;
And we with them will bow before the sceptered wisdom
   of a child.
The trembling broken years shall be restored
And these shall be our offering; for by them we
   shall know
Love has travailed with us all the way.

M. L. (A NUN OF BURNHAM ABBEY)

Keep from me all that I might comprehend!
O God, I ripen toward you in my unknowing.

138

The barely burgeoning leaf on the roadside tree
Limns innocence: here endeth the first lesson.

Keep from me, God, all forms of certainty:
The steady tread that paces off the self

And forms it, seamless, ignorant of doubt
Or failure, hell-bent for fulfilment.

To know myself: is not that the supreme disaster?
To know Thee, one must sink on trembling knees.

To hear Thee, only the terrified heart may truly listen;
To see Thee, only the gaze half-blind with dread.

Though the day darken, preserve my memory
From Your bright oblivion, Erase not my faulty traces.

If I aspire again to make four poor walls my house,
Let me pillow myself on the book of my peregrinations.

God, grant me strength to give over false happiness,
And the sense that suffering has earned us Your regard.

Elohim! Though sorrow fill me to the brim,
Let me carefully bear the cup of myself to Thee.

RACHEL KORN

"Father, into your hands I commend my spirit!"
And into YOUR hands, Jesus Christ,
my most merciful Redeemer,
Infinite Love,
I commend myself in the hour of death:
my body and soul,

my heart and my mind and my will,
all that I have, and all that I am.

Into your hands,
the beautiful hands of a carpenter
with their lines and sinew and muscle,
strong and sensitive hands
nailed to the Cross,
I commend those whom I love.
Hands that can heal the sick,
can give sight to the blind,
hands that can raise the dead
and restore them to life with a touch,
receive those whom I love
receive them and bless them from the Cross:
receive them, comfort them, lead and uphold them,
unite them to yourself
and re-unite them to me
for evermore in your Kingdom,
Jesus, merciful Lord.

CARYLL HOUSELANDER

PART TWO

SUPPLICATION:
THE REQUESTS

*A*fter devotional prayer comes supplicatory prayer, when we have the ear of the Divine through our praise and thanksgiving, through our offerings of love and the time we have already given the Divine. We are prepared and ready to ask, to petition. Supplication prayers are not about needs that we bargain for—e.g., If You give me this, then I'll go to church more. These kinds of bargaining requests we should have left behind in childhood. As Oriah Mountain Dreamer wrote in an essay on prayer, "My prayers for self have changed over the years. When I was a child I asked questions, sought guidance. . . . Now I do not completely trust myself or others when we cannot ask for what our hearts desire."

So for this part of the book I have chosen supplicatory subjects which are of spiritual content and particularly applicable to women. The subjects, I hope, are helpful because they identify where supplication prayer is necessary—spiritually, as opposed to materially. For example, instead of beseeching God to win the lottery, which is not prayer and supposes God to be a wizard, we ask for strength, knowledge, sustenance, support, and inspiration, which is prayer.

God spoke to Julian of Norwich and said,

I am the ground of your beseeching,
First it is My will you have it,

And then I make you will it,
And then I make you beseech it;
And if you beseech it,
How should it then be that you should not have your
  beseeching?"

Too, The Mother said that we can make proposals to
God, "but after all it is only His will that is realized." And
as Julian of Norwich taught, God already knows what we
need, which isn't always what we think we want.

    The grace that comes from any prayer, particularly
in continual perseverance in prayer, prepares us to recognize God's answers and God's messages to us. I quote below an example of this from the nineteenth-century
African American preacher Amanda Berry Smith's autobiography, about her prayers for conversion. She had
been tormented by the Devil, who had suggested that she
give up praying as nothing was happening, at which time
she heard a voice whispering to her to persevere, to "pray
once more."

> Then in my desperation I looked up and said, "O
> Lord, if Thou wilt help me I will believe Thee,"
> and in the act of telling God I would, I did. O, the
> peace and joy that flooded my soul! The burden
> rolled away; I felt it when it left me, and a flood
> of light and joy swept through my soul such as I
> had never known before. I said, 'Why, Lord, I do
> believe this is just what I have been asking for,'
> and down came another flood of light and peace.
> And I said again, 'Why, Lord, I do believe this is
> what I have asked Thee for.' Then I sprang to my
> feet, all around was light, I was new. I looked at
> my hands, they looked new. I took hold of myself
> and said, 'Why, I am new, I am new all over.' I
> clapped my hands; I ran up out of the cellar, I

walked up and down the kitchen floor. Praise the Lord! There seemed to be a halo of light all over me; the change was so real and so thorough that I have often said that if I had been as black as ink or as green as grass or as white as snow, I would not have been frightened. I went into the dining room; we had a large mirror that went from the floor to the ceiling, and I went and looked in it to see if anything had transpired in my color, because there was something wonderful that had taken place inside of me, and it really seemed to me it was outside too, and as I looked in the glass I cried out, "Hallelujah, I have got religion; glory to God. I have got religion!" I was wild with delight and joy; it seemed to me as if I would split! I went out into the kitchen and I thought what will I do, I have got to wait till Sunday before I can tell anybody. This was on Tuesday; Sunday was my day in town, so I began to count the days, Tuesday, Wednesday, Thursday, Friday, Saturday, Sunday. O, it seemed to me the days were weeks long. My! can I possibly stand it till Sunday? I must tell somebody, and as I passed by the ironing table it seemed as if it had a halo of light all around it, and I ran up to the table and smote it with my hand and shouted, "Glory to God, I have got religion!"*

The power of prayer in healing and helping others, of bidding God to intervene on behalf of others for their

---

*Amanda Berry Smith, *An Autobiography* [1893], quoted in the essay "Black Women: From Slavery to Womanist Liberation," by Emilie M. Townes, in *In Our Own Voices: Four Centuries of American Women's Religious Writing*, edited by Rosemary Skinner Keller and Rosemary Radford Reuther (San Francisco: HarperSanFrancisco, 1995).

highest good—or the needs of the world—is also a vital part of supplication. Many people petition saints or other holy people who have passed on to also pray on the behalf of others. On a little card I found extolling the power of prayer, it is written,

The day was long, the burden I had borne,
Seemed heavier than I could longer bear,
And then it lifted—but I did not know
Someone had knelt in prayer;
Had taken me to God that very hour,
And asked the easing of the load, and He,
In infinite compassion, had stooped down
And taken it from me. . . .

Prayers of request and supplication are quoted here under the following subjects and chapters:

Faith and Trust—Chapter 5; Grace—Chapter 6; Mercy—Chapter 7; Patience and Hope—Chapter 8; Humility—Chapter 9; Knowledge, Understanding, and Wisdom—Chapter 10; Strength and Courage, Sustenance and Support—Chapter 11; Peace—Chapter 12; Love, Compassion, Charity, and Kindness—Chapter 13; Comfort—Chapter 14; Inspiration—Chapter 15; Healing Self, Healing Others, Healing the World—Chapter 16; and For Help with Duty, Work, and Family—Chapter 17.

Below is a selection of a few general supplicatory prayers as a form of introduction to the specific chapters that follow.

Why then do you neglect prayer, when without prayer nothing can be obtained?

ANGELA OF FOLIGNO

*In prayer you must ask help from the Lord, for we of
ourselves can do little.*

ST. TERESA OF ÁVILA

*When someone repeats a prayer in the heart by the gift of the
Holy Spirit, those prayers when offered in purity cannot be
hidden, but ascend to God. . . .*

HILDEGARD OF BINGEN

Our God and God of all ages. You are the source of life
and blessing. You gave unexpected joy to Sarah in her old
age. You gave wisdom and insight to Rebecca. You gave
joy to Leah and took pity on the tears of Rachel. Hear
now the voice of their daughters as we call on Your
name. Hold us and sustain us in Your presence like a
mother who holds her child in her arms.

CHERYL WYLEN

You, O Lord, have called us to watch and pray.
Therefore, whatever may be the sin against which I pray,
make me careful to watch against it and so have reason
to expect that my prayer will be answered. In order to
perform this duty aright, grant me grace to preserve a
sober, equal temper, sincerity to pray for Your assistance,
remembering also that sobriety and equality of mind
consist in freedom from all confusion.

SUSANNA WESLEY

Help us, our Father, we pray, to comprehend more fully the prayer Your son taught us. Give us an understanding of every petition.

We have prayed, "Hallowed be Thy name." May we understand that all our relationships, our struggles and temptations, our dreams and desires must be endowed with reverence. Direct our powers in dignity and quietness; may our every action be in Your name.

We have prayed, "Thy kingdom come." Help us to remember that Thy kingdom will come upon the earth as first one soul and then another submits to Thy rules of life. Help us to say, unreservedly, "Here I am, use me."

Our Father, we have prayed, "Thy will be done in earth as it is in heaven." Help us to enter into a new and deeper relationship with You, knowing that only as our small purposes become part of Your great purpose, can we share in Your redemption of the world. May we be willing to say, "Not my will, but Thine be done."

Our Father, we have prayed, "Give us this day our daily bread." Help us to know that You will supply our every need. Above all, we pray for Your rich, unfailing gifts of the living Water and the living Bread.

Our Father, we have prayed, "Forgive us our trespasses as we forgive them that trespass against us." We need to be reminded that our sins are forgiven only as we forgive others, that the gifts we bring to Your altar can be offered only if we are at peace with each other.

Our Father, we have prayed, "Lead us not into temptation, but deliver us from evil." May we know with certainty that in the frictions, the ceaseless demands, the clashes of wills which engulf us we may turn to You as our sure bulwark. Lead us, our Father, out of fear and confusion, into Your peace.

SUE WEDDELL

5

FAITH AND TRUST

*W*ithout faith, it is futile to ask God for anything. So, asking for faith itself is a prayer with which many of us begin. We ask for our faith to continue and deepen. We ask to trust in the ways and goodness of the Divine.

Never forget that you are not alone. The Divine is with you helping and guiding you. He is the companion who never fails, the friend whose love comforts and strengthens. The more you feel lonely, the more you are ready to perceive His luminous Presence. Have faith and He will do everything for you.

THE MOTHER

Faith is nothing other than a proper understanding of our being, with true belief and certain trust, that we are in God.

JULIAN OF NORWICH

I do not pray for riches. But should riches come to me, I pray for generosity so that I would be willing to share with others.

I do not pray for beauty. But should I be fair of face and form, I pray for modesty lest I flaunt my loveliness.

I do not pray for power. But should it be my lot to lead and influence others, I pray for wisdom, lest arrogance take over my nature.

I do not pray for honor. But should honor come to me, I pray for understanding, lest esteem cause me to forget those who need a helping hand.

I do not pray for talent. But should I be gifted, I pray for humility, knowing full-well that all talent comes from You.

I do not pray for trouble. But should trouble come to me, I pray for courage to begin anew and neither whine nor blame.

I do not pray for sorrow. But when grief enters my life, I pray for fortitude to bear my trials with patience and to be a comfort to those around me.

For generosity; for modesty; for wisdom; for understanding; for humility; for courage; for fortitude.

But most of all I pray for faith—faith in Your perfection; faith in the perfection of Your judgments and Your laws.

VIRGINIA MOISE ROSEFIELD

I am apt to query whether I am not deceiving myself, in supposing I am the servant of the Lord, so ill to endure suffering, and to be so anxious to get rid of it; but it has been my earnest prayer that I might truly say, "Not as I will, but as You will." Lord! help me. I pray that I may be enabled to cast all my burden and all my care upon You, that I may rest in the full assurance of faith in Your love, pity, mercy and grace. I pray help me, that my soul may be less disquieted within me, and that I may more trustfully and hopefully go on heavenward. Increase my faith in Your faithfulness gracious Lord, whilst I believe that those who are once in grace are not always in grace; yet help me ever to feel that You are faithful, O Lord! who has called us out of darkness into Your marvellous light, and only You can do it; therefore be pleased to hearken to the prayer of Your poor servant, increase her faith, and be Yourself, for Your own name sake, not only the author, but the finisher of it.

ELIZABETH FRY

O God, who am I now?
Once, I was secure in familiar territory
    in my sense of belonging
unquestioning of
the norms of my culture
the assumptions built into my language
the values shared by my society.
But now you have called me out and away from home
and I do not know where you are leading.
I am empty, unsure, uncomfortable.
I have only a beckoning star to follow.
Journeying God,
pitch your tent with mine

so that I may not become deterred
by hardship, strangeness, doubt.
Show me the movement I must take
    toward a wealth not dependent on possessions
    toward a wisdom not based on books
    toward a strength not bolstered by might
    toward a God not confined to heaven
but scandalously earthed, poor, unrecognized . . .
help me to find myself
as I walk in others' shoes.

KATE COMPSTON

O eternal Trinity,
my sweet love!
You, light,
give us light.
You, wisdom,
give us wisdom.
You, supreme strength,
strengthen us.
Today, eternal God,
let our cloud be dissipated
so that we may perfectly know and follow your truth,
in truth,
with a free and simple heart.

ST. CATHERINE OF SIENA

Send to my heart even now, O blessed Lord!
Of burning faith a ray so fresh and clear
That Thy whole will may grow to me more dear;
As I would serve for love, not for reward.
No bitter drop Thy soothing springs afford,

Whether they meet the eye, or greet the ear;
In beauty clothed do all Thy works appear,
Most bounteous when Thou seem'st the least to accord,
If, as Your servant, I a boon might crave,
This faith would I possess, to warm and shine,
And ever feed the soul with light Divine,
Virtue from Thee goes forth, and if it gave
To roots deep planted a firm hold in me,
Much loving fruit I might return to Thee.

VITTORIA COLONNA

"Lord, that I may see!"
Give me light to see you in my even-Christian,
and to see my even-Christian in you.
Give me faith to recognize you
in those under my own roof.
In those who are with me, day after day,
on the way of the Cross.
Let me recognize you
not only in saints and martyrs,
in the innocence of children,
in the patience of old people
waiting quietly for death.
In the splendour of those
who die for their fellow men;
but let me also discern your beauty
through the uglinesss of suffering for sin
that you have taken upon yourself.
Let me know you in the outcast,
the humiliated, the ridiculed, the shamed.
In the sinner who weeps for his sins.
Give me even the courage
to look at your Holy Face,
almost obliterated,

bruised and lacerated
by my own guilt,
and to see myself!

Look back at me, Lord,
through your tears,
with my own eyes,
and let me see you,
Jesus, condemned to death,
in myself,
and in all men
who are condemned to die.

CARYLL HOUSELANDER

Lord, I believe, help my unbelief. My faith may be the
size of a mustard seed but even so, even aside from its
potential, it brings with it a beginning of love, an inkling
of love, so intense that human love with all its heights
and depths pales in comparison.

DOROTHY DAY

Adored Lord, increase my Faith, perfect it, crown it
    Your own,
Your choicest, dearest gift. Keep me in your fold and lead
    me to eternal life.

ST. ELIZABETH SETON

Dearest Lord, increase my faith more firmly, more fixedly
establish me upon the Rock of Ages, that however the
winds blow, the rains descend, or the floods beat against
me, I may not be greatly moved; and let not any of the
hindering or pulling things of this world lessen my love to
You and to Your cause; or prevent me from going steadily
forward in heights and in depths, in riches and in
poverty, in strength and in weakness, in sickness and in
health; or prevent my following hard after You in spirit,
with a humble, faithful, watchful, circumspect, and
devoted heart.

ELIZABETH FRY

O Jesus, lift my heart up above the worries of little
things, for they, like grains of dust, have great power.
They can stop noble desires and deaden the most ardent
hearts. Let me be small and humble; let me be always
seeking only Your glory. Every little breath I take, I do so
by Your grace only. You hold my very life in Your hands.
How could I then lack trust in You? Inflame my heart
with Your love, the source of all virtue, especially of trust.

CATHERINE DE HUECK DOHERTY

O Lord, whose way is perfect,
Help us, we pray, always to trust in your goodness;
that walking with you in faith, and following you in all
simplicity, we may possess quiet and contented minds,
and cast all our care on you, because you care for us;
For the sake of Jesus Christ our Lord.

CHRISTINA ROSSETTI

6

GRACE

*W*ithout the gift of the Divine's grace, the nourishment that fuels the fires of our souls, nothing in ourselves can be moved, transformed, distilled, or supported. Grace is the pure spirit of God's saving love. It has been associated with symbols such as the fountain and water; it can be poured as blessings to bestow grace upon us. Grace is a spiritual power that transforms us, guides us and connects us to the Truth. When we open in faith to the possibilities of divine intervention, then grace occurs just by this attitude. Catherine de Hueck Doherty prayed, "Your graces are a free gift; not the result of my trying." St. Teresa of Ávila referred to grace as "the sweetest water" in her analogies of her soul to nature. She wrote of the need of her soul, like a plant, to be watered to grow and to "increase the fragrance of the little buds of virtue . . . so that they might bloom to His glory."

The Divine Grace is with us and never leaves us even when the appearances are dark.

For those who have given themselves to the Divine each difficulty that confronts them is the assurance of a new progress and thus must be taken as a gift from the Grace.

THE MOTHER

Grace is God.

JULIAN OF NORWICH

For the action of grace in our hearts is secret and silent.

SIMONE WEIL

Grant us such grace that we may work Your will,
And speak Your words, and walk before Your face,
Profound and calm like waters deep and still;
Grant us such grace.

CHRISTINA ROSSETTI

O God, you have promised me my daily sustenance;
bestow it as You will, upon Your friends or enemies.

RĀBE'AH OF BASRA

Don't let me fall
As a stone falls upon the hard ground.
And don't let my hands become dry

As the twigs of a tree
When the wind beats down the last leaves.
And when the storm raises dust from the earth
With anger and howling,
Don't let me become the last fly
Trembling terrified on a windowpane.
Don't let me fall.
I have asked for so much,
But as a blade of your grass in a distant wild field
Let's drop a seed in the lap of the earth
And dies away,
Sow in me your living breath,
As you sow a seed in the earth.

KADYA MOLODOWSKY

Come, Holy Breath, come. Blow into the dusty rooms of
old. Refresh and make new.

PATRICIA LYNN REILLY

Dear Lord, make me understand that Your graces are a
free gift, not the result of my trying or my goodness.

CATHERINE DE HUECK DOHERTY

O Life, who gives life to all! Do not deny me this sweetest
water that You promise to those who want it. I want it,
Lord, and I beg for it, and I come to You. Don't hide
Yourself, Lord, from me, since You know my need and
that this water is the true medicine for a soul wounded
with love of You. O Lord, how many kinds of fire there
are in this life! Oh, how true it is that one should live in

fear! Some kinds of fire consume the soul, other kinds
purify it that it might live ever rejoicing in You. O living
founts from the wounds of my God, how you have flowed
with great abundance for our sustenance, and how surely
she who strives to sustain herself with this divine liqueur
will advance in the midst of the dangers of this life.

ST. TERESA OF ÁVILA

Living Water,
You well up from the center of the Universe
to nourish your creation.
As the woman of Samaria drew water
    for Jesus, a stranger,
give of Yourself to quench
the thirsting of our souls:
that, satisfied by the nectar of your love,
we reach out in compassion
to all who hunger for You.
Stream of Our Desire,
Pool of Wisdom,
You flow through Time
like a mighty River,
Womangod forever and ever.

MARY KATHLEEN SPEEGLE SCHMITT

My natural Mother, my gracious Mother, my most
precious Mother, have mercy on me. I have made my self
dirty and unlike You, and I may not and cannot make it
better, except with Your secret help and Your grace.

JULIAN OF NORWICH

Help me to wait for Your enabling grace without discouragement.

SUSANNA WESLEY

GRACE IN OUR WAY OF LIFE

Grace transforms our failings full of dread into abundant, endless comfort; grace transforms our failings full of shame into a noble, glorious rising; grace transforms our dying full of sorrow into holy, blissful life.

JULIAN OF NORWICH

O Jesus, it is a hard path for flesh and blood—impossible without Your help. O Jesus, You know I love You! You alone know my sinfulness, my imperfections, faults. Help me, above all, in courage. I want to walk your way. Here I am. Make me a saint even if it breaks me in the making. I want to be filled with You as a cistern is filled with water—clear and cool in the desert of life. I want to fertilize your fields, forever overflowing with Your Spirit, the Spirit which alone can bring men and women to You!

CATHERINE DE HUECK DOHERTY

God, our sustainer,
You have called out your people into the wilderness
to travel your unknown ways.
Make us strong to leave behind false security and comfort,
and give us new hope in our calling;

that the desert may blossom as a rose,
and your promises may be fulfilled in us.
In the name of Jesus Christ. Amen.

O God, the power of the powerless,
you have chosen as your witnesses
those whose voice is not heard.
Grant that, as women first announced the resurrection
though they were not believed,
we too may have courage
to persist in proclaiming your word,
in the power of Jesus Christ. Amen.

O God, our beloved,
born of a woman's body;
you came that we might look upon you,
and handle you with our own hands.
Grant that we may so cherish one another in our bodies
that we may also be touched by you,
through the Word made flesh,
Jesus Christ. Amen.

God our Mother,
you hold our life within you,
nourish us at your breast,
and teach us to walk alone.
Help us so to receive your tenderness
and respond to your challenge
that others may draw life from us,
in your name. Amen.

O God, our deliverer,
you cast down the mighty,
and lift up those of no account;
as Elizabeth and Mary embraced

with songs of liberation,
so may we also be pregnant with your Spirit,
and affirm one another in hope for the world,
through Jesus Christ. Amen.

O God, our soul's desire,
whose integrity is beyond our imagining,
and whose loveliness is more than we can bear,
make our hearts restless to seek your truth
in every part of our life;
that we may look upon your beauty without fear,
and find our rest in you,
through Jesus Christ. Amen.

O God whose Word is life,
and whose delight is to answer our cry,
give us faith like the Syro-Phoenician woman,
who refused to remain an outsider;
that we too may have the wit to argue
and demand that our daughters be made whole,
through Jesus Christ. Amen.

O covenant God,
You call us to the risk of commitment
even from the place of despair.
As Ruth and Naomi loved and held to one another,
abandoning the ways of the past;
so may we also not be divided,
but travel together
into that strange land where you will lead us,
through Jesus Christ. Amen.

God our creator,
You have made us one with this earth,
to tend it and to bring forth fruit;
may we so respect and cherish

all that has life from you,
that we may share in the labour of all creation
to give birth to your hidden glory
through Jesus Christ. Amen.

O God, in whose weakness is our strength,
you have taught us not to trust in armed might,
nor in the weapons of war.
As Jesus also suffered outside the gate,
let us go forth with him;
that the gates of hell may not prevail against us,
and that we may embrace even our enemies,
through Jesus Christ our saviour. Amen.

JANET MORLEY

Mary, our blessed Lady, you had more perfect grace
in you from the time you were conceived in your mother's
womb than did the twelve apostles when they received
the light of the Holy Spirit at Pentecost! This was indeed
necessary, for if God the Son had found so much as the
least spot or stain of vanity in you, he could not have
chosen you to be his mother; yet you were his mother,
and no such spot or stain could have been in you.

I see our Lady standing at the foot of the Cross,
where Jesus suffered for the fault of Adam, repairing more
than was damaged by the original fault, bringing a new life
of grace which our Lady had in the wholeness of her being.

What would you have said to those whose cruelty
caused this suffering? How would you have repaid them
for their sin? If needs be, you would have given your own
life rather than know God could not forgive them their
sin. But this was not necessary, as Christ re-united man
to God in such abundance and such anguish.

In such abundance, because the tiniest drop of his

blood, that would sit on the point of a needle, would have been enough to redeem a hundred thousand worlds, had there been so many. But he gave his blood in such abundance that it has detached me from myself and and made me live in accordance with the divine will.

MARGUERITE PORETE

Lord, You know better than I know myself that I am growing older and will someday be old. Keep me from the fatal habit of thinking I must say something on every subject and on every occasion. Release me from craving to straighten out everybody's affairs, make me thoughtful but not moody: helpful but not bossy. With my vast store of wisdom, it seems a pity not to use it all, but You know Lord that I want a few friends left at the end.

Keep my mind free from the recital of endless details; give me wings to get to the point. Seal my lips on my aches and pains, they are increasing, and love of rehearsing them is becoming sweeter as the years go by. I dare not ask for grace enough to enjoy the tales of other's pains, but help me to endure them with patience.

I dare not ask for improved memory, but for a growing humility and a lessening cocksureness when my memory seems to clash with memories of others. Teach me the glorious lesson that occasionally I may be mistaken.

Keep me reasonably sweet; I do not want to be a Saint—some of them are so hard to live with—but a sour old person is one of the crowning works of the devil. Give me the ability to see good things in unexpected places, and talents in unexpected people. And, give me, O Lord, the grace to tell them so.

ANONYMOUS (SEVENTEENTH-CENTURY NUN)

7

MERCY

*A*sking for mercy or forgiveness enhances our ability to know ourselves, our bodies, our motives, our mistakes. It helps us gain humility. Buddhists believe that our goal in life is to become as perfectly ourselves as we can. To do so, we need to learn to forgive ourselves. Mother Teresa advised that we need to forgive ourselves and forgive others in order for God to forgive us, and that includes forgiving not only what we have done, but what we have failed to do. "Mercy works by turning all things to good for us," wrote Julian of Norwich. St. Catherine of Siena called God's mercy "life-giving."

In many of the writings in this book reference is made to sin, and the need for penance to obtain mercy and purification. Sin can be misconduct or error against God's will, or against our own inner wisdom, intuition, and judgment. We all have experiences of what happens when we act against our intuition or ignore the call of our souls and our bodies. The Catholic writer Mary Jo Leddy wrote of sin, "we speak about sin because we do not

understand why we do what we don't want to do."
She explained, "Sin is precisely what remains inexplicable in our lives. It is this which gives it power over us, which eludes analysis but which remains open to forgiveness."

Confessing or sharing one's errors leads to a purging, a purification, a "sweeping the doorstep" (Sufi Omm Mohammad). A contrite heart allows us to experience the depths—and gifts—of divine mercy.

According to the law of man the guilty ought to be punished. But there is a law more imperative than the human law. It is the Divine Law, the law of compassion and mercy.

It is because of this law that the world is able to endure and progress towards Truth and Love.

THE MOTHER

Mercy is a sweet gracious working of love, mingled with abundant pity. For mercy works by preserving us, and mercy works by turning all things to good for us. Mercy allows us for love, to fail up to a certain point, and insofar as we fail, so far we fall, and insofar as we fall, so far we die, for we must and ought to die insofar as we fail in the sight and feeling of God, Who is our life.

Our failing is full of dread, our falling is full of shame, and our dying is full of sorrow. But still, in all this, the sweet eye of pity and love never departs from us, and the working of mercy does not cease.

JULIAN OF NORWICH

O good and kind Father, teach me what to say according to Your will! O reverend Father, sweet and full of grace, do not forsake me, but keep me in Your mercy.

HILDEGARD OF BINGEN

O Lord, when I meditate upon the wisdom of Your conduct among your creatures, I perceive that Your justice crushes them. Then I reflected upon myself by the vastness of Your mercy and realized that Your effusive grace embraces every being. O Lord, You have delayed chastisement of sinners, so Your lack of haste and granting of respite to them has made them desirous of Your gracious forgiveness. And why should it not be like this, since your bounty and grace towards previous peoples and nations was equally generous.

ANONYMOUS (SUFI WOMAN FROM ARJAN)

Lord of the world, I pray to you, God, as Queen Esther prayed. Lord of the whole world, with your right hand and your left hand, you have created the whole world with both your hands. May you spread your mercies over me.

REBECCA RACHEL LEAH

O eternal Mercy, you who cover over your creatures' faults! It does not surprise me that you say of those who leave deadly sin behind and return to you: "I will not remember that you had ever offended me." O unspeakable mercy! I am not surprised that you speak so to those who forsake sin, when you say of those who persecute you: "I want you to pray to me for them so that I can be merciful to them." What mercy comes forth from your Godhead, eternal Father, to rule the whole world with your power!

By your mercy we were created. And by your mercy we were created anew in your Son's blood. It is your mercy that preserves us. Your mercy made your Son play death against life and life against death on the wood of the cross. In him life confounded the death that is our sin, even while that same death of sin robbed the spotless Lamb of his bodily life. But who was conquered? Death! And how? By your mercy!

Your mercy is life-giving. It is the light in which both the upright and sinners discover your goodness. Your mercy shines forth in your saints in the height of heaven. And if I turn to the earth, your mercy is everywhere. Even in the darkness of hell your mercy shines, for you do not punish the damned as much as they deserve.

You temper your justice with mercy. In mercy you cleansed us in the blood; in mercy you kept company with your creatures. O mad lover! It was not enough for you to take on our humanity: You had to die as well! Nor was death enough: You descended to the depths to summon our holy ancestors and fulfill your truth and mercy in them. Your goodness promises good to those who serve you in truth, so you went to call these servants of yours from their suffering to reward them for their labors!

I see your mercy pressing you to give us even more when you leave yourself with us as food to strengthen our weakness, so that we forgetful fools should be forever reminded of your goodness. Every day you give us this food, showing us yourself in the sacrament of the altar within the mystic body of holy Church. And what has done this? Your mercy.

O mercy! My heart is engulfed with the thought of you! For wherever I turn my thoughts I find nothing but mercy! O eternal Father, forgive my foolish presumption in babbling on so before you—but your merciful love is my excuse in the presence of your kindness.

ST. CATHERINE OF SIENA

Your mercy, Lord, Lord now your mercy show,
On You I lie
To You I fly
Hide me, hive me as Your own,
Till these blasts be overblown,
Which now do fiercely blow.

MARY HERBERT, COUNTESS OF PEMBROKE

O God who is in Heaven, my trust and my hope is fully in you! May you guide me on this long road I have not travelled before! It's often during my life you helped me. Well I know your holy help, because I was often held by sorrow, with no escape. When the need was highest, it was then you would lay your merciful eye on me, and a light like the shining of the sun would come on my worried mind. The clouds of sorrow would be gone without trace; in place there would be some spiritual joy whose sweetness I cannot describe here.

PEIG SAYERS

Come Lord! God's image cannot shine
    Where sin's funereal darkness lowers—
Come! Turn those weeping eyes of thine
    Upon these sinning souls of ours!

And let those eyes with shepherd care
    Their moving watch above us keep;
Till love the strength of sorrow wear,
    And, as Thou weepedst, *we* may weep!

For surely we may weep to know,
    So dark and deep our spirits' stain;
That, had thy blood refused to flow
    Thy very tears had flowed in vain.

ELIZABETH BARRETT BROWNING

O Lord God, as the heavens are high above the earth, so are your ways above our ways, and your thoughts above our thoughts. For wise and holy purposes best known to yourself, you have seen fit to deprive me of all earthly relatives; but when my father and mother forsook me, then you did take me up. I desire to thank you, that I am this day a living witness to testify that you are a God, that will ever vindicate the cause of the poor and needy, and that you have always proved yourself to be a friend and father to me. O, continue your loving kindness even unto the end; and when health and strength begin to decay, and I, as it were, draw nigh unto the grave, O then afford me your heart-cheering presence, and enable me to rely entirely upon you. Never leave me nor forsake me, but have mercy upon me for your great name's sake. And not for myself alone do I ask these blessings, but for all the poor and needy, all widows and fatherless children, and for the stranger in distress;

and may they call upon you in such a manner as to be convinced that you are a prayer-hearing and prayer-answering God; and thine shall be the praise, forever.

MARIA W. STEWART

FORGIVENESS

In [the] place of your retirement to be alone with your conscience, turn your heart toward God to entreat Him with sincerity to assist you, that you may discover all your faults, but do not trouble and torment your mind. Examine yourself seriously, diligently, with a sincere desire to know and confess your sins, but after that, be at rest. God, who sees the bottom of your heart and the sincerity of your intention and endeavors, will forgive them.

ST. ELIZABETH SETON

There is so much suffering in families these days all over the world that it is important to pray, and it is important to forgive.

MOTHER TERESA

All kinds of people have lived next door to me . . .
    a funny old lady who was scared of burglars,
    a toothless woman with bleached hair,
    a lonely divorcée,
    a frail clergy widow,
    a Christian Science family,
    a bitter old couple who wouldn't say "hello,"

a family whose daughter left home because her
   stepmother did not love her,
a husband and wife whom I never saw. . . .

I have watched the news . . . and prayed for war-torn
   countries;
I have heard of the needy . . . and have given money for
   their support;
I have read of prisoners of conscience . . . and have
   written to their governments;
I have seen that help was wanted in a charity shop . . .
   and volunteered.

But how much have I done for the people next door?
   Is it because they live right beside me
   that I have sometimes failed to see their needs?

Lord, forgive me for being caught up in a whirl of
   Christian activity
and not have enough time for my neighbours;
forgive me for bearing the burden of the world,
and neglecting the people on my doorstep.

JEAN HACKETT

The shadows are lengthening, God.
The sun is sinking lower and lower on this Yom Kip-
   pur Day.
It won't be long now before our final prayers are said,
And we go home,
To friends and family,
When we reunite with them
After our self-imposed estrangement on this solemn day.

And now, although it is late,
I must ask:
Did I fully repent, God?
Did I examine my life enough?
Did I take the whole year into account?
All my deeds and misdeeds,
    were they atoned for?

This has been the hardest Yom Kippur so far.
Before this year, I seemed to sail through the ten days
    between Rosh Hashanah and Yom Kippur.
I was concerned with impressions I made on others,
With friends I was to visit,
With messages sent out and messages received.
But I wasn't concerned with the me that is deep inside.

This year, God, somehow you got to me.
Somehow, amid the rushing and the excitement of the
   season,
Somehow in the days of self-examination,
I truly began to examine me.
Finally, what has been expected of every Jew,
I began to expect of myself.
And now I ached.
How I looked forward with longing, real longing,
    for the approaching conclusion of Yom Kippur,
And for the release from my own introspection.

Looking at myself is no pleasure, God.
Looking and seeing all that is within me,
All that makes me do what I do,
And think what I think.
I know I'm not what You expect me to be.

Sometimes I wish the world wasn't the way it is.
Sometimes I wish I could be someone else,

At some other time.
I'm tired of apologizing over and over again
For the same mistakes.
How can I truly believe I will change,
When deep inside I know I can't,
And even more,
That sometimes I won't.

I am me, God,
With all my failings
And my half-promised vows.
I am me
Even when I say I will improve,
      and I know I won't.
I can only say that I'll try, God.
I can only say
That trying will have to be good enough for You.

You have given me the key to Your gates, My God.
You have provided me with the way
To be the best I can.
So why must I knock on those gates?
If I have in my possession
The means,
Why must I stand as a beggar,
Waiting for permission to enter?

Even as I ask, I know the answer.
The permission to enter comes
Not from You,
But can only come from me.
Only when I feel strong enough to open the gates can I
      enter.
Only when persistence and yearning accompany me
Can I push through to Your forgiveness.

And now, even as the sun sets,
I don't know if I'm ready.
I don't know if I've made an inventory complete enough.
I don't know if I can open those gates, God.
I need Your help.
I think I really need Your help.
If I can manage to push
Even the littlest bit from my side,
Will you pull on Yours?
If I say I'll try, God,
Will You accept that?
Will Your gates then open for me?

MIRIAM S. BIATCH

Before the beginning Thou hast foreknown the end,
Before the birthday the death-bed was seen of Thee:
Cleanse what I cannot cleanse, mend what I cannot
    mend,
O Lord All-Merciful, be merciful to me.

CHRISTINA ROSSETTI

O Lord, I swept my door-step, now You sprinkle the water.

OMM MOḤAMMAD

8

PATIENCE AND HOPE

*G*od imposes the lessons of patience on us regularly. Julian of Norwich said that we are inclined towards two kinds of sickness when God tests our patience. The first is "impatience or sloth because of which we bear our hard labor and our pain with depression." The second is "despair or dread full of doubt." But when we learn to practice what St. Elizabeth Seton called "the virtue of the perfect," we find that "true patience kills every fear" (St. Catherine of Siena). English religious Maria Boulding once wrote, "in the winters of your prayer, when there seems to be nothing but darkness and a situation of general frozenness, hold on, wait for God. He will come."

Patience is the key to endurance in faith, and leads to the deeper experience of that which follows: hope.

PATIENCE

The things we cannot realise today we shall be able to realise tomorrow. The only necessity is to endure.   .

THE MOTHER

The sea does not reward those who are too anxious, too greedy, or too impatient. To dig for treasures shows not only impatience and greed, but lack of faith. Patience, patience, patience, is what the sea teaches. Patience and faith. One should lie empty, open, choiceless as a beach—waiting for a gift from the sea.

ANNE MORROW LINDBERGH

Patience is a queen who stands guard upon the rock of courage. She is an invincible victor. She does not stand alone, but with perseverance as her companion.

ST. CATHERINE OF SIENA

Courage and patience, these I ask
Dear Lord, in this makest strait;
For hard I find my ten years' task,
Learning to suffer and to wait.

Life seems so rich and grand a thing,
So full of work for heart and brain,
It is a cross that I can bring,
No help, no offering, but pain.

The hard-earned harvest of these years
I long to generously share;

⊛ 177

The lessons learned with bitter tears
To teach again with tender care;

To smooth the rough and thorny way
Where other feet begin to tread;
To feed some hungry soul each day
With sympathy's sustaining bread.

So beautiful such pleasures show,
I long to make them mine;
To love and labor and to know
The joy such living makes divine.

But if I may not, I will only ask
Courage and patience for my fate,
And learn, dear Lord, Thy latest task—
To suffer patiently and wait.

LOUISA MAY ALCOTT

Beloved, You know my impatience. You know how
quickly I tire of all resolutions; how impatient I am about
lack of progress; how tired I become the moment the
work I have started begins to run smoothly; how green
distant grass looks to me!

O Jesus, help me to be patient, to plod and not to
be always snatching at stars. Teach me to plod daily
through small irritations, discouragements, knowing it is
for You.

CATHERINE DE HUECK DOHERTY

My soul is sorrowful—my spirit weighed down to
the dust. It cannot utter one word to You, my heavenly

Father—but still it seeks its only refuge and law at Your feet and waits for its deliverance in Your good time, when it shall please the Lord. Then will my bonds be loosed and my soul be set at liberty.

O, whatever is Your good pleasure, Your blessed will be done! Let me have only one wish—to please You—but one fear—that of offending You, never forgetting the comparison of my own unworthiness with Your goodness. Let my soul wait with patience and glorify You for Your patience with me.

ST. ELIZABETH SETON

Give me that tranquil courage which is content to await your gift. I live by what comes to me from you. Your word proceeding forth from my mouth, at your own time, in your own way, not by my deliberate self-occupied use of the power you give. Sometimes my need and exhaustion seem very great, and you seem very silent: surrounding conditions seem very stony, and hard. Those are the moments when my faith is purified, when I am given my chance of patience and fortitude and tranquility; abiding among the stones in the wilderness and learning the perfection of dependence on you.

EVELYN UNDERHILL

Grant to us all,
Lord Jesus,
that in the soul's long winters
we may wait patiently,
grow imperceptibly,
in the rhythms and seasons of your love
and so enter into your peace.

Give us grace
to wait patiently,
without doubt,
without impatience,
without anxiety,
for the morning of resurrection.

May every little death in life
teach us how to die
the last death that is the beginning of true life.
Be our life to us
on earth, Lord Jesus,
and our Everlasting Life.

CARYLL HOUSELANDER

HOPE

All through those weary first days in jail when I was in solitary confinement, the only thoughts that brought comfort to my soul were those lines of the Psalms that expressed the terror and misery of man suddenly stricken and abandoned.

The blackness of hell was all about me. The sorrows of the world encompassed me. I was like one gone down into the pit. Hope had forsaken me. . . .

And yet if it were not the Holy Spirit that comforted me, how could I have been comforted, how could I have endured, how could I have lived in hope?

DOROTHY DAY

O glorious resurrection! God of Abraham and all
our Fathers, in all the centuries during which the

believers have placed their hope in Thee, none has ever
been deceived. Therefore my hope also is in Thee.

IDA CALVIN

Lord, let me know the power of the spirit; O Lord, let
  me know
If in its darkest hour on the prisoning earth below,
The spirit be captive and bound with the body, to beat at
  its walls
Till, deaf with the clamor of sound, it shall hear not the
  heaven that calls.
Shall it sink in the darkness and fail, and be joined to the
  ruin of life?
Is the striving of none avail, and the hope that lives in
  the strife?
What of the spirit, O Lord? Shall it wait and be never
  aware?
Will Thou not send it a word from the highest where
  Truth is laid bare?
For Hope that has no defender lives on for a word
  from Thee;
O God! it will never surrender, 'tis mighty and sure
  and free.

NINA DAVIS SALAMAN

9

HUMILITY

*T*he state of humility is a spiritual skill, which needs to be mastered. It is selflessness and lowliness; it requires no encouragement, extolling, or admiration. When pride and the expectations of the ego fall away humility steps in to aid the soul in spiritual growth. And it is usually through circumstances beyond our control that we learn it. Elizabeth of the Trinity said that to be "plunged into humility is to be plunged into God." And it is by being humble before God that we learn more of God. British writer Caryll Houselander wrote of the difficulty of being stripped "of all pretence," and like many Christian women, looked to the example of the humility of Christ.

Humility, the most beautiful of all the virtues.

SIMONE WEIL

How much good is accomplished by humility! It renders
peaceful and quiet the souls of those who are filled with it.

ANGELA OF FOLIGNO

Humility is to have place
deep in the secret of God's face

where one can know, past all surmise,
that God's great will alone is wise.

JESSICA POWERS (*Humility*)

Clothe me in Thy holiness
Thy meek humility;
Put on me my glorious dress,
Endue my soul with Thee;
Let thine image be restored,
Thy name and nature let me prove;
With Thy fullness fill me, Lord,
And perfect me in love.

I have much need of humbling myself before You,
the great and holy God, because of the sins that I am
daily guilty of in thought, word and deed against Your
divine majesty. Help me to overcome habitual levity in
my thoughts and to shun vain and impure thoughts
which, though they do not take up their abode in my
mind for any long period of time, yet, in their passing
through, often leave a tincture of impurity. Enable me to
keep my heart with all diligence, my thoughts and
affections, for out of them are the issues of life. How
often have I offended in this kind! Cleanse me from
secret faults, for out of the abundance of the heart the

mouth speaks. Help me to guard against vain and unnecessary words, and to speak of You, my God, with that reverence, that humility, that gravity that I ought.

SUSANNA WESLEY

Gracious God, who does, with the most inestimable gift of Your love, freely give all things which we need, O give me more and more the lovely ornament of humility! Enable me to meditate with delightful attention on the excellencies of my Saviour and ardently desire to be more like him in this engaging virtue! O how bright it shone in every scene of His astonishing abasement! And did not the holy Jesus, the Lord of Lords and King of Kings, condescend to innumerable instances of benevolence to poor sinners! Did he not even stoop to wash the feet of His disciples, to teach them a lesson of affectionate humility! And shall not I, a poor sinful creature, rejoice to be able to administer any comfort or assistance to the meanest of His servants? Transform me, blessed Saviour, into Your own lovely image, and make me meek and lowly.

ANNE STEELE

Jesus
Stripped of your garments
upon Calvary,
give me the courage
and the humility,
to be stripped before the world
of all pretence.
To show myself,
even to that one whom I love

and whose good opinion of me
is vital to my happiness,
just as I am,
naked,
stripped of everything
that could hide
the truth of my soul,
the truth of myself from them.

CARYLL HOUSELANDER

Deliver me, O Jesus,
From the desire of being loved,
From the desire of being extolled,
From the desire of being honoured,
From the desire of being praised,
From the desire of being preferred,
From the desire of being consulted,
From the desire of being approved,
From the desire of being popular,
From the fear of being humiliated,
From the fear of suffering rebukes,
From the fear of being calumniated,
From the fear of being forgotten,
From the fear of being wronged,
From the fear of being ridiculed,
From the fear of being suspected.

MOTHER TERESA AND THE MISSIONARIES OF CHARITY

10

KNOWLEDGE, UNDERSTANDING, AND WISDOM

*W*e have knowledge, reason, and the intellect not only to evaluate ourselves and contribute to our communities but to know and love God. Usually we start this process within ourselves with self-knowledge. Self-knowledge can be viewed in different ways by women. Marguerite Porete spoke of the "dark night" she needed to enter to find a "greater knowledge of myself," because it is only in the darkness that we truly see, while Hildegard of Bingen referred to "the gifts of light from within" as that which enlightens—the sparks of infinite knowledge. St. Catherine of Siena wrote in her *Dialogue* (which records a conversation with God) that love follows upon understanding; in essence, she was told by God that the more we know the more we love, and the more we love the more we know.

Wisdom is the highest peak of knowledge and understanding. It is referred to so aptly in the Old Testament scriptures as Lady Wisdom, e.g., "She hastens to make herself known to those who desire her," or "Her radiance never ceases." Wisdom is the knowledge of good, which is found in ourselves and in nature. Christina Rossetti wrote of seeing this knowledge of good within the seed of a tree, the egg of a bird, the shroud of a butterfly. Meinrad Craighead defined her path to wisdom in herself, as taken through her own interior consciousness and not through the more masculine ways of the logical mind. "My sleeping is my dreaming, my dreaming is my thinking, my thinking is my wisdom," she wrote.

KNOWLEDGE

The Knowledge of God

. . . she oversees all people and all things in heaven and earth. And she is so bright and glorious that you cannot look at her face or her garments for the splendor with which she shines. For she is terrible with the terror of the avenging lightning, and gentle with the goodness of the bright sun; and both her terror and her gentleness are incomprehensible to humans, the terror of divine brilliance in her face and the brightness of her beauty in her garments, as the sun cannot be looked at in its burning face or its beautiful clothing of rays. But she is with everyone and in everyone, and so beautiful is her secret that no person can know the sweetness with which she sustains people, and spares them in inscrutable mercy; spares even the hardest stone, which is a hard and incorrigible person who never wants to turn aside from evil, until it can be penetrated no farther.

HILDEGARD OF BINGEN

The Divine's words comfort and bless, soothe and illumine, and the Divine's generous hand lifts a fold of the veil which hides the infinite knowledge.

THE MOTHER

The Knowledge of Self

At the same time, this matter of self-knowledge must never be neglected. No soul on this road is such a giant that it does not often need to become a child at the breast again. For there is no state of prayer, however sublime, in which it is not necessary often to go back to the beginning. And self-knowledge with regard to sin is the bread which must be eaten with food of every kind, however dainty it may be, on this road of prayer: without this bread we could not eat our food at all. But bread must be taken in moderate proportions.

ST. TERESA OF ÁVILA

Try to be wise enough to know that you do not know. Then the Divine can lead you forward into true knowledge, calmly, stage by stage. Give me your mind without fear and I will expand it. When the heart suffers, it is easy to transform its suffering into joy, but when the mind creates and lives by a fantasy, it is extremely hard to change it. So be very careful. Do not let your mind become your worst enemy.

MOTHER MEERA

Glory of Yahweh,
invisible yet known and felt,
You cover us with mists of time,
and draw us close beneath the canopy
    of your sacred space.
Open our hearts and minds to knowledge of You:
that, luminous with the power of your love,
we embody your goodness to all the earth.
Ancient Mother,
Beloved Companion,

You are the Fire of Eternity.

MARY KATHLEEN SPEEGLE SCHMITT

I count the stars, I wait for one pin of light.

MEERA

Lord, make me like a crystal that your light may shine
through me.

KATHERINE MANSFIELD

Please listen to me,
Great Repa Yogi, the accomplished one.
When I look at human lives
They remind me of dew on grass.
Thinking thus, my heart is full of grief.

When I see my friends and relatives,
They are as merchants passing in the street.
Thinking thus, my heart is grieved and sad.

Because of my good deeds in former lives,
I was born this time a human being.
My past life drives me from behind,
Cooking and household duties pull me on.
I draw closer to death every minute.
This decaying body
At any time may fall.
My breath, like morning-fog,
At any time may disappear.
Thinking thus, I cannot sleep.

Thinking thus, my heart is sad.

Oh, my Father Jetsun,
For the sake of Dharma I visit you.
Pray bless, protect, and pity me,
And grant me the holy Teachings!

SAHLE AUI

Lord Jesus, merciful and patient, grant us grace, we
beseech You, ever to teach in a teachable spirit; learning
alone with those we teach, and learning from them
whenever You so please; that we and they may all be
taught of God.

CHRISTINA ROSSETTI

UNDERSTANDING

I lie on the earth,
I kneel
In the ring of my horizons,
And stretch my hands
With an entreaty
To the west, when the sun sets,
To the east, when it rises there,
To each spark
To show me the light
And give light to my eyes,
To each worm that glows in the darkness at night,
That it shall bring its wonder before my heart
And redeem the darkness that is enclosed in me.

KADYA MOLODOWSKY

Lord, purge our eyes to see
Within the seed a tree,
Within the glowing egg a bird,
Within the shroud a butterfly.
Till, taught by such we see
Beyond all creatures, Thee
And hearken to Thy tender word
And hear its "Fear not: it is I."

CHRISTINA ROSSETTI

In the Hands of God

I am Yours and born for you,
What do You want of me?

Majestic Sovereign,
Unending wisdom,
Kindness pleasing to my soul;
God sublime, one Being Good,
Behold this one so vile.
Singing of her love to you:
What do You want of me?

Yours, you made me,
Yours, you saved me,
Yours, you endured me,
Yours, you called me,
Yours, you awaited me,
Yours, I did not stray.
What do You want of me?

Good Lord, what do You want of me,
What is this wretch to do?
What work is this,
This sinful slave, to do?
Look at me, Sweet Love,
Sweet Love, look at me,
What do You want of me?

In your hand
I place my heart,
Body, life and soul,
Deep feelings and affections mine,
Spouse—Redeemer sweet,
Myself offered now to you,
What do You want of me?

Give me death, give me life,
Health or sickness,
Honor or shame,
War or swelling peace,
Weakness or full strength,
Yes, to these I say:
What do You want of me?

Give me wealth or want,
Delight or distress,
Happiness or gloominess,
Heaven or hell,
Sweet life, sun unveiled,
To you I give all:
What do You want of me?

Give me, if You will, prayer,
Or let me know dryness;

An abundance of devotion,
Or if not, then barrenness.
In you alone, Sovereign Majesty,
I find my peace:
> What do You want of me?

Give me then wisdom,
Or for love, ignorance;
Years of abundance,
Or hunger and famine.
Darkness or sunlight,
Move me here or there:
> What do You want of me?

If You want me to rest,
I desire it for love;
If to labor,
I will die working:
Sweet Love say
Where, how and when:
> What do You want of me?

Calvary or Tabor give me,
Desert or fruitful land;
As Job in suffering
Or John at Your breast;
Barren or fruited vine,
Whatever be Your will:
> What do You want of me?

Be I Joseph chained
Or as Egypt's governor,
David pained
Or exalted high,
Jonas drowned,

Or Jonas freed:

>What do You want of me?

Silent or speaking,
Fruitbearing or barren,
My wounds shown by the Law,
Rejoicing in the tender Gospel;
Sorrowing or exulting,
You alone live in me:

>What do You want of me?

>Yours I am, for You I was born:
>What do You want of me?

>St. Teresa of Ávila

I beseech you, my Lord, give me understanding, that
by my account I may be able to make known these
mystical things; forsake me not, but strengthen me by the
daylight of Your justice, in which Your son was
manifested. Grant me to make known the divine
counsel, which was ordained of old, as I can and
should. . . .

>Hildegard of Bingen

Wisdom

The truth is neither in separation nor in uniformity.
The truth is in unity manifesting through diversity.

The Mother

Lover of Weeds,
You created the wildflowers and the beasts of the field.
From your Body, the Universe,
evolved all living things,
and there is no creature in heaven or earth whom You do
    not love.
Teach us the Wisdom of valuing all of life:
that, leaving behind the dualisms of worlds past,
we enter into unity with You and all Creation;
Spiritwoman who draws all into one,
You are our Living Body,
and our World without End.

Mary Kathleen Speegle Schmitt

O fire of the Paraclete,
the life of every creature's life:
you are holy in giving life to forms;

You are holy in anointing
the severely injured,
holy in cleansing
loathsome wounds.

O vent of holiness,
fire of charity,

O sweet taste in our bodies
and infusion in our hearts
of the fragrance of all virtues.

O clearest fountain,
in which is shown
how God gathers together those who wander
and seeks those who are lost.

O shield of life
and hope of all our limbs' union,
O belt of honor:
save those who are blessed.

Guard those who have been imprisoned
by the enemy,
release those in bondage
whom divine power wills to save.

O boldest path,
penetrating into all places,
on high and on earth,
and in every abyss:
you fit and gather all together.

From you the clouds issue and the air soars,
the rock have their humors
and the waters bring forth their streams
and the earth sweats out green things growing.
And always you teach the learned,
those made happy by the inspiration of Wisdom.

So let there be praise to you
who are the sound of all praise
and the joy of life,
who are hope and powerful honor,
granting the gifts of light.

Hildegard of Bingen

11

STRENGTH AND COURAGE, SUSTENANCE AND SUPPORT

*T*hese prayers introduce a variety of needs. One of the most poignant is Mother Tessa Bielecki's plea for divine strength when she is in a place of administrative burnout from life's demands, and suffering "chronic weariness." American Benedictine Joan Chittister's litany to Judeo-Christian holy women is a wonderful honoring of the courage of those who went before us. The 1991 Nobel Peace Prize recipient, Burmese Aung San Suu Kyi, who lived for many years under house arrest, asked that we not let fear dictate our actions, even though this is, sadly, a common occurrence.

Lady Jane Grey, Queen of England for nine days in 1553, wrote her mature prayer for strength and courage when she was only fifteen and confined to prison for treason. Her words as she faced her impending execution offer an example of faith, patience, surrender, and courage.

STRENGTH

All our strength is with the Divine. With Him we can surmount all the obstacles.

THE MOTHER

Lord, strengthen our souls, so that so many firm resolutions may be more than mere words.

ST. ELIZABETH SETON

Lord, be pleased so to help and strengthen me in this that for Your own cause's sake, for my own soul's sake, my beloved family's and the Society's sake, I may in no way be a cause of reproach; but in my life, conduct and conversation glorify Your great and excellent name. In all my perplexities be pleased to help me and make a way, where I see no way.

ELIZABETH FRY

My Lord and My God, My Love and My All—walking the dangerously thin line between complaint and lament, with the holy audacity of Saint Teresa, I say: "If this is the way You treat Your friends, no wonder You have so few!" But then, along with that wild woman of Ávila, I pray that since You have so few friends, we few had better be good ones! Make me one of Your *good* friends.

I am not who I was when You first called me in all my naïve enthusiasm. With wide-open eyes and a broken heart, I am far more sobered and yet more intoxicated than ever, more realistic and yet more romantic, more sorrowful and ever more joyous.

What an arduous business to balance all Your paradoxical demands on the tightrope of life: solitude and togetherness, fast and feast, love and detachment, work and prayer. I do not ask for a lightening of the burden, but only for greater strength to bear the weight, and greater wisdom to bear it creatively. Or, if it be Your will to have it crucify me, then grant me the grace to go gladly, not merely with resignation, but rollicking with laughter.

I wouldn't mind a cross of wood so much, but being nailed to a desk and buried alive under mounds of paper and telephone calls is an ignominious way to go! But this is the way You have chosen for me. Do I need a better system or more surrender?

Your answer lies in the secret of Saint Ignatius: to work as though everything depends on me, and pray as though everything depends on You. I've pulled off one or the other over the years, but now I beg You to help me live out a better balance between the two. And if I can't, then burn my files or consume me with Your flames!

I am a bow in Your hands, Lord, and I am being overdrawn. Help me to discern when that overdrawing comes from my own drivenness and I need more stillness, more secretarial help, and time-management—and when that overdrawing is You and all I need is the willingness to say yes.

Whenever You move me into the public eye, strengthen Your interior hold on me. Keep me buried in the hiddenness of Your heart. As the demands of my life grow greater and my patience thins, help me to go the distance and live out my exile in this crucified paradise. And when I have given You my all, may I say, "I have only done my duty" (Luke 17.10).

Make me more Your fool, more Your spouse, more Your slave. Plunge me ever more deeply into a life of self-spending service, and despite my chronic weariness, let me never count the cost or measure the length of the arrow that pierces my heart.

I am Your tragic-merry woman and lay down my life in union with You, my Suffering Servant, my Crucified Clown, My Bridegroom and my King.

MOTHER TESSA BIELECKI

O God! if this indeed be all
That Life can show to me;
If on my aching brow may fall
No freshening dew from Thee;

If with no brighter lamp than this
The lamp of hope may glow
And I may only *dream* of bliss,
And wake to weary woe;

If friendship's solace must decay,
When other joys are gone,
And love must keep so far away,
While I go wandering on,—

Wandering and toiling without gain,
The slave of others' will,
With constant care and frequent pain,
Despised, forgotten still;

Grieving to look on vice and sin,
Yet powerless to quell
The silent current from within,
The outward torrent's swell;

While all the good I would impart,
The feelings I would share,
Are driven backward to my heart,
And turned to wormwood there;

If clouds must *ever* keep from sight
The glories of the Sun,
And I must suffer Winter's blight,
Ere Summer is begun:

If Life must be so full of care—
Then call me soon to Thee;
Or give me strength enough to bear
My load of misery.

ANNE BRONTË

God harden me against myself,
This coward with pathetic voice
Who craves for ease, and rest and joys:

Myself, arch-traitor of myself,
My hollowest friend, my deadliest foe,
My clog whatever road I go.

Yet One there is can curb myself,
Can roll the strangling load from me,
Break off the yoke and set me free.

CHRISTINA ROSSETTI

God, at this time of the year, as we celebrate Purim, we
are reminded of the important role women have played
throughout our history.

Because of Esther's determination she was able to
   succeed in her difficult task,
Because of her intelligence she found a solution to the
   Jews' predicament.
Because of her courage, she was able to approach
   Ahasuerus even though her own position was in
   jeopardy.

These qualities and the many others Esther possessed are
   qualities that were found in Jewish women from the
   past and are woven throughout the personalities of our
   modern day heroines.

May we approach the challenges that face us in our
   homes, in our Temple and in our community with the
   same tenacity and wisdom of Esther, and with your
   guidance may we go from "strength to strength."

GOLDIE J. KATZ

Dear God, creator of women in your image,
born of a woman in the midst of a world half women,
carried by women to mission fields around the globe,
made known by women to all the children of the earth,
give to the women of our time
      the strength to persevere,
      the courage to speak out,
      the faith to believe in you beyond
      all systems and institutions
so that your face on earth may be seen in all its beauty,
so that men and women become whole,
so that the church may be converted to your will in
   everything and in all ways.

We call on the holy women who went before us,
channels of Your Word in testaments old and new,
to intercede for us
so that we might be given the grace
to become what they have been
for the honor and glory of God.

Saint Esther, who pleaded against power for the
   liberation of the people,)
Saint Judith, who routed the plans of men and
   saved the community,)
Saint Deborah, laywoman and judge, who led
   the people of God,)
Saint Elizabeth of Judea, who recognized
   the value of another woman,)
Saint Mary Magdalene, minister of Jesus,
   first evangelist of the Christ,)   Pray
Saint Scholastica, who taught her brother
   Benedict to honor the spirit above
   the system,)
Saint Hildegard, who suffered interdict for the
   doing of right,)   for
Saint Joan of Arc, who put no law above the
   law of God,)
Saint Clare of Assisi, who confronted the pope
   with the image of woman as equal,)
Saint Julian of Norwich, who proclaimed for all
   of us the motherhood of God,)
Saint Thérèse of Lisieux, who knew the call to
   priesthood in herself,)
Saint Catherine of Siena, to whom the pope
   listened,)   us
Saint Teresa of Ávila, who brought women's
   gifts to the reform of the church,)
Saint Edith Stein, who brought fearlessness

to faith,   ) Pray
Saint Elizabeth Seton, who broke down boundaries
   between laywomen and religious by wedding
   motherhood and religious life,   ) for
Saint Dorothy Day, who led the church to a
   new sense of justice.   ) us

Mary, mother of Jesus, who heard the call of God and
   answered,
Mary, mother of Jesus, who drew strength from the
   woman Elizabeth,
Mary, mother of Jesus, who underwent hardship bearing
   Christ,
Mary, mother of Jesus, who ministered at Cana,
Mary, mother of Jesus, inspirited at Pentecost,
Mary, mother of Jesus, who turned the Spirit of God into
   the body and blood of Christ, pray for us.

JOAN CHITTISTER

FOR COURAGE

*Courage is a sign of the soul's nobility. But courage must be
calm and master of itself, generous and benevolent.
   There is no greater courage than to be always truthful.*

THE MOTHER

*Fearlessness may be a gift but perhaps more precious is the
courage acquired through endeavour, courage that comes
from cultivating the habit of refusing to let fear dictate one's
actions, courage that could be described as "grace under*

pressure"—grace which is renewed repeatedly in the face of harsh, unremitting pressure.

AUNG SAN SUU KYI

May it please His Majesty to give us the courage so that we may merit to service Him.

ST. TERESA OF ÁVILA

O merciful God, consider my misery best known unto you; and be now to me a strong tower of defence, I humbly require you. . . . For You know better what is good for me than I do; therefore do with me in all things what you will, and plague me what way you will. Only, in the meantime, arm me, I beseech you, with your armour, that I may stand fast, my loins being girded about with verity, having on the breast-plate of righteousness, and shod with the shoes prepared by the gospel of peace; above all things, taking to me the shield of faith, wherewith I may be able to quench all the fiery darts of the wicked; and taking the helmet of salvation, and the sword of your spirit, which is your most holy word; praying always, with all manner of prayer and supplication, that I may refer myself wholly to your will, abiding your pleasure, and comforting myself in those troubles that it shall please you to send me; seeing such troubles as profitable for me, and seeing I am assuredly persuaded all you do cannot but be well. Hear me, O merciful Father, for his sake, whom should be a sacrifice for my sins; to whom with you and the Holy Ghost be all honour and glory.

LADY JANE GREY

O my Lord, you only are our king; help me, who am alone and have no helper but you, for my danger is in my hand. Ever since I was born I have heard in the tribe of my family that you, O Lord, took Israel out of all the nations, and our ancestors from among all their forebears, for an everlasting inheritance, and that you did for them all that you promised. . . .

Remember, O Lord; make yourself known in this time of our affliction, and give me courage, O King of the gods and Master of all dominion! Put eloquent speech in my mouth before the lion, and turn his heart to hate the man who is fighting against us, so that there may be an end of him and those who agree with him. But save us by your hand, and help me, who am alone and have no helper but you, O Lord.

QUEEN ESTHER (ESTHER 14: 3–5, 12–14, ADDITION C)

FOR SUSTENANCE AND SUPPORT

Heaven to me a mystic Erin is,
God's sea-encircled dwelling, wholly lit
by its own inner and eternal day,
and all my birds of longing nest in it.

I pray to Patrick of the Trinity
to gain for me this isle of the Triune.
Grant me to turn my prow into its port
before the cycle of the next new moon.

I pray to Brigid, Mary of the Gael,
so clothe me with the Virgin it may be
that when my mantle sweeps against the waves
they may take heed to her tranquility.

Brendan the Voyageur I too implore:
through these dark waters take me to my goal.
As once you found my earthland, find for me
the unimagined homeland of my soul.

Have pity, saints of Erin; help my ship
out to the blessed isle! And till I be
anchored in God my postexilic Good,
O Columbkill the exile, pray for me.

JESSICA POWERS (*The Far Island*)

You angel of God who has charge of me
From the fragrant Father of mercifulness,
The gentle encompassing of the Sacred Heart
To make round my soul-shrine this night,
    Oh, round my soul-shrine this night.

Ward from me every distress and danger,
Encompass my course over the ocean of truth,
I pray you, place your pure light before me,
O bright beauteous angel on this very night,
    Bright beauteous angel on this very night.

Be Yourself the guiding star above me,
Illume me to every reef and shoal,
Pilot my barque on the crest of the wave,
To the restful haven of the waveless sea,
    Oh, the restful haven of the waveless sea.

ANN MACDONALD

I have made truce with Time. The hours stand still
That once so quickly fled on winged feet,
Moments too fluid cannot now fulfill
Their destined passage where the planets meet
Infinity. For all is infinite waste,
Vastness and stillness and a withering
Of flowered things, no loitering and no haste,
No blight of winter and no tryst with spring.

For I have sworn a truce and planted high
The signal of distress. Time cannot pass,
Any more than stars can leave their native sky,
Or earth prevent the quiet, pushing grass;
Over my life Time has no more command.
O Lord, reach out Your strong, sustaining hand!

ANN BATCHELDER

12

PEACE

*T*o be at peace is everyone's greatest need. The only way to find peace and experience it is through and from the Divine. The state of peace "which the world can neither give nor take away" (St. Elizabeth Seton) is attained through the spiritual equation of silence and love: silence + love = peace. God speaks in the silence of our hearts. Catherine de Hueck Doherty wrote of her need for stillness, to be able to "listen to the great silence in which You whisper in my heart."

The Buddhist women here also share the equation; they found their steps to peace through the teachings of the Buddha, which involve silence, detachment, and the practice of compassion.

Peace is not found in those who do not with Him go.

ST. CATHERINE OF GENOA

The Divine's Presence gives us peace in strength, serenity in action and an unchanging happiness in the midst of all circumstances.

Nowhere will you be able to find peace unless you have peace in your heart. Look for the inner causes of disharmony much more than the outer ones. It is the inside which governs the outside.

THE MOTHER

Meditate on the unconditioned.
Get rid of the tendency
to judge yourself
above, below, or
equal to others.
By penetrating deeply
into judgment
you will live at peace.

ABHIRUPA-NANDA

O God, by the bond of trust I have in You, give me peace of heart. Placate all my thoughts with contentment in You. Do not allow my lot to be distanced from You, O desire of all who yearn.

ḤAYYUNA

O peace, dear object of my heart! O God, who is my peace, who makes us at peace within ourself, with all the world, who by this means pacifies heaven and earth! When shall I, my God, when shall I, by the tranquillity of my conscience, by a sweet confidence in Your power, by

an entire acquiescence, or rather an attachment to, a
delectation in Your eternal will in all the events of this
life, possess that peace which is in You, which comes
from You, and which You Yourself are?

EUGÉNIE DE GUÉRIN

I want to be very still, not even praying with my
lips—just to sit at Your feet, my God, and listen to the
great silence in which You seem to whisper to my heart.

There are so many things I want to hear from You in
that silence; yet I must go back into the rush and turmoil
of life. But, as I think of it, I see a way out. And this is to
keep deep in my soul—within the rush and turmoil—the
great silence and peace in which alone we poor mortals
can clearly hear Your quiet voice. We are so weak that
alone we can do nothing, not even keep silent in our
souls in order to hear Your voice.

CATHERINE DE HUECK DOHERTY

I do not ask, O Lord, that life may be
A pleasant road;
I do not ask that Thou wouldst take from me
Aught of its load;

I do not ask that flowers should always spring
Beneath my feet;
I know too well the poison and the sting
Of things too sweet.

For one thing only, Lord, dear Lord, I plead,
Lead me aright—

Though strength should falter, and though heart
should bleed—
Through Peace to Light.

I do not ask, O Lord, that Thou shouldst shed
Full radiance here;
Give but a ray of peace, that I may tread
Without a fear.

I do not ask my cross to understand,
My way to see—
Better in darkness just to feel Thy hand
And follow Thee.

Joy is like a restless day; but peace divine
Like quiet night:
Lead me, O Lord—till perfect Day shall shine,
Through Peace to Light.

ADELAIDE ANNE PROCTER

O my God, Trinity whom I adore, help me to forget
myself entirely that I may be established in You as still
and as peaceful as if my soul were already in eternity.
May nothing trouble my peace or make me leave You, O
my Unchanging One, but may each minute carry me
further into the depths of Your Mystery. Give peace to
my soul; make it Your heaven, Your beloved dwelling and
Your resting place. May I never leave You there alone but
be wholly present, my faith wholly vigilant, wholly
adoring, and wholly surrendered to Your creative Action.

ELIZABETH OF THE TRINITY

Eternal wellspring of peace—
May we be drenched with the longing for peace
that we may give ourselves over to peace
until the earth overflows with peace
as living waters overflow the seas.

MARCIA FALK

The Buddha taught
seven qualities of enlightenment.
They are ways to find peace
and I have developed them all.

For I have seen the Blessed One.
This is my last body,
and I will not go
from birth to birth again.
This is my last rebirth.

JENTI

May peace be within us.
May peace be around us.
May peace be beside us.
May peace be between us.
May we walk peacefully with Mother Earth.
May peace fill our days and our nights.
May peace fill the earth.

DIANN L. NEU

13

LOVE, COMPASSION, CHARITY, AND KINDNESS

*T*he thirteenth-century mystic Hadewijch of Brabant called love "the mother of all virtues." God is love, and love is God; the words are interchangeable. For God said to Hildegard of Bingen, "I am love."

The love of God and the Divine is never ending; it is the virtue we carry with us through life and beyond. When love is embraced, its vitalness is revealed. "Outside it now I dare not live," wrote Jean Sophia Pigott.

"The thirst for affection and love is a human need," wrote The Mother, "but it can be quenched only if it turns towards the Divine. As long as it seeks satisfaction in human beings, it will always be disappointed or wounded."

Many Christian saints and mystics attained a deeper understanding of Christ's love through suffering by studying His Passion; it led to a comprehension of what it means to be "crucified by love" (Elizabeth of the Trinity). It is the way in which we love when we suffer that enables us to be able to love others when they suffer. It is not about how many times we suffer, but how much we learn about love through our suffering.

The need for a personal love is the most prevalent need of human beings. Alone, we can experience God's love for us through prayer and contemplation, but because God and love are contained within each other, we also find God through our active love of the people around us. As we come to experience love with another and accept love from another, we can enter the realm of the divine. In the section here called "Love of Others" The Mother advises us how to love. Julian of Norwich teaches that by deliberately choosing love, we are assured we are loved without end. In giving you receive.

LOVE

Love is like a tree whose planting is bitterly painful, but the fruit of which is sweet and palatable.

ANONYMOUS (SUFI WOMAN)

I drew so close to Love
That I began to understand
How great the gain of those
Who give themselves wholly to Love:
And when I saw this for myself,
What was lacking in me gave me pain.

HADEWIJCH OF BRABANT

In all that she does, love strives only for the purity, the nobility and the highest excellence which she herself is, which she possesses and enjoys within herself, and it is this same striving which love teaches to those who seek to follow her.

BEATRICE OF NAZARETH

The soul drew close to love,
Greeted her reverently
And said: God greet you, Lady Love!

Love: May God reward you, dear Queen.

Soul: Lady Love, you are most perfect.

Love: O Queen, that is why I rule all things. . . .

Soul: Lady Love, you have taken from me all that I ever possessed on earth.

Love: But Lady Queen, what a blessed exchange!

Soul: Lady Love, you took from me my childhood.

Love: Lady Queen, in return I give you heavenly freedom.

Soul: Lady Love, you took from me all my youth.

Love: Lady Queen, in return I gave you many holy virtues.

Soul: Lady Love, you took from me my family and my friends.

Love: O dear! What a pitiful lament, Lady Queen.

Soul: Lady Love, you took from me worldly honours, worldly wealth and the whole world.

Love: Lady Queen, I shall make good your loss with the Holy Spirit in a single hour, according to your wish.

Soul: Lady Love, you overwhelmed me so completely that my body writhed in a strange sickness.

Love: Lady Queen, in return I gave you sublime knowledge and profound thoughts.

Soul: Lady Love, you have consumed all my flesh and blood.

217

Love: Lady Queen, you have been purified and drawn up to God.

Soul: Lady Love, you are a thief; you must give me yet more in return.

Love: Lady Queen, then take me myself!

Soul: Lady Love, now you have repaid me with a hundredfold on earth.

Love: Lady Queen, now you may ask that God and all His riches be given you.

MECHTHILD OF MAGDEBURG

Love—do not name it, O innocent one.

Strange is the path of love—set foot there, your body wastes away.

If you desire to love, be ready to give up your head.

Love—as the moth loves the lamp—revolve round it, surrender your body.

Love—like the deer hearing the horn come forth, give up your life.

Love—as the *chakor* loves the moon—consume fiery coals.

Love—as the fish loves the water—die rather than be parted.

Love—as the bee loves the lotus—die enclosed within it.

MEERA

LOVE OF GOD AND THE DIVINE

It is only through love and harmony that you can reach God.

THE MOTHER

Love is God.

ELIZABETH BARRETT BROWNING

I learned that love was our Lord's meaning. And I saw full surely that because God made us he loved us, which love was never slack nor ever shall be. And in this love he has done all his works; and in this love he has made all things profitable to us; and in this love our life is everlasting. In our making we had beginning; but the love wherein he made us was in him from without beginning; in which love we have our beginning. And all this shall we see in God, without end.

JULIAN OF NORWICH

Take Thine own way with me, dear Lord,
Thou canst not otherwise than bless;
I launch me forth upon a sea
Of boundless love and tenderness.

I could not choose a larger bliss
Than to be wholly thine; and mine
A will whose highest joy is this
To ceaselessly unclasp in Thine.

I will not fear Thee, O my God!
The days to come can only bring

❀ 219

Their perfect sequences of love,
Thy larger, deeper comforting.

Within the shadow of this love,
Loss doth transmute itself to gain;
Faith veils earth's sorrows in its light,
And straightway lives above her pain.

We are not losers thus; we share
The perfect gladness of the Son.
Not conquered—for, behold, we reign;
Conquered and Conqueror are one.

Because we have not reached thy heart;
Not venturing our all on Thee,
We may not know how good Thou art.

JEAN SOPHIA PIGOTT

Before there was a trace of this world of men,
I carried a memory of a lock of your hair,
A stray end gathered within me, though unknown.

Inside that invisible realm,
Your face like the sun longed to be seen,
Until each separate object was finally flung into light.

From the moment of Time's first-drawn breath,
Love resides in us,
A treasure locked into the heart's hidden vault.

Before the first seed broke open the rose bed of Being,
An inner lark soared through your meadows,
Heading toward Home.

What can I do but thank you, one hundred times?
Your face illumines the shrine of Hayati's eyes,
Constantly present and lovely.

BIBI ḤAYĀTI

I'm the woman of love
for my lord, white as jasmine.

• • •

Like a silkworm weaving
her house with love from her marrow,
and dying in her body's threads winding tight,
round and round,
I burn desiring what the heart desires.

Cut through, O Lord,
my heart's greed,
and show me your way out.

O Lord, white as jasmine.

MAHĀDĒVIYAKKA

O adorable Face of Jesus, sole Beauty
that ravishes my heart, deign to impress
your Divine Likeness on me, so that you
can no longer look upon the soul of your little spouse
without seeing Yourself.

O my Beloved, for love of you, I accept not to see your
tender sweet Glance
here below, nor to feel your lips' indescribable Kiss.

Rather I beseech you to inflame me with your love, so
    that it may rapidly
consume me and soon bring into your presence.

ST. THÉRÈSE OF LISIEUX

O Beloved, I love, love, love You. Give me light to love
You more.

CATHERINE DE HUECK DOHERTY

O, Omnipotent Jesus, give me what Yourself
command, for though to love You be of all things most
sweet, yet it is above the reach and strength of Nature.
But I am inexcusable if I do not love You, for You grant
Your love to all who desire or ask it. I cannot see without
Light, yet if I shut my eyes to the noon day Light, the
fault is not in the sun but in me.

ST. ELIZABETH SETON

O my beloved Christ, crucified by love, I wish to be
a bride for Your Heart; I wish to cover You with glory; I
wish to love you . . . even unto death! But I feel my
weakness, and I ask You to "clothe me with Yourself," to
identify my soul with all the movements of Your Soul, to
overwhelm me, to possess me, to substitute Yourself for
me that my life may be but a radiance of Your Life. Come
into me as Adorer, as Restorer, as Savior. O Eternal
Word, Word of my God, I want to spend my life in
listening to You, to become wholly teachable that I may
learn all from You. Then, through all nights, all voids, all
helplessness, I want to gaze on you always and remain in

Your great light. O my beloved Star, so fascinate me that I may not withdraw from Your radiance.

O consuming Fire, Spirit of Love, "come upon me," and create in my soul a kind of incarnation of the Word: that I may be another humanity for Him in which He can renew His whole Mystery. And You, O Father, bend lovingly over Your poor little creature; "cover her with Your shadow," seeing in her only the "Beloved in whom You are well pleased."

O my Three, my All, my Beatitude, infinite Solitude, Immensity in which I lose myself, I surrender myself to You as Your prey. Bury Yourself in me that I may bury myself in You until I depart to contemplate in Your light the abyss of Your greatness.

ELIZABETH OF THE TRINITY

LOVE OF OTHERS

"You must love with the same pure love with which I love you. But you cannot do this for me because I love you without being loved and without any self-interest. And because I loved you without being loved by you, even before you existed (in fact it was love that moved me to create you in my own image and likeness), you cannot repay me. But you must give this love to other people, loving them without being loved by them. You must love them without any concern for your own spiritual or material profit, but only for the glory and praise of my name, because I love them. In this way you will fulfill the whole commandment of the Law, which is to love me above all things and your neighbour as your very self."

THE DIVINE VOICE IN ST. CATHERINE OF SIENA'S THE DIALOGUE

Only he who loves can recognise love. Those who are incapable of giving themselves in sincere love, will never recognise love anywhere, and the more the love is divine, that is to say, unselfish, the less they can recognise it.

THE MOTHER

If you look to something outside yourself for an increase in love, you will see shadows in the flickering flames. But if you burn with the pure fire of love, without looking for anything outside to add to it, you will see things clearly as they are.

MARGUERITE PORETE

Lord, I see clearly that any affection which I have ever had is scarcely as one drop in the vast ocean of all the seas, when compared with the tenderness of Your divine Heart towards those whom I love. . . . Therefore I cannot even by one thought wish anything other than that which Your almighty wisdom has appointed for each of them. . . . Lord, bless Your special friends and mine, according to the good pleasure of Your divine goodness.

ST. GERTRUDE THE GREAT AND
MECHTHILD OF MAGDEBURG

Eternal goodness,
you want me to gaze into you
and see that you love me,

to see that you love me gratuitously
so that I may love everyone
with the very same love.
You want me, then,
to love and serve my neighbors gratuitously,
by helping them
spiritually and materially
as much as I can. . . .

God, come to our assistance!

ST. CATHERINE OF SIENA

O powerful love of God . . . Your love seeks nothing but
company.

ST. TERESA OF ÁVILA

Oh, move us—Thou hast power to move—
    One in the one Beloved to be!
Teach us in the heights and depths of love—
    Give Thine—that we may love like Thee!

ELIZABETH BARRETT BROWNING

From the prison confines of darkness
From the turbid cesspool of the world
Hear my needful clamor,
O able, unique God.

Rend this veil of blackness, and
Perhaps you'll see within my breast

The source and substance
Of sin and corruption.

The heart you gave me, it isn't a heart
Beating in blood; free it, or
Keep it empty of carnal desires,
Or encumber it with affection and fidelity.

Only you are aware and only you know
The secrets of that first sin;
Only you are capable of granting
To my soul the original bliss.

O Lord, O Lord, how can I tell you
Of my weariness with my own body and my vexation?
Every night on the threshold, as it were, of your glory
I have the hope of another body.

From my eyes snatch
The eagerness to run to another;
O God, have mercy, and teach my eyes
To shy away from the shining eyes of others.

Give me a love that will shape me
Like the angels in your heaven,
Give me a friend, a lover in whom I might see
A glimpse of the bliss of your being.

Some night rub from the state of my mind
The image of love and the picture of its treachery;
In avenging faithlessness
I want victory over its rival in a fresh love.

O Lord, O Lord, whose powerful hand
Established the foundation of existence,

Show your face and pluck from my heart
The zest for sin and lust.

Don't be satisfied with an insignificant slave's
Rebelliousness and seeking of refuge in another;
Don't be satisfied with the flood of her tears
At the foot of a wine cup.

From the prison confines of darkness,
From the turbid cesspool of the world
Hear my needful clamor,
O able, unique God.

FURUGH FARRUKHZAD

COMPASSION AND CHARITY

The important thing is not to think much but to love much; and so do that which best stirs you to love.

ST. TERESA OF ÁVILA

It is not how much we do, but how much love we put into the doing.

MOTHER TERESA

Charity owns no master but love, possesses nothing and asks nothing for herself; looks after others, not herself, asking nothing in return; she knows neither shame nor fear nor unease, flinching from nothing that might befall her.

227

Charity takes no heed of anything under the sun; the whole world is her domain. She gives freely to all anything she may possess of value, her own self included. Her generosity can lead her to promise things she does not possess, yet she is shrewd enough to win where others lose out. Her works lead to the highest degrees of the spiritual life, and to perfection in charity.

MARGUERITE PORETE

May my body be a prayerstick for the world.

JOAN HALIFAX

Sweet Jesus, give me that infinite charity so necessary, so beautiful, to love my neighbour for You. I love You, my sweet Lord. Perfect my charity. Make it really simple and good. Especially may it be pure in intention. Keep me from vanity, from trust in myself. Keep my sins and my selfishness before me. Help me to burn with love for You and, through you, for others.

CATHERINE DE HUECK DOHERTY

How long, Mother of All,
will your daughters be cast into the darkness of poverty,
left alone to survive without the resources to care for
    their children?
How long will these little ones, if they go to school at all,
    go without breakfast,
to come home to an empty room or stay with loveless
    strangers?

How long will You allow their grandmothers to be cast
    into the streets to wander with their garbage bags,
their beat-up shopping carts, rusted from days and nights
    of exposure to the elements,
parked near the doorway where their owners curl up to
    sleep on concrete,
huddling against cold rock to warm their old bones?
How much longer will your daughters sit on curbsides,
their hands stretched out in supplication,
their voices bleeding with sorrow
in the hope of receiving a few cents to tide them over
    one more day?
How long will women creep in pre-morning gloom to
    cross the bridge to a foreign city
where they work in the homes of the wealthy
for less than the children they care for receive for their
    weekly spending money?
How long must they sew for no money,
hunched over their pedal-driven machines in rooms with
    inadequate light,
wearing out their eyes to live in blindness in their old age?
The woman who peddles papayas in the village
    restaurant,
even yet is shooed into the streets, ignored, unheard and
    unpaid.

O Poorest of the Poor, You yourself lived in poverty
and knew the weight of the oppression of your people!
You had compassion for the widows and the orphans,
and gave your life for the cause of justice for those in
    need.
You raised from death the son of the widow of Nain
so that she might have comfort and support.
You cared for your widowed mother and at the time of
    your death

sought protection for her in the home of your beloved
   disciple.

Have compassion, then, on all who are poor!
Prevent us from judgment or contempt!
Enable us to look beyond the satisfactions we manage for
   ourselves to the vulnerability of our very being.
Teach us to live with less in order that the poor have
   more.
Let us be the vehicles of your desire to empower all who
   must depend upon others for their subsistence;
make us enablers of their journey to dignity and self-
   reliance.

For You, Mother, have given birth to everything that is;
You are the Breadmaker of the World;
and your Spirit longs to bring each of your children to
   the warmth of your hearth,
and to the nourishment of the banquet You have
   prepared for us in the Land of the Living, world
   without end.

                              MARY KATHLEEN SPEEGLE SCHMITT

Father, do not let me find consolation
in sensible devotion
to the person of Jesus Christ,
while Jesus Christ passes me by
unrecognized,
unknown,
unsought,
uncomforted
on the Via Crucis
we travel together.
Do not let my heart

be moved to pity
for the painted Christ on the wall,
while it remains a stone,
hard, insensitive
to Christ suffering alone
in the ugliness
of shame and disgrace,
in the outcast,
the shunned,
the forgotten,
in mental sufferers
hidden away in hospitals,
in prisoners serving life sentences,
in people wrestling with bitterness
and despair behind the Iron Curtain,
in those fighting a losing fight
with human weakness and degradation—
in the unhelped,
the uncomforted,
the unloved.

CARYLL HOUSELANDER

Holy God, as you have touched us, may we
now touch others with your love

The oppressed and the persecuted,
crying out for the liberating touch of justice
    Touch them with your justice in us

The poor and the outcast,
crying out for the life-giving touch of compassion
    Touch them with your compassion in us

The battered victims of war and violence,
crying out for the healing touch of peace
    Touch them with your peace in us

The lost and the lonely,
crying out for the welcoming touch of friendship
    Touch them with your friendship in us

The prisoners of their own fear and cruelty,
crying out for the generous touch of mercy
    Touch them with your mercy in us

And those we love
crying out for the continuing touch of love
    Touch them with your love for us

May our lives be the place where you touch us,
and we touch others in your name,
for you are the source of our life and love.

KATHY GALLOWAY

God, the Father of mankind, who in your great love
made all the peoples of the world to be one family, help
those of different races and religions to love, understand
and accept one another. Take away all hatred, jealousy,
and prejudice so that all may work together for the
coming of your kingdom of righteousness and peace;
through Jesus Christ our Lord.

EVELYN UNDERHILL

KINDNESS

Kindness has converted more people than zeal, science, or eloquence.

MOTHER TERESA

Keep us, O God, from all pettiness,
let us be large in thought, in word, in deed.

Let us be done with fault finding and leave off all
   self-seeking.

May we put away all pretense and meet each other face
   to face
without self-pity and without prejudice.

May we never be hasty in judgment and always generous.

Let us take time for all things, and make us to grow calm,
   serene, and gentle.

Teach us to put into action our better impulses,
straightforward and unafraid.

Grant that we may realize that it is the little things of life
   that create differences,
that in the big things of life, we are as one.

And, O Lord God, let us not forget to be kind!

MARY STUART, QUEEN OF SCOTLAND

Oh God, who has given us the privilege of choosing good over evil, grant me, I pray, one attribute above all others—Grant me kindness.

If I am kind, I cannot do unto others that which I would not have done unto me.

If I am kind, I cannot be selfish and grasping, but must share Your bounty with others, causing joys, both great and small, by thoughtful deeds and gifts.

If I am kind, I cannot dishonor my parents by harsh word or wicked deed.

If I am kind, I cannot carry hurtful gossip to break another's heart, nor could I bear false witness against my neighbor.

If I am kind, I cannot take another's possessions for my own. I cannot steal that which another holds dear and has labored to obtain.

If I am kind, I cannot covet that which belongs to my neighbor, longing to deprive him of his loved ones, his home, his possessions, and to take them for my own. . . . Rather would I rejoice in his good fortune.

If I am kind, above all, I cannot kill—I cannot harm or hurt the weak, the poor, the young, the old. I cannot cause a little child to cry nor mistreat a helpless creature. I cannot take pleasure in the weeping of women nor the despair of men. I cannot hate. I cannot revile. I cannot ignore the needs of others.

And so I pray, Oh, God: grant me kindness—Your all-encompassing kindness.

VIRGINIA MOISE ROSEFIELD

14

COMFORT

"*Y*ou make all things bearable," wrote St. Catherine of Genoa, who ran a hospital. We are never alone in our pain or distress if we only remember to share—share with God, and with others. Suffering alone never brings comfort. There are some examples here of prayers for comfort with spiritual pain. In one prayer Marion Woodman expresses the fear she feels as she confronts cancer and appeals to the loving motherhood of Sophia. Many women beseech Mary, the mother of Jesus, in their grief, sorrow, and loss, relying on Mary's obvious understanding and her own life experience. There also are petitions here for healing after a miscarriage and other family tragedies. The Mother's stark instruction that all suffering, illness, and hardships can be taken as blessings is a tried-and-true formula; when we understand this, there's comfort in the knowing.

IN SUFFERING

When you are afflicted and tested within and without, it is most certainly a sign that you are among the loved ones of the Beloved.

There are three things which these most holy, and misunderstood, tribulations accomplish in the soul. First, they make the soul turn to God, or if it has already done so, they prompt it to greater conversion and closer adherence to him. Second, tribulations make the soul grow. When rain comes on well-prepared soil, it germinates and bears fruit; so, likewise, when tribulations come, the soul grows in virtue. Third, tribulations purify, comfort, and quiet the soul, and give it peace and tranquility.

ANGELA OF FOLIGNO

If the Lord wills for you a hardship, do not protest. Take it as a blessing and indeed it will become so.

THE MOTHER

Ah, Lord Jesus, King of bliss, how shall I be eased? Who will teach me and tell me what I need to comprehend if I cannot see it in You at this time?

JULIAN OF NORWICH

Spirit of comfort and longing,
enfold my fear,
unclothe me of my pride,
unweave my thoughts,
uncomplicate my heart,

and give me surrender:
that I may tell my wounds,
lay down my work,
and greet the dark.

JANET MORLEY

Dear Jesus, must my soul always be steeped in suffering? Again, yesterday and today, it came over me like a wave. So many things seem so difficult—poverty, insecurity, the terrible injustice done to me. Jesus, my love, can I go on?

O, I know the problems of suffering. I know the mystery of success through failure. But tell me, Beloved, why am I so terribly lonely, so tragically lonely? Why must I always be in pain and live the way I do? No friends—really, no one loves me. People ask so much and give so little!

Beloved of my soul, why? Why is life such a lonely thing? It seems to me, at times, an unbearable burden. I come to You; I pray. But my own sinfulness stands in the way. It is as if my window were opaque and would not let the sun through.

I am so alone at times when You are far, Beloved. Today is a day like that. I feel tortured with fire and pains of such strange, inexplicable tortures that I want to scream. Instead, I am silent. O Jesus, have mercy on me. For today I am in such darkness, such spiritual sorrow, such pain. I want to cry. O Beloved, have pity on me a sinner. I cry to You out of the desert of my life.

CATHERINE DE HUECK DOHERTY

Dear Sophia, loving Mother
  You who give life
  And take life away,
      Hold your terrified daughter in the blood-warm
        curve of your arms,
      Cherish the whole of me,
  In your mercy, give me strength to hold my eyes
    open in this darkness,
          steadfastness to reject sentimentality,
          faith to endure the paradox of death and life,
          grace to surrender every particle of my Being
            to the wave of your love,
          Oh pour your love over my family and
            friends.
              Into thy hands I commend my Spirit.

MARION WOODMAN

Let every suffering and pain be welcome that comes from
  God's will,
for you have illuminated me, O Lord,
for the last thirty-six years or so.
For your sake I have always sought to suffer,
within as well as without.
And this desire has never let me suffer greatly.
On the contrary, all those things that I have undergone
that seemed intense suffering
were, because of your will, sweet and consoling.
Now that I am at the end
and seem to be in such pain from head to toe
that it would seem that the body could not endure it
and would be about to die and be quite annihilated,
I see that you who rule over all things with your will
do not want me to die as yet.

So that in the midst of the pain my body endures,
without comfort of any kind,
I still cannot say that I am suffering.
You make all things bearable,
and my joy is such that it cannot be imagined or expressed.

ST. CATHERINE OF GENOA

O my Lord, I am in a dry land, all dried up and
cracked by the violence of the north wind and the cold;
but as you see, I ask for nothing more; you will send me
both dew and warmth when it pleases you.

ST. JANE FRANCES DE CHANTAL

IN GRIEF, SORROW, AND LOSS

Spill tears if you have grief
As tears of grief provide relief.
Strive to be straight
Try to be upright upon the Path
To fast and heave sighs of burning grief.
For the way of those acquiescent to God
Is to live with sights and burning grief.

SHA'WANA

It is suffering that exists,
suffering that endures,
suffering that disappears.

Nothing but suffering exists.
Nothing but suffering comes to an end.

VAJIRA

Please, Arya Tara,
Please grant your blessings, Mother of Dakinis.
You are the Lord of Death who knows karma!
I have not done anything bad, and I have even helped
    many people with my compassion.
I know that if one is born one must die,
So I am not attached to my body.
I have known that all possessions are impermanent,
So I have given many away.
I know that at the time of death,
One is separated even from the closest of kin,
So even to them I have not been attached.
I have not even got angry with my enemies.
Please be compassionate to me!

NANGSA OBUM

O Mary, our Mother, lead us with you on the way of
sorrow our Jesus has traced out; keep your heart united
with your pains, that at last we may share your glory. Let
us remain with you at the foot of the cross and at least
share your sorrows; let the wounds and death of our Jesus
at least obtain for us true contrition of heart after sharing
so much in the cause of them.

Your child left to you by your Jesus, unworthy as I
am, I cast myself with confidence in your arms. You are
the refuge of sinners; to the bosom of your mercy, I

241

commit myself in His merits. You will not reject the child
of His tears and blood.

ST. ELIZABETH SETON

Healing after a Miscarriage

Nothing helps. I taste ashes
in my mouth. My eyes are flat,
dead. I want no platitudes,
no stupid shallow comfort.
I hate all pregnant women,
all new mothers, all soft babies.

The space I'd made inside myself
where I'd moved over
to give my beloved room to grow—
now there's a tight angry
bitter knot of hatred there instead.

What is my supplication?
Stupid people and new mothers,
leave me alone.
Deliver me, Lord,
of this bitter afterbirth.
Open my heart
to my husband-lover-friend
that we may comfort each other.
Open my womb
that it may yet bear
living fruit.

MERLE FELD

You cry out, "My son!"
You don't know his coming and going.
You grieve,
but who knows where he came from?

Everything alive is like this,
You wouldn't grieve
about his coming and going
if you understood.

He came unasked.
He left,
and there is nothing you could do;
he must have come from somewhere
and he lived just a few days.

He came by one road,
he is leaving by another;
he has gone from the human world,
and his journey will go on.
He came. He went.
What is there to cry about?

She pulled out the arrow
hidden in my heart,
that grief for my son.
I was helpless with grief.
She has thrust it away.
Today it is gone;
I am free and want nothing.

I take refuge in the Buddha-sage,
the Dharma, and the Sangha.

PANCASATA PATACARA

(Kisagotami:)
　　　The Guide of a restless,
　　　passionate humanity has said—
　　　to be a woman is to suffer.
　　　To live with co-wives is suffering.
　　　Women can give birth
　　　and, becoming depressed,
　　　cut their throats.
　　　Beautiful young women eat poison,
　　　but both will suffer in hell
　　　when the mother-murdering fetus
　　　comes not to life.

(Patacara:)
　　　On a journey, near to childbirth
　　　I found my husband dead
　　　and gave birth on the road;
　　　I hadn't reached my family's home.
　　　I lost both sons
　　　and my husband dead on the road,
　　　then mother, father, brother
　　　burning on one pyre.

(Buddha or an enlightened nun:)
　　　(Miserable woman,
　　　your family is destroyed,
　　　this pain can't be measured,
　　　and your tears have been falling
　　　for thousands of lives.)

(Patacara:)
　　　I have seen the jackals
　　　eating the flesh of my sons
　　　in the cemetery.
　　　My family destroyed,
　　　my husband dead,

despised by everyone,
I found what does not die.

(Kisagotami:)
I have practiced the Great
Eightfold Way
straight to the undying.
I have come to the great peace
I have looked into the mirror
of the Dharma.

The arrow is out.
I have put my burden down.
What had to be done has been done.

Sister Kisagotami
with a free mind
has said this.

PATACARA AND KISAGOTAMI

Eternal God, as you created humankind
in your image, women and men, male and female,
renew us in that image;
God, the Holy Spirit, by your strength and love,
comfort us as those whom a mother comforts;
Lord Jesus Christ, by your death and resurrection,
give us the joy of those for whom pain and suffering
become, in hope, the fruitful agony of travail;
God, the Holy Trinity, grant that we may together
enter into a new life, your promised rest of
achievement and fulfilment—world without end.

WORLD COUNCIL OF CHURCHES

15

INSPIRATION

*W*e need the spirit of inspiration, as it is the very necessary source of our creativity. From the conception of our thoughts and ideas, to our instincts and intuitions, we rely on inspiration as our interior guide. Our talents, skills, and abilities are inspired by the gifts of the spirit.

In praying for inspiration, the women here commonly petition the Holy Spirit as not only fire ("the fire of genius") but as wind, sun, moon, honey, and flower.

The heavens were opened and a blinding light of exceptional brilliance flowed through my entire brain. And it so kindled my whole heart and breast like a flame, not burning but warming.

HILDEGARD OF BINGEN

O Holy Spirit, come;
Rest on these inarticulate hands and dumb!

Be fire
For my elate desire.

Be wind
To quicken the still music of my mind.

Be the heard
Utter, ineffable word.

Teach, Holy One, with Your love's art
My hands, my heart.

Yours be the tongue
In which the songs of my desire are sung.

SISTER MARY MADELEVA

Dear Heart of the Eternal Rose—
    O Many-coloured Heart of Fire—
That in our Lord's green garden grows,
    Come, Holy Ghost, our souls inspire.

Sweet Honey of the heavenly flowers,
    Distilled from the white lily's heart,
Drip on these thirsty lips of ours—
    Thou the anointing Spirit art.

O Wind, down heaven's long lanes ablow,
    Warm, perfume-laden Breath of Love,
O Sweetness, on our hearts bestow
    Your blessed unction from above.

O Sun, in the mild skies ashine,
    O Moon, bewitching all the night,
These dark and groping ways of mine
    Enable with perpetual light.

Dear Absolution of the Sun,
    Dear Quickener of the meadow's grace,
When the day's course of toil is run,
    Anoint and cheer our soiled face.

When evening falls and darkness creeps,
    And the long starry hours have come,
And all the world is tired, and sleeps,
    Keep far our foes, give peace at home.

O Sun, O Wind, O Flower, O Fire! . . .
Come, Holy Ghost, our souls inspire!

SHEILA KAYE-SMITH

Fire of the Spirit, life of the lives of creatures,
spiral of sanctity, bond of all natures,
glow of charity, lights of clarity, taste
of sweetness to sinners, be with us and hear us . . .

Composer of all things, light of all the risen,
key of salvation, release from the dark prison,
hope of all unions, scope of chastities, joy
in the glory, strong honour,
be with us and hear us.

HILDEGARD OF BINGEN

248 ✿

16

HEALING SELF, HEALING OTHERS, HEALING THE WORLD

*S*ickness is, in most cases, a spiritual gift of purification, transformation, or enlightenment. We are frequently given sickness as a call to listen to the messages from our bodies and from God. The healing of sickness also is a divine process, and prayer as an instrument of that healing has proven to be more powerful than any traditional medicine. Be it through personal petition or collective intercession, partnership with the Divine's healing grace is an experience of love.

Mechthild of Magdeburg's prayer about losing health is an example of how, in loss, we make space for the gifts of receiving compassion and help. Simone Weil offers that when the acts of compassion and gratitude (i.e., giving and receiving) are exchanged, God is present. In the section "Healing Others," St. Teresa of Ávila prays for us to be used by God and the Divine as healers on God's behalf. We all must do our part, however small. We need to "trouble mankind for its human heart" (Jessica Powers). Being with the pain of others—"to suffer for them / and with them" (Caryll Houselander)—instead of trying to make things better or removing ourselves from painful situations brings us the opportunity to offer what Katie Riley calls "the warmth of our spirit."

There are prayers here too for healing and protection of the world. Peace, not war, is the most commonly prayed-for state, as well as relief for the hungry, the prisoners, and the afflicted. In the end, peaceful action is suggested as the healer of the world.

HEALING SELF

God is my repairer of fences, turning my paths into rest.

JESSICA POWERS (*Repairer of Fences*)

Suffering borne with courage means to the devout mind a participation in the sufferings of Christ and, if bravely endured, can lighten the sufferings of others.

DOROTHY DAY

O God,
Giver of Life
Bearer of Pain
Maker of Love,
you are able to accept in us what we cannot even
   acknowledge;
you are able to name in us what we cannot bear to speak of,
you are able to hold in your memory what we have tried
  to forget;

you are able to hold out to us the glory that we cannot
   conceive of.
Reconcile us through your cross
to all that we have rejected in our selves,
that we may find no part of your creation to be alien or
   strange to us,
and that we ourselves may be made whole.

Through Jesus Christ, our lover and our friend.

JANET MORLEY

We wear our everyday work clothes when we are healthy.
And, when we are ill, our bridal dress.

Lord, I am grateful to You
that in Your mysterious love
You have taken away from me
all earthly wealth,
and that You now clothe and feed me
through the kindness of others.

Lord I am grateful to You
that since You have taken away from me
the sight of my eyes,
You care for me now
through the eyes of others.

Lord, I am grateful to You
that since you have taken away from me
the strength of my hands and heart,
you care for me now
through the hands and hearts of others.

Lord, I pray for them,
that You will reward them in Your love,
that they may continue to faithfully serve and care
until they come to a happy end
in eternity with You.

MECHTHILD OF MAGDEBURG

Lord, undertake Yourself for me;
Your arm of power can alone heal, help and deliver;
and in You do I trust, and hope, though at times deeply
    tried and cast down before You;
yet, O Lord! You are my hope,
and be therefore entreated of Your poor sorrowful and
    often afflicted servant,
and arise for my help.
Leave not my poor soul destitute, but through the
    fullness of Your own power, mercy and love, keep me
    alive unto Yourself, unto the end!
that nothing may separate me from Your love, that I may
    endure unto the end;
and when the end comes, that I may be altogether Yours,
    and dwell with You,
if it be but the lowest place within the gate, where I may
    behold Your glory and Your holiness;
and for ever rest in You.

ELIZABETH FRY

Dear God,
Be my redeemer, my internal teacher, my divine
    physician.
Thank you for Your presence in my life.

I surrender to You all I am, all I think, all I feel, and all I
   have.
I recognize in this moment that Yours is the power to
   heal and to make whole.
You who have the power to work miracles, You who
   rule time and space, please take me in Your arms and
   hold me.
Dear Lord, please lift me up and heal me.
Cast out of my mind all thoughts that are not of You.
Cast out of me all harsh and critical nature.
Cast out of me all violence and all anger.
Cast out of me all demons from my past.
For I would be made new.
I wish to walk so close to You that we might be as one.
I ask for new life, new mind, new body, new spirit.
Dear God, please come into me and release me from
   this pain.

MARIANNE WILLIAMSON

HEALING OTHERS

*On February 7, 1837, God spoke to me and called me to
His service.*

FLORENCE NIGHTINGALE

*Christ has no body now on earth but yours,
no hands but yours,
no feet but yours.
Yours are the eyes through which Christ's compassion must
   look out on the world.*

✿ 253

Yours are the feet with which he is to go about doing good.
Yours are the hands with which he is still to bless.

ST. TERESA OF ÁVILA

God is present at the point where the eyes of those who give
and those who receive meet.

SIMONE WEIL

Worse than the poorest mendicant alive,
the pencil man, the blind man with his breath
of music shaming all who do not give,
are You to me, Jesus of Nazareth.

Must You take up Your post on every block
of every street? Do I have no release?
Is there no room of earth that I can look
to Your sad face, Your pitiful whisper "Please"?

I seek the counters of time's gleaming store
but make no purchases, for You are there.
How can I waste one coin while you implore
with tear-soiled cheeks and dark blood-matted hair?

And when I offer You in charity
pennies minted by love, still, still You stand
fixing Your sorrowful wide eyes on me.
Must all my purse be emptied in Your hand?

Jesus, my beggar, what would You have of me?
Father and mother? the lover I longed to know?
The child I would have cherished tenderly?
Even the blood that through my heart's valves flow?

I too would be a beggar. Long tormented,
I dream to grant You all and stand apart
with You on some bleak corner, tear-frequented,
and trouble mankind for its human heart.

JESSICA POWERS (*The Master Beggar*)

Lord, the one that I love is sick and in great pain;
out of your compassion heal him and take away his pain.
It breaks my heart to see him suffer;
may I not share his pain if it is not your will that he be
    healed?
Lord, let him know that you are with him;
support and help him that he may come to know you
    more deeply as a result of his suffering.
Lord be our strength and support in this time of dark-
    ness and give us that deep peace which comes from
    trusting you.

ETTA GULLICK

Dearest Lord, may I see you today and every day in the
person of your sick, and, whilst nursing them, minister
unto you.

Though you hide yourself behind the distressing
disguise of the irritable, the exacting, the unreasonable,
may I still recognize you, and say: "Jesus, my patient, how
sweet it is to serve you."

Lord, give me this seeing faith, then my work will
never be monotonous. I will ever find joy in humouring
the fancies and gratifying the wishes of all poor sufferers.

O beloved sick, how doubly dear you are to me,

when you personify Christ; and what a privilege is mine
to be allowed to tend you.

Sweetest Lord, make me appreciative of the dignity
of my high vocation, and its many responsibilities. Never
permit me to disgrace it by giving way to coldness,
unkindness, or impatience.

And O God, while you are Jesus my patient, deign
also to be to me a patient Jesus, bearing with my faults,
looking only to my intention, which is to love and serve
you in the person of each one of your sick.

Lord, increase my faith, bless my efforts and work,
now and for evermore.

MOTHER TERESA

Desperately we commit to your care the years of our
life that are before us. Give us strength to be of service to
our fellows. May our lives shine so that others feel the
warmth of your spirit. It is the warmth of our spirit
overflowing among others who seek, who are ill, who are
lonely, for which we pray. We would become people who
add to this small world's knowledge of Truth. People
whose very presence heals. Tranquil people, in whom the
loneliness of others is stilled.

We see through a glass darkly, but may we be given
a vision that enables us to transmit through our
personality what we see of permanence and of value. We
realize that the meditations of our hearts influence not
only ourselves but others. We pray that our thoughts
shall be pure, that their very purity may bring healing to
ourselves and to others.

Often we lie in bed and toss and turn. May we be
enabled to reach out to Christ, the centre of centres, and
find rest and stillness, and having found it may we be
enabled to radiate this stillness to others.

We pray from the depths of our hearts that we may be more worthy followers of you. We pray to be absorbed—to be made one—with all the goodness in the world. We know we are surrounded by the ocean of darkness but we know that there is an ocean of light. It is into this ocean of light that we desire to move and into which we would carry our sick friends.

Help us, O God, to identify ourselves with all who suffer. Yet help us to move forward with a gladness that is infectious. We pray that we may discover how to remain young, gay, enthusiastic, full of enterprise. A smile inward and outward; a means of facing with sweetness and gentleness whatever befalls us.

KATIE RILEY

Mother of Christ,
Help me to be willing
to accept the suffering
that is the condition of love.

Help me to accept
the grief
of seeing those whom I love suffer,
and when they die
let me share in their death
by compassion.

Give me the faith
that knows Christ in them,
and knows that his love is the key
to the mystery of suffering.

Help me,
Blessed Mother,

to see with your eyes,
to think with your mind,
to accept with your will.

Help me to believe that it is Christ
who suffers in innocent children,
in those who die in the flower of manhood,
in those whose death is an act of reparation,
in those who are sacrificed for others.

Remind me
that their suffering is Christ's love
healing the world,
and when I suffer for them
and with them
I, too, am given the power
of his redeeming love.

CARYLL HOUSELANDER

HEALING THE WORLD

What we would like to do is change the world—make it a little simpler for people to feed, clothe, and shelter themselves as God intended them to do. And to a certain extent, by fighting for better conditions, by crying out unceasingly for the rights of the workers, of the poor, of the destitute—the rights of the worthy and the unworthy poor, in other words—we can to a certain extent change the world; we can work for the oasis, the little cell of joy and peace in a harried world. We can throw our pebble in the pond and be confident that its ever-widening circle will reach around the world.

DOROTHY DAY

Will you not open slowly,
your lotus shaped bell like eyes,
eyes like the sun,
the moon,
and look on us,
so that all maledictions
may be destroyed?

ANDAL

God, who cares for us,
The wonder of whose presence fills us with awe.
Let kindness, justice and love shine in our world.
Let your secrets be known here as they are in heaven.
Give us the food and the hope we need for today.
Forgive us our wrongdoing
as we forgive the wrongs done to us.
Protect us from pride and from despair
and from the fear and hate which can swallow us up.
In you is truth, meaning, glory and power,
while words come and go.

ST. HILDA COMMUNITY

Lord, make us channels of your peace. . . .

Wherever in your world we find hatred—
      the hatred that hurts and divides
      nations and communities and families;
      the hatred that dehumanizes
      and destroys;
      —enable each one of us to bring love;
          love like your love for us,
          that keeps no score of wrongs and that never
          gives up.

❁ 259

Wherever in your world we find the injured—
    victims of famine and war;
    of want or of plenty;
    the handicapped or the disadvantaged;
    —enable each one of us to bring love;
      love like your love for us,
      that is very patient and kind.

Wherever in your world we find despair—
    on account of alienation;
    or unemployment;
    or bad housing, or childlessness;
    on account of loneliness or fear;
    —enable each one of us to bring love,
      love like your love for us,
      to lift their spirits and bring them hope.

Wherever in your world we find darkness—
    because of superstition;
    of ignorance;
    or because people love evil rather than good;
    —enable each one of us to let our light shine,
      that others may turn to the Light
      that has never been extinguished.

Wherever in your world we find sadness—
    because of bereavement;
    or the evaporation of dreams;
    or because of unachieved ambition;
    or on account of others;
    —enable each one of us to spread joy;
      the joy that comes from knowing
      that we are never abandoned.

Lord, make us channels of your peace.
In giving, may we also receive;
In losing our lives in the service of others,
     may we find them anew in you.

JESSIE CLARE

Spirit of the universe, who has bound the world together
through laws of justice, given us insight to comprehend
them, a creative sense of work and readiness for deeds of
love. . . .
     Oh that the sound of the Shofar might rouse the
congregation, that secular writings no longer obstructed
the path of women, that the spectre of the great death
would disappear, and that a generation would arise, born
of strength and love and reverence for the holy
Schechina [sic], who blesses those who live and govern
with a pure heart.

BERTHA PAPPENHEIM

Dear Lord, your lovely world is full of pain,
Injustice, greed, and hunger mar our day,
We turn in penitence to you again,
And for our sister-nations humbly pray.

So many Lord, have not enough to eat,
Though crops are bountiful, and transport good,
While you intended all should be replete,
And live in quiet trust and brotherhood.

The captives still cry out for their release;
The blind, in millions, wait on us for sight;

The agony of conflict pleads for peace,
As those who live in darkness long for light.

Make us aware that you are with us still;
That love and comfort, health and honesty,
Shall overcome the evil and the ill,
Of worldly wisdom and rapacity.

Fill us with kindly caring sympathy,
And multiply our gifts a hundredfold,
Rouse us from selfishness and apathy,
And your whole church into your likeness mould.

Grant that by peaceful action we may change
The dreary outlook of the helpless poor,
Through prayer and ingenuity arrange
That food shall be delivered to their door.

Bring back the beauty and the joy of life,
Dear Lord and Saviour of your family;
Reverse the order of all wrong and strife,
And your fair world return to harmony.

E. Gwendoline Keevil

Spirit of love
That flows against our flesh
Sets it trembling
Moves across it as across grass
Erasing every boundary that we accept
And swings the doors of our lives wide—
This is a prayer I sing:
Save our perishing earth!

Barbara Deming

Aphrodite Columba, Great Goddess, Holy Dove of Peace, hear Your daughters as they call to You again after the turning of centuries; for they are humanity's lifegiving mothers. They know the toil of birthing and nurturing. They know war to be a waste of their precious toil, and a desecration of Your earth. Kindly Mother, give Your daughters power to oppose the forces of war, to prevent aggressive destruction, to establish Your laws of peace and kindship. Help women raise their children with teachings of peace. Help men resist the myths of glory in conflict. Help us all to respect life more than conquest. Let the return of the Divine Mother image usher in a new era, as the women of all nations reach out to one another with understanding, under Your symbol. Let those who do not comprehend motherhood hear and obey those that do. Aphrodite Columba, Sacred Dove, let the spiritual needs of those who yearn for You be served at last. May our prayer rise to You as the white dove rises on her wings. Blessed Be.

BARBARA G. WALKER

Virgin Goddess,
complete within your Self,
You yet desire to be One
with all that You have created.
From the depths of your belly
speak to us of your love:
that, made new by the knowledge
of your great regard for us,
we seek to nurture every element of this earth.
Birth-Giving Mother,

Awakening Child,
the flow of your compassion
is the consummation of the Universe.

MARY KATHLEEN SPEEGLE SCHMITT

17

FOR HELP WITH DUTY, WORK, AND FAMILY

*T*he monotheistic religions believe that our life purpose and our responsibilities are dictated by the Divine, as God created everything. In widely practiced Eastern religions, one's duty is to live one's life as dictated by one's karma, or "to exceed ourselves" (The Mother). In doing so, The Mother writes, that one attains the Divine. The *Woman's Evangel Journal* published a piece which stressed that women have been given the capacity for doing some kind of work in the world. It acknowledged that women who have begun the work before us—those who emancipated, evangelized, educated, nursed, and healed— should arouse us to our duty. However, women who work for purely economic reasons at unrewarding jobs do damage to their souls. Dorothy Day offered a drastic prayer that supports this belief: "[if] our jobs do not contribute to the common good, we pray God for the grace to give them up."

As I wrote in the introduction, the work many women in this book did, and still do, involves perseverance, hardship, courage, enormous faith, and great love. "To work without love is slavery," said Mother Teresa. St. Elizabeth Seton exclaimed with certainty that "God calls us to a holy life." And Catherine de Hueck Doherty felt that praying during one's duties offers the opportunity "to let Your light shine before the world."

Women who pray recognize the results of their labor as only the evidence of God's intervening grace. Yet women's work is not without torment; there is always fatigue to combat, and there are priorities to be recognized. Elizabeth Fry, mother of eleven children, asked God to direct her in the lessons of prioritizing by giving her the wisdom to know "what to do and what to leave undone."

In the "Family and Motherhood" section, the challenges of motherhood are seen. Yet mother Christine Gellie wrote, "You reward each moment I give for love." There are prayers about childlessness, as well as about raising a child, whether as a single mother or as a parental team.

DUTY

The aim of ordinary life is to carry out one's duty; the aim of spiritual life is to realise the Divine.

THE MOTHER

The notion of vocation was like this for me. I saw the carrying out of a vocation differed from the actions dictated by reason or inclination in that it was due to an impulse of an essentially and manifestly different order; and not to follow such an impulse when it made itself felt, even if it demanded impossibilities, seems to me the greatest of all ills.

Simone Weil

There is nothing in the universe that I fear, but that I shall not know my duty, or shall fail to do it.

Mary Lyon

Malach homowes (Angel of Death), I have called You in days that were long for me. Nevertheless you approach me gently and unexpected. Your wing had grazed me softly, when you paused in your approach. What signal did you follow when, although conscious of your eternal and universal triumph, you yielded for a while?

Is there still a mission for me to perform, which accomplished, shall complete the significance of my life? If so I shall rally and seek strength for it and pull myself together to accomplish whatever is commanded.

Bertha Pappenheim

Blessed Lord, can we be forgetful of our duty to You, You who have purchased all for us? O, strengthen us, pity our weakness, be merciful to us, and as Your Holy Angels always do You service in heaven, give us grace to serve You so faithfully while on earth that we may hereafter be received into their blessed society and join their everlasting hallelujas in Your Eternal Kingdom.

St. Elizabeth Seton

Lord, be with me, and help me by Your Spirit, to perform all my duties to Your praise. I pray You be very near to us all; protect us by Your providential care over us, and above all, further visit us by Your love, power, and Spirit. Oh Lord! turn us, and we shall be turned; help us, and we shall be helped; keep us, and we shall be kept.

ELIZABETH FRY

WORK

Our mission is to become flexible instruments in God's hands and to effect His work to which He leads us. If we fulfill our mission, we do what is best for ourselves, for our immediate environment, and together with it, what is best for the entire nation.

EDITH STEIN (St. Teresa Benedicta of the Cross)

If our jobs do not contribute to the common good, we pray God for the grace to give them up. Have they to do with shelter, food, clothing? Have they to do with the Works of Mercy? Everyone should be able to place his job in the category of the Works of Mercy.
. . . Whatever has contributed to the misery and degradation of the poor may be considered a bad job, and not to be worked at.

DOROTHY DAY

If you are really in love with Christ, no matter how small your work, it will be done better; it will be wholehearted. Your work will prove your love.

You may be exhausted with work, you may even kill yourself, but unless your work is interwoven with love, it is useless. To work without love is slavery.

Mother Teresa

God give me work
Till my life shall end
And life
Till my work is done.

Winifred Holtby

Oh, may your Spirit guide my feet,
In ways of righteousness;
Make every path of duty plain
And straight before my face.
Since I'm a stranger here below,
Let not my path be hid;
But mark the road my feet should go,
And be my constant guide.

Zilpha Elaw

Jesus, how often I wander far from You even when working for You. Look at me shouting, doing, talking, teaching, feeling proud and good! Am I doing anything? Who can say? I am not doing the principal thing: praying and being quiet. How much better would I see things if I prayed to You more, my Lord. Help me to understand.

❀ 269

Help me to see that often it is in doing nothing that one does most.

Jesus, my God! Teach me to be a lamp with You as the oil. Help me always to shine brightly for others to see. Help me.

CATHERINE DE HUECK DOHERTY

Woman Laborer,
You rise before sunup
and return home after nightfall;
You stoop with the weight of your work; your spirit faints.
Be in our day-to-day struggle to survive:
that, strengthened by your presence with us,
we are freed to work for justice and human dignity.
Mother of the World,
Woman Carpenter,
You are the Courage of the poor and downtrodden!

MARY KATHLEEN SPEEGLE SCHMITT

I mourn over myself for being so much engrossed by the cares of this life; I fear that my heart may be overcharged by them. Be pleased, O Lord! to grant a little help in this respect, and let not Your servant, who loves You, who has sought to serve You, and trust in You, now in her latter days, have Your work marred in her, by her heart being overcharged with the cares of this life.

ELIZABETH FRY

FAMILY AND MOTHERHOOD

Life began
in the womb of an African woman
life continued
with food from mother nature
and the growth that each new day brings
she makes her appearance into the world
        into the world
an African child is born
as delicate as the petals of a rose .
fresh as the morning dew
God's gift, God's wonderful gift
welcome to the world.

PAULINE CRAWFORD (AFOLASHADE)

Blessed Trinity have pity!
    You can give the blind man sight,
Fill the rocks with waving grasses—
    Give my house a child tonight.

You can bend the woods with blossom,
    What is there you cannot do?
All the branches burst with leafage,
    What's a little child to you?

Trout out of a spawning bubble,
    Bird from shell and yolk of an egg,
Hazel from a hazel berry—
    Jesus, for a son I beg!

Corn from shoot and oak from acorn
    Miracles of life awake,

Harvest from a fist of seedlings—
    Is a child so hard to make?

Childless men although they prosper
    Are praised only when they are up,
Sterile grace however lovely
    Is a seed that yields no crop.

There is no hell, no lasting torment
    But to be childless at the end,
A naked stone in grassy places,
    A man who leaves no love behind.

God I ask for two things only,
    Heaven when my life is done,
Payment as befits a poet—
    For my poem pay a son.

Plead with Him O Mother Mary,
    Let Him grant the child I crave,
Womb that spun God's human tissue,
    I no human issue leave.

Brigid after whom they named me,
    Beg a son for my reward,
Let no poet empty-handed,
    Leave the dwelling of his lord.

GIOLLABHRIGHDE MACCONMIDHE

Down by the rushes I paused and bent—
I bent with a sudden lovely pang of joy,
And I knew that my hope was true. . . .
Lord God of our fathers, if you send me a son
He shall be bred in your fear,

But if you send me a daughter
She shall be bred in your love.
Lord, I pray you, send me a girl.

Sheila Kaye-Smith

O God, it might seem odd to some to pray for someone
not yet born—but not to you and not to me.

In these nine months of womanly patience, I have
learned more than ever to marvel at your creative
plans—and our part in them.

I rejoice that the fashioning of a baby, and the
founding of a family, requires the gifts of body, mind and
spirit you have given to us each.

Bless these days of waiting, of preparation, of tender
hope. Let only things and thoughts that are clean and
strong and glad be about us.

I give you thanks that from childhood till this
experience of maturity, you have made it both beautiful
and natural for me to give love and to receive it.

In this newest experience, hold us each safe,
relaxed, and full of eager hope—even as you count each
life in your presence, precious.

Rita Snowden

. . . How dark was everything around me but a few
hours ago; anxiety filled my heart, and I was afraid of the
results of my fears and pain. But when I called in my
woe, the Lord heard me, and saved me from my troubles.
The hours of anxiety have passed, and now joy and light
surrounded me. You, O God! have safely led me through
the dangers of the hours of delivery, You have done more
unto me than I ventured to hope; You have fulfilled my

273

prayer, You have given me a dear, healthful, well-formed child. Therefore, I praise Your mercy, and shall never forget Your benefits; my heart and mouth shall ever overflow with thanks and praises of Your supreme power and loving-kindness.

And with filial confidence in Your mercy I commit all my cares to You, trusting that You will accomplish the work of grace which You have begun. You will renew my strength, that I may be able to fulfil the duties of a good and faithful mother.

My God and Lord! Bestow Your protection also upon my newborn infant, that it may thrive and grow, and be healthful in body and soul, to be a pleasure unto You, a delight unto me and my beloved husband, an honour unto all men. Yea, Eternal One, in You I place my trust, I wait upon Your help; he who trusts in You shall never be put to shame.

FANNY NEUDA

Mother/Father-God
As my door opens and she is brought to me
I rejoice in gratitude
At this tiny miracle
Wrapped in a blanket,
Eyes closed inward in sleep,
So as to prolong her dream.
Here in the curve of my arm
I soon must wake and nurse her.
Yet I too wait to gaze,
Hushed, in awe;

As wave on wave of joy sweep over me,
I marvel at my baby's starfish hands
Shell-like ears and moss-soft hair

That frames her tiny star-shaped face;
Reminders that she came from me,
But her soul traveled through sky and many waters.
She is a mystery that landed here,
And soon will wake, hungry and eager,
For new life in our world.

Great Creator—Parent of Compassion,
You have entrusted your masterpiece
To my unskilled care—Empower and ready
Me, I pray—and mostly
Let my love that welcomes and enfolds her
Grow as she grows,
So both of us and all of us may
Know and trust and always turn to You,
Source of all Love.

Anita Wheatcroft

For Children and Parenting

God help you, mothers, to do right.

Julia A. J. Foote

Sometimes the only thing that keeps a woman going is the necessity of taking care of her young. She cannot sink into lethargy and despair because the young ones are dragging at her skirts, clamoring for something—food, clothing, shelter, occupation. She is carried outside herself. She is saved by childbearing, as it says in the Old Testament; she has a rule of life which involves others and she will be saved in spite of herself.

Dorothy Day

With a new awareness, both painful and humorous, I begin to understand why the saints were rarely married women. I am convinced it has nothing inherently to do, as I once supposed, with chastity or children. It has to do primarily with distractions. The bearing, rearing, feeding and educating of children; the running of a house with its thousand details, human relationships with their myriad pulls—woman's normal occupations in general run counter to creative life, or contemplative life, or saintly life.

ANNE MORROW LINDBERGH

A Mother's Prayer

Lord,
I was dreaming of success and power,
money and glory,
and here I am immersed,
sometimes trapped,
in my daily routine mothering a family,
feeding, caring for, consoling, listening to . . .
those you entrusted to me,
with machines continuously full of clothes
that have to be emptied,
and refrigerators continuously empty
that have to be filled . . .
So many little deaths to myself,
to my serenity,
to my freedom.
   But you are here!
   alive at the very core of my life
   and you reward each moment I give for love.
An unexpected smile, a look,

and your joy erupts within me
to brighten the thousand daily actions
woven by the thread of life.
Lord, stay with me,
and let the little deaths of each day
lead me along the path
of eternal life.

CHRISTINE GELLIE

Oh, You to whom in vain no suppliant bows
Whose good dispensing hand does never close
Deign now to listen to a Parent's Prayer
And grant that this Your holy Book may prove
The choicest present of maternal love!

When dawning reason opens on her Soul
And youthful passions need some strong control
In these blest precepts may she seek the road
Which terminates in bright eternal good.

Here as she views the glorious prospect shine
Of life and Immortality divine,
O, may the boundless hopes inspire her youth
To listen to, and love the voice of truth!

Here, too, while studying the holy Word,
The pure religion of her Blessed Lord
May the remembrance of the life He gave
To pain and death a fallen world to save
Touch her young heart, and all her bosom move
With Faith, Obedience, gratitude and love.

ST. ELIZABETH SETON

Dear God,

There are no words for the depth of our love for this
  child.
We pray for her care and her protection.
We surrender her into Your hands.
Please, dear God, send Your angels to bless and surround
  her always.
May she be protected from the darkness of our times.
May she always see You at the center of her life.
May her heart grow strong,
To love You and serve You.
We surrender, dear God, our parenthood to You.
Make us the parents You want us to be.
Show us how to love most patiently, to be there for her
  most fully,
To understand profoundly who she is and what she
  needs.
May this family be a blessing unto her now and forever.
May she learn her values and principles of love and
  righteousness.
May she learn from us kindness.
May she learn from us strength.
May she learn from us the lessons of power:
That she has it,
That she must surrender it to You to be used for Your
  purposes throughout her life
For thus shall You be gladdened,
And thus shall she be free,
To live most fully and love most deeply.
That is our wish.
That is our prayer for her and for us forever.

MARIANNE WILLIAMSON

Spirit-Filled One, your grandma is God and so are your favorite star and rock. God has many names and many faces. God is Mother, Daughter, and Wise Old Crone. She is found in your mothers, in your daughters, and in you. God is the God of Sarah and Hagar, of Leah and Rachel; She is Mother of All Living, and blessed are her daughters. You are girl-woman made in her image. You can run fast, play hard, and climb trees. You are Batwoman, firewoman, and Goddess. The Spirit of the Universe pulsates through you. Be full of yourself. You are good. You are very good.

PATRICIA LYNN REILLY

Heavenly Father in the stillness I call on you. Come to my aid and see me through these difficult times. As I strive to be Father and Mother to this child, give me courage and patience to cope with the problems of each day. You are the great provider, in you all our needs are met. Teach me to trust and wait on you as you work your purpose out. I know you have a divine plan which you will reveal to me in your own time. Dear God keep my child from bad company and ever guard and protect him/her from wrongdoing. Make this child aware that I am doing the very best I know how in the present situation, and help me to show my love in more ways than I do now. Help me with calm confidence to be a good parent.

JUNE ISAACS-MASCOLL

Now the children are asleep, my Lord.
I am tired and would spend a half hour in stillness with
   You.

I want to bathe my soul in Your infinity, like the
workingmen who plunge into the surf to shed the dust
and heat of their bodies.

Let my burning heart feel Your ever-renewing power;
Let my clouded spirit be lost in the crystal clarity of Your
wisdom;
Heal my unworthy love in the waters of Your love which
is so true, steady and deep.

O Lord, I would not stand to be a mother one more day,
if I thought I had to account for all my faults; I am all
sin.
My love walks over my wisdom, but I love my children.
I know that their little seeing eyes see through me, right
to my soul, that they imitate me.

Help me, O Lord, to be good in the deepest of my
intentions, good in all my desires.
Make of me what I wish my children to be, with a heart
that is strong, true and great.
Help me not to be annoyed by the little things.

Give me the large view of things, a sense of proportion so
that I can truly judge what is important, what is not.
Lend me strength to be a real mother to my children,
knowing how to turn right their souls and their
imaginations, knowing how to help them unfold their
dreams and care for their bodies.

Guard them against evil and let them grow up healthy
and pure.

This I ask in the name of our Lord Jesus Christ.

ANONYMOUS (AFRICAN WOMAN)

O Lord! What a great favour You grant to those children whose parents love them so much as to want them to possess their estates, inheritance, and riches in that blessed life that has no end! ... Open the eyes of parents, my God. Make them understand the kind of love they are obliged to have for their children so that they do not do these children so much wrong and are not complained about before God in that final judgement where, even though they may not want to know it, the value of each thing will be understood.

St. Teresa of Ávila

Give, I pray You, to all children grace reverently to love their parents, and lovingly to obey them. Teach us all that filial duty never ends or lessens; and bless all parents in their children, and all children in their parents.

Christina Rossetti

Heavenly Father, You have given us a model of life in the Holy Family of Nazareth. Help us, O loving Father, to make our family another Nazareth where love, peace and joy reign.
May it be deeply contemplative, intensely Eucharistic, and vibrant with joy.
Help us to stay together in joy and sorrow through family prayer.
Teach us to see Jesus in the members of our family, especially in His distressing disguises.
May the Eucharistic Heart of Jesus make our hearts meek

and humble like His and help us to carry out our family
  duties in a holy way.
May we love one another as God loves each one of us
  more and more each day, and forgive each other's
  faults as You forgive our sins.
Help us, O loving Father, to take whatever You give and
  to give whatever You take with a big smile.
Immaculate Heart of Mary, cause of our joy, pray for us.
Saint Joseph pray for us.
Holy Guardian Angels be always with us, guide and
  protect us.

MOTHER TERESA

18

GIVING THANKS
FOR PETITIONS

*I*t is important to always give thanks to the Divine
for hearing our petitions and our pleas. And when evidence is given that our prayers have been heard, then we
should *really* give thanks with an honoring ceremony; the
lighting of candles; or by giving alms or doing charity work.

The women below who honor the Divine for hearing
their petitions now find, in hindsight, that their words or
acts of gratitude only led them towards a higher level of
prayer, which is that of surrender.

We thank You with all our hearts for every gracious
    dispensation,
for all the blessings that have attended our lives,
for every hour of safety, health and peace,
of domestic comfort and innocent enjoyment.
We feel that we have been blessed far beyond anything
    that we have deserved;

and though we cannot but pray for a continuance of all
   these mercies, we acknowledge
our unworthiness of them and implore You to pardon the
   presumption of our desires.

JANE AUSTEN

Dear Lord, I thank You, that I did not get
   An answer to my prayer of long ago.
In looking back, I see I asked amiss
   In praying for the things I longed for so.
I should have prayed to trust Your wisdom more.
   To know Your ways were better far than mine.
How blind we are, when stubborn human will
   Obscures the perfect plan of Love's design!

I thank You that in spite of my mistakes
   Your hand was always there to bring me through,
And keep me steady, when my wayward feet
   Brought me in greater danger than I knew.
Oh, keep me from our own undoing, Lord!
   So many times we might have slipped, and gone,
So many times we might have missed the way,
   Had not Your tender mercy led us on.

I thank You that a prayer which is not right
   Love does not answer; for, if what seems best
To blind, misguided sense, should have its way,
   One might be ruined at his own request!
That futile, selfish prayer of long ago
   Was never prayer at all, as now I see.
Today I have but one supreme desire,
   To go with joy where'er God leads me.

For now each hour His purposes unfold
        Like flower petals smiling in the sun.

LOUISE WHEATLEY COOK HOVNANIAN

Are you not weary of our selfish prayers?
Forever crying, "Help me, save me, Lord!"
We stay fenced in by petty fears and cares,
Nor hear the song outside, nor join its vast accord.

And yet the truest praying is a psalm:
The lips that open in pure air to sing
Make entrance to the heart for health and balm;
And so life's urn is filled at heaven's all-brimming spring.

Is not the need of other souls our need?
After desire the helpful act must go,
As the strong wind bears on the winged seed
To some bare spot of earth, and leaves it there to grow.

Still are we saying, "Teach us how to pray"?
O teach us how to love! and then our prayer
Through other lives will find its upward way,
As plants together seek and find sweet life and air.

Your large bestowing makes us ask for more,
Prayer widens with the world where through love flows.
Needy, though blest, we throng before Your door:
Let in Your sunshine, Lord, on all that lives and grows!

LUCY LARCOM

Govern all by Your wisdom, O Lord, so that my soul may always be serving You as You will, and not as I may choose. Do not punish me, I beseech You, by granting that which I wish or ask, if it offend Your love, which would always live in me. Let me die to myself, that so I may serve You; let me live to You, who in Yourself are the true life. Reign and let me be the captive, for my soul covets no other freedom.

ST. TERESA OF ÁVILA

And now, Lord, what wait I for? My hope is in you. Do more for me than I can possibly ask or think, and finally receive me to yourself.

MARIA W. STEWART

Oh, God help me, how little we desire to reach Your grandeurs, Lord! How miserable we would remain if Your giving were in conformity with our asking!

ST. TERESA OF ÁVILA

PART THREE

SURRENDER:
THE RESPONSES

$\mathcal{B}$eing in the place of surrender is the next stage of prayer. It is a more advanced stage and one that takes most of our lives to achieve. Yet it forms the essence of the flowering and the maturing of the soul. It is not easy to master: it requires consciousness, discipline, and commitment. But in spiritual life there is no other road to take. This view has been taught not only in the Western religions, but in all Eastern practices as well. Yet there is a difference; in the monotheistic traditions, we submit and surrender to the purpose and idea of God, as all-knowing, all-loving. In the Eastern religions, Taoists submit to more contemplation, and surrender to nothingness and perfection to the Tao (the Way); the Buddhists seek the relinquishment of all desires and longings, so that one can be free; Hindus (and particularly those who follow the yogic way) wish to complete their individual karma on earth in this lifetime and be purified in Self and in God.

There are a number of levels in the practice of surrender. The beginning stage is that of intention; the intermediate one is to "make space" for the divine will to work through us and in our lives; and the advanced one is a state of total Abandonment, of the freedom that comes in giving everything to the Divine's intention. This section provides the prayers of women who struggle to live in surrender, who have found their way in it, who seek divine love at the end of their lives, and who have entered the infinite—the heavenly realms—while still on earth.

19

Your Will Be Done, Not Mine

*T*he first stage of surrender requires us to contemplate what "Your will be done" means in our lives. It usually asks us to change many ways in which we operate; we need to say good-bye to our ego and pride, to become humble and be guided in love. We need to commit ourselves to God's guidance. St. Teresa of Ávila called God her "infinite wisdom." However, Simone Weil explains that when we say "Your will be done" we have to have in mind "all possible misfortunes added together," for God's will is not necessarily ours.

The supreme example of this is in the death of Jesus Christ two thousand years ago. Perceived then as one of the greatest misfortunes, it was later revealed to be miraculous—a redemption that reached all the corners of the world through the growth, devotion, and practice of Christianity. Christ cried out in his agony, "not mine, but Your will be done." We too can come to accept God's will, to the point where when something happens that, in the past we may have perceived as unfortunate or disastrous, it makes no difference to our prayerful state of love for and trust in God.

In the second stage of surrender, "making space," we are to make room in our lives for God's life, spirit, and intention—and not ours. Emptying ourselves of our imperfections—our needs, fears, desires, anxieties, expectations of outcomes, wants—makes space for us to obey God's will. Mother Teresa taught that "God cannot fill what is already full." St. Teresa of Ávila wrote, "and if you should desire to please me by fulfilling all that my desire seeks, I see that I would be lost." The Mother likened this state of surrender to being like a "page perfectly blank" for God to etch on. Christine Bull offers a meditation of silence so that we can have the ability to carry a "Felt awareness" for "your will / Expressed in me."

In the stage of abandonment, we are carried away to "dying in God" (Catherine de Hueck Doherty). Human needs are completely removed to allow the soul—the essence of the Self—to become central in all that we do. This elevation to true joy and freedom is the advanced form of surrender, when all experiences—good or bad—are welcomed as gifts of joy and love from the Divine. The state of abandonment allows us the capability of living in real peace, a peace that exists in our center and cannot be disturbed by exterior activity. French mystic Marguerite Porete claimed that when "love and will," died in her, she found freedom.

GOD'S WILL

*The Lord is not an all-powerful automaton that human
beings can move by the push-button of their will. And yet
most of those who surrender to God expect that from Him.*

THE MOTHER

What pleases Him does not always please us. He wills us to enter in the way of suffering, and we desire to enter in action. We desire to give rather than receive and thus do not purely seek His will.

ST. ELIZABETH SETON

Every time we say "your will be done" we should have in mind all possible misfortunes added together.

SIMONE WEIL

Lord, you know what I want, if it be your will that I have it, and if it be not your will, good Lord, do not be displeased, for I want nothing which you do not want.

JULIAN OF NORWICH

Too long and too often, O my God, have I listened to the dictates of ingratitude and disobedience—but after Your example, my soul desires humbly and blindly to submit—to submit in the most contradictory circumstances and painful reverses, in necessities, under all the miseries of life, the repugnances, and oppositions of the heart, and rebellion of the passions.

In the midst of darkness, discouragement and desolation, after your example, my soul desires to submit wholly and entirely to Your dispensation, even in the least particular. This, Lord, is the submission I owe You, and from which I cannot depart without forgetting who You are and what I am.

ST. ELIZABETH SETON

*I began to meditate on the need to mould my will to his,
without seeking favours in return, and my meditation went
like this:*
—If you would rather I had never existed, so that I could
never have offended you, then so would I;
—If you wish to send me all the torments you can to
avenge my faults, then this is what I want;
—If I could be like you, without fault, and then suffer
the poverty and humiliation and pain that Christ did, out
of his goodness and wisdom and power, then I should like
to be;
—If I could be as worthy in myself as you are in yourself,
so that none of my worth could be taken from me
without my willing it to be, then I should place all this
worth in you and become nothing rather than keep
anything of myself that did not come from you;
—If all this worth belonged to me of right, then I should
rather lose it all beyond hope of recovery than have it
when it did not come from you. And if I had all the
torments you can send, then I should prefer these to any
glory that did not come from you, even though it might
last for ever;
—Rather than do anything to displease you, I should
prefer to see your human nature suffering on the Cross as
much as you did suffer for me—so much do I not want to
displease you;
—If I knew that the whole of your creation, myself
included, would be destroyed unless I offended against
his will, then I would rather see it destroyed;
—If I knew that I would have such everlasting torment
as you have everlasting goodness unless I offended you,
then I would choose the everlasting torment rather than
offend you;
—If you were to give me as much of your goodness as

you have everlasting value, I should value it only for your sake; if I lost it, I should lament the loss only for your sake; if you gave it back to me, I should rejoice in it only for your sake. And if you would rather I became nothing than received your goodness, then nothing it shall be;
—If it were possible for me to have as much of you in me as you have in yourself, and if I saw that it would please you better for me to suffer as much as you are good, then I would rather have the sufferings than you in me;
—If I knew that Jesus in his manhood and the Virgin Mary and all the saints in heaven were pleading that I should have you in me rather than the sufferings, and you were to say to me: "I will give you the gift of my being in you, if you want it, because these my friends in heaven have pleaded with me, but without their pleading I would not be giving it to you; so if you want it, take it!," then I would suffer the torments for ever rather than take this gift from you knowing it did not come from your will alone. If the humanity of Christ, and the Virgin Mary, and all the saints prayed for it to be given to me, I would not have it unless it came from the sheer goodness and goodwill and love that a lover has for his love.

MARGUERITE PORETE

O my God and my infinite Wisdom, measureless and boundless and beyond all the human and the angelic intellects! O love that loves me more than I can love myself or understand! Why, Lord, do I want to desire more than what You want to give me? Why do I want to tire myself in asking You for something decreed by my desire? For with regard to everything my intellect can devise and my desire can want You've already understood my soul's limits, and I don't understand how my desire will help me. In this that my soul thinks it will gain, it will perhaps lose. For if I ask You to free me from a trial, and the purpose of that trial is my mortification, what is it that I'm asking for, my God? If I beg You to give the trial, it perhaps is not a suitable one for my patience, which is still weak and cannot suffer such a forceful blow. And if I suffer it with patience and am not strong in humility, it may be that I will think I've done something, whereas You do it all, my God. If I want to suffer, but not in matters in which it might seem unfitting for Your service that I lost my reputation—since as for myself I don't know of any concern in me about honor—it may be that for the very reason I think my reputation might be lost, more will be gained on account of what I'm seeking, which is to serve You.

I could say many more things about this, Lord, in order to explain that I don't understand myself. But since I know You understand these things, why am I speaking? So that when I awaken to my misery, my God, and see my blind reason, I might be able to see whether I find this misery in what I write. How often I see myself, my God, so wretched, weak, and fainthearted. For I go about looking for what your servant has done, since it already seemed to her she had received favors from You to fight against the tempests of this world. But no, my God, no: no more trust in anything I can desire for myself. Desire from me what You want to desire, because this is what I want; for all my good is in pleasing You. And if You, my God, should desire to please me by fulfilling all that my desire seeks, I see that I would be lost.

ST. TERESA OF ÁVILA

O Parent of parents, and friend of all friends,
Your desires for me were not what I had imagined,

For without my asking, You took me into your care
And by degrees led me from everything else,
So that I might finally see and be grounded in you.
What had I ever done to please you?
Or what was there in me with which to serve you?
I could never do anything to deserve your choice of me.
O happy beginning of freedom, the source of all good
   things for me,
And more worth to me than anything else in the whole
   world.
If I had never got in the way of your desires and gifts,
How much better my relationship with you would now be!
It is now more than nineteen years since I first
recognized you as the centre of my life, and where am I?
My Jesus, forgive me. Remember what you have done
   for me,
And how far you have brought me.
And in response to your great goodness and love,
Do not permit me to block your dream and desire
   for me.

MARY WARD

Each morning as I lift my eyes to the rising sun,
And softly whisper, "Thy will be done."
All I ask for, I may not receive;
Help me not to murmur, not to grieve,
But bless Thee for the gift of sight
To see the radiance of the sunlight.

As I go about my daily task,
For strength, dear God, of Thee I'll ask;
Help me to scatter happiness along the way,
And gather the tears that fall each day;

When my daily chores are sincerely done,
I'll bless the Lord, through Jesus Christ the Son.

LYN MARTIN

Dear God,

I surrender to You my doings this day.
I ask only that they serve You and the healing of the
    world.
May I bring Your love and goodness with me, to give
    unto others wherever I go.
Make me the person You would have me be.
Direct my footsteps, and show me what You would have
    me do.
Make the world a safer, more beautiful place.
Bless all Your creatures.
Heal us all, and use me, dear Lord, that I might know the
    joy of being used by You.

MARIANNE WILLIAMSON

Help me, O Master. Look not at the unworthiness of
Your servant but only on her desire to serve You.
Enkindle that desire until, as a flame, it consumes me
entirely! Bless all the things I do in Your name. Give me
understanding of what I should do and what I should run
away from. Give me Your love! In temporal things, give
me my daily bread, and the rest as You will. Your will be
done, not mine.

CATHERINE DE HUECK DOHERTY

Lord, I hereby surrender my will and my love; you have brought them to the point of surrender. I had thought that my calling was always to live in love through the promptings of my will. But now both love and will— which brought me out of my spiritual childhood—are dead in me, and in this death I find my freedom.

MARGUERITE PORETE

I desire in my heart to say "Not as I will, but as You will." I think none of my friends need fear (as I believe they used to do) my being exalted by the good opinion of my fellow mortals. May my Lord, whom I have loved and sought to serve, keep me alive unto Himself.

ELIZABETH FRY

MAKING SPACE

There must be emptying before there can be any true filling.

FRANCES RIDLEY HAVERGAL

I went away full, but the Lord has brought me back empty.

NAOMI (FROM THE BOOK OF RUTH 1:21)

Those who want only God's will want nothing for themselves, except to carry out God's will for themselves and for others.

But those who operate through their own wills leave no space for God.

Marguerite Porete

We must lie before the Divine always like a page perfectly blank, so that the Divine's will may be inscribed in us without any difficulty or mixture.

The Mother

The unbearable is bearable in you, Lord. I am putting myself totally in your hands, Beloved. For I know now even better than I have known it for fifty years, that you are the only one. I love you. Here I am, Lord.

For I foresee that days ahead of me will be days of pain and joy in you. I understand now a little better what total surrender means. I realize what silence encompasses. It encompasses, among other things, total forgiveness. This I ask of you for this year, or part of it, as it pleases you.

Now I must enter the tunnel of your loneliness in earnest. I sense I will find also your joy, but it will be a little further on; and for me one step on your way is like the mileage between here and the moon.

Catherine de Hueck Doherty

In stillness
And silence
I know
You are my God
And I love you

silence

There is no
Felt awareness
But deeper inside
Than I knew existed
I am with you

silence

All else
Is of no account
My pride, self-doubt
Inhibitions
Washed aside

silence

Held in being
Loved into life
Delicately balanced
Joy transcending
Aching anguish

silence

Called by name
Compelled by love
Desiring nothing
Except your will
Expressed in me

CHRISTINE BULL

I gave up my house
and set out into homelessness.
I gave up my child, my cattle,
and all that I loved.
I gave up desire and hate.
My ignorance was thrown out.
I pulled out craving
along with its root.
Now I am quenched and still.

SANGHA

ABANDONMENT

First, entire abandonment; and second, absolute faith.

HANNAH WHITALL SMITH

*The deepest longing of woman's heart is to give herself
lovingly, to belong to another, and to possess this other being
completely. This longing is revealed in her outlook, personal
and all-embracing, which appears to us as specifically
feminine. But this surrender becomes a perverted self-
abandon and a form of slavery when it is given to another
person and not to God; at the same time, it is an unjustified
demand which no human being can fulfill. Only God can
welcome a person's total surrender in such a way that one
does not lose one's soul in the process but wins it.*

EDITH STEIN (St. Teresa Benedicta of the Cross)

Wild Nights—Wild Nights!
Were I with thee
Wild Nights should be
Our luxury!

Futile—the Winds—
To a Heart in port—
Done with the Compass—
Done with the Chart!

Rowing in Eden—
Ah, the Sea!
Might I but moor—Tonight—
In Thee!

EMILY DICKINSON

Grant, I pray, O Lord, that with that lowliness of
mind that befits my humble condition, and that
elevation of soul which Your majesty demands, I may
ever adore You; may I continually live in that fear which
Your justice inspires, in that hope which Your clemency
permits. May I submit myself to You as all-powerful, leave
myself in Your hands, as all-wise, and turn unto You as
all-perfect and good. I beseech You, most merciful Father,
that Your most vivid fire may purify me, that Your
clearest light may illuminate me, and that purest love of
Yours may so advance me that, held back by no mortal
influence, I may return safe and happy to You.

VITTORIA COLONNA

303

My God, I surrender myself to Your providence! Let my parents, my children and myself perish, If You have so ordained it! I care not. My only desire, in time and eternity, is to obey You and serve Your Divine Majesty.

Of what, my God, am I afraid? What can I fear? Your kind foresight extends to the lilies of the field and the birds of the air. Can You then refuse it to Your humble servants? It is enough for us to seek Your Kingdom and its justice. All the rest will be added unto us.

ST. JANE FRANCES DE CHANTAL

O my Lord and my All! How can You wish us to prize such a wretched existence? We could not desist from longing and begging You to take us from it, were it not for the hope of losing it for Your sake or devoting it entirely to Your service—and above all, because we know it is Your will that we should live. Since this is so, "Let us die with You!" as St. Thomas said, for to be away from You is but to die again and again, haunted as we are by the dread risk of losing You for ever!

ST. TERESA OF ÁVILA

Father, since you are the Good and I am mediocrity, rend this body and soul away from me to make them into things for your use, and let nothing remain of me, forever, except this rending itself, or else nothingness.

SIMONE WEIL

Young,
intoxicated by my own
lovely skin,
my figure,
my gorgeous looks,
and famous too,
I despised other women.

Dressed to kill
at the whorehouse door,
I was a hunter
and spread my snare for fools.
And when I stripped for them
I was the woman of their dreams;
I laughed as I teased them.

Today,
head shaved,
robed,
alms-wanderer,
I, my same self,
sit at the tree's foot;
no thought.

All ties
untied,
I have cut men and gods
out of my life,

I have quenched the fires.

VIMALA

20

AT THE END
OF LIFE

*W*omen's prayers towards the end of their lives are very specific. The ultimate surrender is to let oneself go into God through death, and the themes in these prayers are of the process of moving from what Emily Brontë once described as her "outward sense gone" into her "inward essence seeking its wings of freedom." Meera wrote of looking for her home with God; Mother Teresa always said that she was going home to Jesus when she died. Therefore, the spiritual reaction to death is that there is nothing to mourn, and that one should celebrate this coming together. Sufi mystic Rabe'ah referred to death as traveling the "bridge between friends."

Some of the prayers in this chapter express women's longings to finally see the face of the Divine in death: "Longing to see you, death I desire" is written like a mantra by St. Teresa of Ávila. Emily Dickinson's future is taken with surety of steps; she "climbs the stair" to "Eternity." "I'm coming—Sir, Saviour," she cries, "I've seen the face—before!" In the end it is love again that is longed for; it is love that we surrender to in death—the ultimate love, the Divine's love. Our whole lives have been in preparation for this act to step into "the secret word of love which holds us in his arms from the beginning" (Simone Weil).

I have gathered here too a section of final words written by women who have intuited their imminent death. St. Thérèse of Lisieux expressed her great love by praying for those she would leave behind. And women's thoughts about the "other side" are gathered in "Afterwords." The afterwords are written by those left behind when others pass on. There is the belief that for all, new life follows death, that no-one's life is wasted; and that everything is remembered in our bodies and our souls.

O life at enmity with my good; who has leave to bring you to an end? I bear with you because God bears with you; I maintain you because you are His; do not be a traitor or ungrateful to me. Nonetheless, woe is me, Lord, for my exile is long!

ST. TERESA OF ÁVILA

Life after life
I stand by the road
and look for a home

with my Lord.

MEERA

Upon this earth of lonely exile, we are mere guests, waiting in expectation for a response from our Host.

BARDAH-YE ṢARIMIYAH

Death is a bridge between friends. The time now nears that I cross that bridge, and friend meets Friend.

RĀBEʿAH OF BASRA

I am not ready to die,
But I am learning to trust death
As I have trusted life.
I am moving
Toward a new freedom
Born of detachment,
And a sweeter grace—
Learning to let go.

I am not ready to die.
But as I approach sixty
I turn my face toward the sea.
I shall go where tides replace time,
Where my world will open to a far horizon
Over the floating, never-still flux and change.
I shall go with the changes,
I shall look far out over golden grasses
And blue waters.
There are no farewells.

Praise God for His mercies
For His austere demands,
For His light
And for His darkness.

MAY SARTON

Dark hair and ruddy face—
How long do they last?
In a moment the gray hairs
Are strewn about like thread.
Opening the blinds, I glimpse
The bloom of the apricot blossom:
Here is the scenery of spring—
Don't allow delay.

CUI SHAOXUAN

In the autumn of my sixty-sixth year, I've already lived a
    long time—
The intense moonlight is bright upon my face.
There's no need to discuss the principles of kōan study;
Just listen carefully to the wind outside the pines and
    cedars.

RYŌNEN GENSO

I do not know, O God, what may happen to me today, I
only know that nothing will happen to me but what has
been foreseen by you from all eternity, and that is
sufficient, O my God, to keep me in peace. I adore your
eternal designs. I submit to them with all my heart. I
desire them all and accept them all. I make a sacrifice of
everything. I unite this sacrifice to that of your dear Son,
my Saviour, begging you, by His infinite merits, for the
patience in troubles, and the perfect submission which is
due to you in all that you will and design for me.

ÉLISABETH DE FRANCE

I thank You, God, that I have lived
In this great world and known its many joys;
The song of birds, the strong, sweet scent of hay
And cooling breezes in the secret dusk,
The flaming sunsets at the close of day,
Hills, and the lonely, heather-covered moors,
Music at night, and moonlight on the sea,
The beat of waves upon the rocky shore
And wild, white spray, flung high in ecstasy:
The faithful eyes of dogs, and treasured books.
The love of kin and fellowship of friends,
And all that makes life dear and beautiful.
I thank You, too, that there has come to me
A little sorrow and, sometimes, defeat,
A little heartache and the loneliness
That comes with parting, and the word "Goodbye,"
Dawn breaking after dreary hours of pain,
When I discovered that night's gloom must yield
And morning light break through to me again.
Because of these and other blessings poured
Unasked upon my wondering head,
Because I know that there is yet to come
An even richer and more glorious life,
And most of all, because Your only Son
Once sacrificed life's loveliness for me—
I thank You, God, that I have lived.

ELIZABETH, COUNTESS OF CRAVEN

O loving God, fiery within, radiant without, now
that You have given this even to me, so undeserving,
hunger wakes in me for that life You have given to Your
chosen ones. To that end I would gladly suffer longer

here. For no soul can or may receive this greeting till it
has utterly conquered self: but in this greeting will I, yet
living, die. . . .

Love without Knowledge
Is darkness to the wise soul.
Knowledge without revelation
Is as the pain of Hell.
Revelation without death,
Cannot be endured.

MECHTHILD OF MAGDEBURG

O God, I am so weary of life, that if I found
someone selling death I would buy it out of my
ardent longing to behold God and witness the
vision of His Face.

ANONYMOUS (SUFI WOMAN)

My God, how sad is
Life without You!
    Longing to see You,
    Death I desire.

This earth's journey
How long it is;
A painful dwelling,
An exile drear.
Oh, Master adored,
Take me away!
    Longing to see You,
    Death I desire.

❀ 311

Dismal is life,
Bitter as can be:
The soul lifeless,
Apart from You.
O my sweet Goodness,
How sad am I!
> Longing to see You
> Death I desire.

O kind death
Free me from trials!
Gentle are your blows,
Freeing the soul.
Oh, my Beloved, what joy
To be oned to You!
> Longing to see You,
> Death I desire.

To this life
Worldly love adheres;
Love divine
For the other sighs.
Eternal God, without You,
Who can live?
> Longing to see You,
> Death I desire.

Unending sorrow
Is this earthly life;
Life that is true
In heaven alone is found.
My God, allow
That there I may dwell.
> Longing to see You.
> Death I desire.

Who fears
The body's death
If one then gains
Pleasure so great?
Oh, yes, in loving You,
Forever, my God!
> Longing to see You,
> Death I desire.

Afflicted, my soul
Sighs and faints.
Ah, who can stay apart
From her Beloved?
Oh! end now,
This is my suffering.
> Longing to see You,
> Death I desire.

The fish caught
On the painful hook,
In death's embrace
Its torment ending.
Ah, how I suffer,
Without You, my Love.
> Longing to see You,
> Death I desire.

Master, my soul
In vain seeks You!
Always unseen
You leave me anxiously longing.
Ah! the very longing inflames
Until I cry out:
> Longing to see You,
> Death I desire.

When at last
You enter my heart,
My God, then at once
I fear your leaving.
The pain that touches me
Makes me say,
    Longing to see You,
    Death I desire.

Lord, end now
This long agony.
Comfort your servant
Sighing for You.
Shatter the fetters
Let her rejoice.
    Longing to see You,
    Death I desire.

Ah, no, Beloved Master,
It is only that I suffer
My sins to atone
My guilt unbounded.
Ah, may my tears gain
Your listening to me:
    Longing to see You,
    Death I desire.

ST. TERESA OF ÁVILA

A Wife—at Daybreak I shall be—
Sunrise—Hast thou a Flag for me?
At Midnight, I am but a Maid,
How short it takes to make a Bride—
Then—Midnight, I have passed from thee
Unto the East, and Victory—

Midnight—Good Night! I hear them call,
The Angels bustle in the Hall—
Softly my Future climbs the Stair,
I fumble at my Childhood's prayer
So soon to be a Child no more—
Eternity, I'm coming—Sir,
Savior—I've seen the face—before!

EMILY DICKINSON

By hours of night—that when the air
    Its dew and shadow yields,
We still may hear the voice of God
    In silence of the fields.

Oh! then sleep comes on us like death,
    All soundless, deaf and deep:
Lord, teach us to watch and pray,
    That death may come like sleep.

Abide with us, abide with *us*
    While flesh and soul agree;
And when our flesh is only dust,
    Abide our souls with *Thee*.

ELIZABETH BARRETT BROWNING

Our wealth has wasted all away,
    Our pleasures have found wings;
The night is long until the day;
    Lord, give us better things—
A ray of light in thirsty night
    And secret water-springs.

Our love is dead, or sleeps, or else
    Is hidden from our eyes:
Our silent love, while no man tells
    Or if it lives or dies.
Oh give us love, O Lord above,
    In changeless Paradise.

Our house has left us desolate,
    Even as Your word hath said:
Before our face the way is great;
    Around us are the dead.
Oh guide us, save us from the grave,
    As You Your saints have led.

Lead us where pleasures evermore
    And wealth indeed are placed,
And home on an eternal shore,
    And love that cannot waste:
Where joy You are unto the heart,
    And sweetness to the taste.

CHRISTINA ROSSETTI

Each of us is alone at the end.
First, you say goodbye to those
you love, then you walk the
narrow sword-blade of reality and
face the evil and weakness in
yourself. Then you hear the voice
of God and the voice of God tells
you, "you will never know or
understand, you can only love."

SVEVA CAETANI

The gold that was my hair has turned
silently to gray. Don't pity me!
Everything's been realized,
in my breast all's blended and attuned.

—Attuned, as all of distance blends
In the smokestack moaning on the outskirts.
And Lord! A soul's been realized:
The most deeply secret of your ends.

MARINA TSVETAEVA

Ah, that my soul might go up with my blessed
Lord—that it might be where He is also. Your *will* be
done; my *time* is in Your hands.
But, O my Savior, while the pilgrimage of this life
must still go on to fulfill your gracious purpose, let the
spirit of my mind follow You to Your mansions of glory; to
You alone it belongs; receive it in mercy; perfect it in
truth, and preserve it unspotted from the world.
Heaven cannot separate You from your children;
nor can earth detain them from You; raise us up, O Lord,
by a life of faith with You.

ST. ELIZABETH SETON

Dear Lord, as the years go on I begin to realize the
beauty and terrible joy of death. It is the opening of a
door to You; it is the return home.

CATHERINE DE HUECK DOHERTY

FINAL WORDS

It seems to me as though something were telling me to go. As I am perfectly sure that this is not just emotion, I am abandoning myself to it. I hope that this abandonment, even if I am mistaken, will finally bring me to the haven.

SIMONE WEIL

O Lord, God Almighty! My life is nigh unto its end. Strengthen me and hearken unto me and pity me and those who stand grieving round about me, and show unto me Your mercy even as unto all those who have been well pleasing unto You. And I pray, Lord, do not desert me because my father and my mother have forsaken me, but, O Lord, my God, raise me up.

And guard me in the short time of this life, and guide me into the haven of Your intent.

JULIANA OF NICODEMIA

O Lord, my God, my hope is in Thee;
O Jesus, my dear one, do now set me free.
Bound to hard chains, in misery of grief
I still yearn for Thee.
Languishing, moaning, down on my knees
I worship and beg Thee to liberate me!

MARY STUART, QUEEN OF SCOTLAND

Dear Jesus, I don't know how long it will be before my banishment comes to an end; there may be many evenings yet that will find me telling the tale of your mercies, still in exile. But for me, too, there will be a last evening; and then, my God, I would like to be able to offer to you the same prayer. I have exalted your glory on earth, by achieving the task which you gave me to do. I have made your name known to those whom you have entrusted to me; they belong to you, and now they are mine by your gift. Now they have learned to recognise all the gifts you have given me as coming from you; I have given them the message which you gave me, and they, receiving it, recognised it for truth that it was you who did send me. I am praying for those whom you have entrusted to me; they belong to you. I am remaining in the world no longer, but they remain, while I am on my way to you. Holy Father, keep them true to your name, your gift to me. Now I am coming to you, and while I am still in the world I am telling them this, so that the joy which comes from you may reach its full measure in them. I am not asking that you should take them out of the world, but that you should keep them clear of what is evil. They do not belong to the world, as I, too, do not belong to the world. It is not only for them that I pray; I pray for those who are to find faith in you through their word. This, Father, is my desire, that all those whom you have entrusted to me may be with me where I am, and that the world may know that you have bestowed your love upon them, as you have bestowed it upon me.

St. Thérèse of Lisieux

Oh, my dear Lord, help and keep your servant!

Elizabeth Fry
(LAST WORDS)

My Lord, it is time to move on.
Well then, may Your will be done.
O my Lord and my Spouse,
the hour that I have longed for has come.
It is time for us to meet one another.

ST. TERESA OF ÁVILA

AFTERWORDS, ON THE DEATH OF OTHERS

*If we have the crown of thorns in this world, will we not have
the roses in the next?*

ST. ELIZABETH SETON

Lord Jesus, today we accept from your merciful
hands what is to come. The times of trial in this world,
the suffering of our death, the sorrow and loneliness of
our last hours upon earth, the purifying, unknown pains
of our purgatory. Into your hands, O Lord, into your
hands, we commit our living and dying, knowing that
you are the dawn of eternal day, the burning light of the
morning star.

CARYLL HOUSELANDER

My God, it is better, O son, that I sent you along
ahead of me, rather than after me. Waiting patiently for
you is better than worrying about you. Though being

away from you grieves me, expecting God to reward you
is to be preferred.

MANQUSA
(ON THE DEATH OF HER SON)

A Rose—a budding Rose—
Blasted before its bloom,
Whose innocence did sweets disclose
Beyond a flower's perfume.
From pain and sorrow now relieved,
Immortal blooms in Heaven.

ST. ELIZABETH SETON
(ON THE DEATH OF HER SIXTEEN-YEAR-OLD DAUGHTER)

A funeral/plainsong from a younger woman to an older woman

i will be your mouth now, to do your singing
breath belongs to those who do the breathing.
warm life, as it passes through your fingers
flares up in the very hands you will be leaving

you have left, what is left
for the bond between women is a circle
we are together within it.

i am your best, i am your kind
kind of my kind, i am your wish
wish of my wish, i am your breast
breast of my breast, i am your mind
mind of my mind, i am your flesh

i am your kind, i am your wish
kind of my kind, i am your best

now you have left you can be
wherever the fire is when it blows itself out.
now you are a voice in any wind
    i am a single wind
now you are any source of a fire
    i am a single fire

wherever you go to, i will arrive
whatever i have been, you will come back to
wherever you leave off, i will inherit
whatever i resurrect, you shall have it

you have right, what is right
for the bond between women is returning
we are endlessly within it
and endlessly apart within it.
it is not finished
it will not be finished

i will be your heart now, to do your loving
love belongs to those who do the feeling.

life, as it stands so still along your fingers
beats in my hands, the hands i will, believing
that you have become she, who is not, any longer
somewhere in particular

we are together in your stillness
you have wished us a bonded life

love of my love, i am your breast
arm of my arm, i am your strength

breath of my breath, i am your foot
thigh of my thigh, back of my back
eye of my eye, beat of my beat
kind of my kind, i am your best

when you were dead i said you had gone to the mountain

the trees do not yet speak of you

JUDY GRAHN

On Her Passing Beyond

You being dead, I, willful, lay alive,
A cerement in your charnel; and kiss your feet,
The warmth pervading to your heart,—a beat
Decay repressing: I composed survive;
Trusting an equal fragrance of no breath;
Deeming your life more lovely in your death.
Beloved, live in me and never die:
Bid me with all vicissitudes comply;
To be your light, and voice, and taste, and smell,
Your emotion, and the beating of your pulse,
Your aspirations, deepest thoughts that dwell
Beyond the conscious of you; your revulse
Towards evil: to be your soul's keen strife,
Delight, peace, movement, sleep:—your life in life.

K. C. LEWIS

Little One, come, I will teach you the song of distance
whereby to flee this peacelessness and din.
Turn from the earth as stranger and begin:
     My soul is out on paths that have no ending

and no return. Where the noon kneels to pray
love guides my steps, ascending and descending.
Out through the sleeping solitudes I stray
    O far
           O far away.
Morning and evening do not mark this day.

O Little One, believe that earth is alien.
Let its concerns all unremembered lie.
Say to the storm or sweetness passing by:
    My soul is out on paths that have no ending
    and no return. A light blurs out my way.
    I am with God and toward my godhood tending.
    I near the foothills of eternal day
        O far
           O far away.
God speaks to me. Earth has no more to say.

JESSICA POWERS (*The Song of Distance*)

21

DIVINE UNION

*T*he most advanced stage of surrender—that which belongs to the "Upper School" of the spiritual life—is the death of Self. This death needs to happen for the soul to be absorbed in divine union. While written experiences and teachings of the passage that the soul takes to divine union are scarce, we can gain an understanding of the stages on the journey through the experience and writings of the Christian women mystics and the Sufi and Hindu bhakta (devotional) saints.

Understanding this mystical and unitive experience that was and is shared by women of so many different faiths, can lead to a bond among all religions. England's Evelyn Underhill, renowned lecturer, writer, and mystic, wrote that a mystic is someone whose life and beliefs are based on firsthand personal knowledge, and that mysticism is the "direct intuition or experience of God." She called it a "science of ultimates, the science of union," and the expression of it "the innate tendency of the human spirit towards complete harmony with the transcendental order."

The process of mystical development, although extremely personal in every instance, follows a circular logic. Evelyn Underhill explained it as follows.

First, there is the "awakening of the Self to consciousness of Divine Reality." Then comes the Self's awareness "for the first time of Divine Beauty" and glimpse of the "immense distance which separates it from the One." This requires the soul to attempt to "eliminate by discipline and mortification all that stands in the way of its progress towards union with God" (known in mystical terms as Purgation). Thereafter, when by Purgation the Self has become detached from the "things of sense," it begins to acquire the virtues which are the "ornaments of the spiritual marriage." And then comes the final purification, which is called "mystic pain," or the Dark Night of the Soul (when the absence of God is felt). Then ecstatic union takes place. This painful process is perceived as the necessary rite of passage to the ultimate.

What is interesting to note in the women mystics' writings in this chapter is that because there are undertones of real sensuality and eroticism in the expressions of love, the Divine is referred to in purely masculine terms—probably because of many women's need to experience union with contra-gender (even in the marriage of their souls!). And, if one looks at this from an Eastern point of view, it is perfectly natural for the yin to want to unite fully with the yang.

There are six parts in this chapter. The first is "The Soul's Search" for "that all-comprehending love of him by whom she loves all things" (Beatrice of Nazareth). St. Catherine of Genoa refers to the Self during the search as being pulled up "to that pure state from which it first issued." Evelyn Underhill wrote that here the mystics' one passion "appears to be . . . to find a 'way out' or a 'way

back' to some desirable state in which alone they can satisfy their craving for absolute truth." In its transforming,
the soul or Self becomes subject to a kind of alchemy. The
soul or Self is brought within the sphere of influence of
the eternal light, commonly referred to as the Sun.

St. Catherine of Genoa wrote, "These rays purify
and then annihilate. / The soul becomes like gold / that
becomes purer as it is fired, all dross being cast out." She
goes on to say that "gold cannot be purified any further
[having come to the point of 24 carats]; and this is what
happens to the soul in the fire of God's love." Angela of
Foligno referred to this stage as being transformed: "set
ablaze by divine love, the soul is transformed by the
power of love into God. The soul becomes as a hot
iron which, when put into the fire, takes on the form of
fire—its heat, colour, power, force—and almost becomes
fire itself."

The Taoist women masters were advanced practitioners of spiritual alchemy. In her short meditation here,
Sun Bu-er describes how, through secret use of language
(the way in which Taoist women taught and practiced
spiritual alchemy), the "immortal and mortal are separated" and then become one not so much through ab-
sorption into heat and fire, but "coolly cross the ocean"
between the two realms. Taoist visionaries see that the
ch'i is like a stream of water that winds its way from nature into human form and back again in a cycle towards
immortality.

The second part of this chapter is "Love." In the
sphere of mystical union, love is the center of everything,
and by joining love with Love (that which is of the Divine), a link is made between the finite and infinite
worlds. Mechthild of Magdeburg's marvelous dialogue
here between God and soul (where God refers to her soul
as "my Queen," and the soul to God as "Lord") draws the
vulnerable "naked soul" towards the deific. The treasure

the soul is offering is "the heart's desire"—withdrawn now from the world—to be laid in God's "own Divine Heart."

Evelyn Underhill said, "The completed mystical life is more than intuitional; it is theopathetic. In the old, frank language of the mystics, it is the deified life." And this, the mystics know, is home. No more are they living in their native land, but in a "returned exile" (Underhill). This returned exile leads to the "twofold intercourse" which can never die (Mechthild). Some mention a "wonderful sweetness" when the Divine enters the soul. There is much eroticism here.

All of this leads to "The Unitive Experience." In many cases, this occurs in a state of rapture. St. Teresa of Ávila once wrote that rapture "comes in general as a shock, quick and sharp, before you can collect your thoughts, or help yourself in any way; and you see and feel it as a cloud, or a strong eagle rising upwards and carrying you away on its wings." What happens is usually a complete suspension of the faculties, or a stillnesss of the physical body which resembles death, while the soul unites with its Divine. Those who witnessed St. Catherine of Siena's quite frequent raptures described her body as lifeless and unaware of its physical surroundings. Bibi Ḥayāti has explained that when she is in unconscious ecstasy she is just "intoxicated with God."

When mystics come out of raptures, they have difficulty describing, in finite terms, what they experienced in the infinite. Some, however, have attempted it. Mechthild wrote that she saw in ecstasy "all things in God and God in all things." Angela of Foligno said, "My soul sees nothing whatever that can be told of the lips or the heart, she sees nothing and she sees All." "God's lovemaking" is vastly different from human lovemaking. In her book *The Feminist Mystic* (New York: Crossroad, 1982), Mary E. Giles wrote that in divine unity, the Lover is also the Supreme teacher. "To be loved by God was to be enraptured by love . . . but also to experience profoundest learning."

After raptures of ecstasy, many mystics behave strangely, as though they have difficulty returning to the finite world. And they enter a place of "Pain" (the fourth part of this chapter) and darkness, a place where love and pain are mingled together; many mystics liken this to Christ's experiences on the cross. Underhill wrote, "Transcendence is a painful process at the best," and "No progress without pain . . . Birth pangs must be endured in the spiritual as well as in the material world; that adequate training must always hurt the athlete." This Dark Night of pain is an aspect of "the transition from multiplicity to Unity; of that mergence and union of the soul with the Absolute, which is the whole object of the mystical evolution of man. It is the last painful break with the life of illusion, the tearing away of the self from that World of Becoming in which all its natural affections and desires are rooted, to which its intellect and senses correspond, and the thrusting of it into that World of Being where at first, weak and blinded, it can but find a wilderness, a 'dark' " (Underhill). This is referred to as God's "hide and seek" game, the game of infinite love. Mechthild prayed that in God's absence "one hour is already too long, / A day is a thousand years." These dark nights, however, provide a place where the Self "struggles between her low and higher personality" (Underhill)—a very necessary part of transformation.

Once the soul has readied itself in the darkness, "taking more and more strongly possession of all her being; (she) little by little receives a new life, never again to be lost" (Madame Guyon du Chesnoy); God returns, and it is in stillness and "Solitude" (part five of this chapter) that divine betrothal is made. St. Teresa of Ávila calls this the Prayer of Quiet; Rābe'ah exclaimed, "Now with You I am at last secluded." Underhill wrote that it is in this most hidden cell of solitude, a place where any soul in the Upper School needs to go, that "the noises of the world are never heard, and the great adventures of the spirit take place."

"The Spiritual Marriage" is the biggest adventure, and the ultimate union. There is no longer any separation; one is only totally in God. Rābe'ah explained, "I do not belong to myself. I am His possession." Underhill stated that there are no more "rapturous satisfactions, no dubious spiritualizing of earthly ecstasies, but a life-long bond that shall never be lost or broken, a close personal union of will and of heart, between the free self and that "Fairest in Beauty." The language of the mortal marriage—of bride with bridegroom—is common, especially among the Christian mystics. They borrowed much of it from the language of divine betrothal portrayed in Solomon's Song of Songs. Then the married soul, having become one in spirit in eternal fidelity, moves into her new abode, to the home of Truth, where no division of realms or realities exists.

The self slides gently, almost imperceptibly, from the old universe to the new.

EVELYN UNDERHILL

". . . let the one who sees with watchful eyes and hears with attentive ears welcome with a kiss My mystical words, which proceed from Me Who am life."

HILDEGARD OF BINGEN

I have separated myself from all created beings,
My hope is for union with You, for that is the goal of my
   desire.

RĀBE'AH OF BASRA

THE SOUL'S SEARCH

*The soul seeks God in his majesty; she follows him there
and gazes upon him with heart and spirit. She knows him, she
loves him and she so burns with desire for him that she cannot
pay heed to any saints or sinners, angels or creatures, except
with that all-comprehending love of him by whom she loves
all things. She has chosen him alone in love above all,
beneath all and within all, and so she desires to see God, to
possess and to enjoy him with all the longing of her heart
and with all the strength of her soul.*

BEATRICE OF NAZARETH

*An aurorial breeze wafted to my soul where the
whiteness of the sun of the true dawn broke. The sun of his
loveliness, in whose atmosphere the bird of my soul soared like
a moth of dancing light, suddenly shone forth. My outcast eye
opened to the light of his world-adorning countenance.*

BIBI ḤAYĀTI

When God sees the Soul pure as it was in its origins,
He tugs at it with a glance,
draws it and binds it to Himself with a fiery love
that by itself could annihilate the immortal soul.

     ❁ 331

In so acting, God so transforms the soul in Him
that it knows nothing other than God;
and He continues to draw it up into his fiery love
until He restores it
to that pure state from which it first issued.

These rays purify and then annihilate.
The soul becomes like gold
that becomes purer as it is fired,
all dross being cast out.

Having come to the point of twenty-four carats,
gold cannot be purified any further;
and this is what happens to the soul
in the fire of God's love.

ST. CATHERINE OF GENOA

At the right time, just out of the valley
You rise lightly into the spiritual firmament.
The jade girl rides a blue phoenix,
The gold boy offers a scarlet peach.
One strums a brocade lute amidst the flowers,
One plays jewel pipes under the moon.
One day immortal and mortal are separated,
And you coolly cross the ocean.

SUN BU-ER

Is this then the night of Power
Or merely—your hair,
Is this the dawnbreak, or your own face?
In the divan of Beauty

Is it an immortal first distich?
Or a mere couplet,
Inscribed from your eyebrow?

Boxwood from the orchard,
Or cypress from the rosegarden . . . ?
Is it the tuba tree, date-bearing in paradise
Or your own stature—elegant, empathic . . . ?
Is it that odor of musk carried by Chinese deer,
Or rosewater's delicate scent?
Is it the rose's wafted breath,
Or the qualities of your perfume?

Is this a scorching lightning bolt,
Or fire radiant from Mt. Sana'i?
Or my burning sigh,
Or your innate character?

Is this Mongolian musk,
Or unadulterated ambergris?
Is it your hyacinth curl
Or your braided tress?

Is this a chalice of the red wine of dawntide
Or White Magic?
Your narcissus-like eye, in a drunken stupor
Or your sorcery?

Is it the garden of Eden
Or an earthly paradise—?
Is it a Ka'ba of the heart's masters
Or your back street?

> Everyone faces to pray
> A *qibla* of adobe and mud,

The *gibla* of Hayati's soul
Is turned towards your face.

BIBI ḤAYĀTI

O, my Lord, you were within my heart, and you
asked of me only that I should return within, in order
that I might feel your presence. O, Infinite Goodness,
you were so near, and I, running here and there to seek
you, found you not!

MADAME GUYON DU CHESNOY

Soul, you must seek yourself in Me
And in yourself seek Me.

With such skill, soul,
Love could portray you in Me
That a painter well gifted
Could never show
So finely that image.

For love you were fashioned
Deep within me
Painted so beautiful, so fair;
If, my beloved, I should lose you,
    Soul, in yourself seek Me.

Well I know that you will discover
Yourself portrayed in my heart
So lifelike drawn
It will be a delight to behold
Yourself so well painted.

And should by chance you do not know
Where to find Me,
Do not go here and there;
But if you wish to find Me,
  In yourself seek Me.

Soul, since you are My room,
My house and dwelling,
If at any time,
Through your distracted ways
I find the door tightly closed,

Outside yourself seek Me not,
To find Me it will be
Enough only to call Me,
Then quickly will I come,
  And in yourself seek Me.

St. Teresa of Ávila

O You, my Friend, my ecstasy and aspiration,
Besides You, my heart spurns all other love.
O Beloved, my long-enduring ambition and
  yearning is to behold You.
Among all the pleasures of Paradise
Only union with You do I wish.

Reyhāna

LOVE

*The Sun sends, by means of love, the knowledge that
His Majesty is indescribably close.*

*But how can we possess, my God, a love in conformity
with what the Beloved deserves, if Your love does not join love
with itself?*

ST. TERESA OF ÁVILA

No, my Love, you are neither fire nor water nor
anything we could say of you. You are what you are in
your glorious eternity. You are: this is your essence and
your name. You are life, divine life, living life, unifying
life. You are all beatitude. You are superadorable oneness,
ineffable, incomprehensible. In a word, you are Love,
my Love.

BLESSED MARIE OF THE INCARNATION

Go on, Lord
Love me into wholeness.
Set me free
To share with you
In your creative joy;
To laugh with you
At your delight
In me,
Your work of art.

ANN LEWIN

God:

> You hunt sore for your love,
> What have you brought Me, my Queen?

Soul:

> Lord! I bring You my treasure;
> It is greater than the mountains,
> Wider than the world,
> Deeper than the sea,
> Higher than the clouds,
> More glorious than the sun,
> More manifold than the stars,
> It outweighs the whole earth!

God:

> O You! image of My Divine Godhead,
> Enobled by My humanity,
> Adorned by My Holy Spirit—
> What is your treasure called?

Soul:

> Lord! it is called my heart's desire!
> I have withdrawn it from the world,
> Denied it to myself and all creatures,
> Now I can bear it no longer,
> Where, O Lord, shall I lay it?

God:

> Your heart's desire you shall lay nowhere
> But in mine own Divine Heart
> And on My human breast,
> There alone will you find comfort
> And be embraced by My Spirit.

Soul:
    Fish cannot drown in the water,
    Birds cannot sink in the air
    Gold cannot perish
    In the refiner's fire,
    This has God given to all creatures
    To foster and seek their own nature,
    How then can I withstand mine?
      I must to God—
    My Father through nature,
    My Brother through humanity,
    My Bridegroom through love,
    His am I for ever!
      Do you think that fire must utterly slay my soul?
    No! Love can both fiercely scorch
    And tenderly love and console.
    Therefore don't be troubled!
    You shall still teach me.
    When I return
    I will need teaching
    For the earth is full of snares.

      Then the beloved goes into the Lover, into the
secret hiding place of the sinless Godhead. . . . And
there, the soul being fashioned in the very nature of God,
no hindrance can come between it and God.
Then our Lord said—
    Stand, O Soul!

Soul:
    What do you will, Lord?

The Lord:
    Your SELF must go!

Soul:
  But Lord, what shall happen to me then?

The Lord:
  You are by nature already mine!
  Nothing can come between Me and you!
  There is no angel so sublime
  As to be granted for one hour
  What is given you for ever.
  Therefore you must keep yourself from
  Fear and shame and all outward things.
  Only that which you are sensible by nature
  Shall you wish to be sensible in Eternity.
  That shall be your noble longing,
  Your endless desire,
  And that in My infinite mercy
  I will evermore fulfill.

Soul:
  Lord! now am I a naked soul
  And you a God most Glorious!
  Our two-fold intercourse is Love Eternal
  Which can never die
  Now comes a blessed stillness
  Welcome to both. He gives Himself to her
  And she to Him
  What shall now befall her, the soul knows:
  Therefore am I comforted.
  Where two lovers come secretly together
  They must often part, without parting.

  Dear friend of God! I have written down this, my
way of love, for may God give it to you in your heart.

MECHTHILD OF MAGDEBURG

My Lord, I do not ask You for anything else in life but that You kiss me with the kiss of Your mouth, and that You do so in such a way that although I may want to withdraw from this friendship and union, my will may always, Lord of my life, be subject to Your will and not depart from it; that there be nothing to impede me from being able to say: "My God and my Glory, indeed Your breasts are better and more delightful than wine."

ST. TERESA OF ÁVILA

Moon-faced, my Saqi carries,
Two ruby-shaded chalices of wine in hand;
From His lips two kisses I steal,
From His palm two flasks.

O, my inner state and my Beloved
Are as one soul cast into two bodies.
How fantastic this fleshly difference,
One individual called by two names!

Your tresses, hanging from either side,
Snare the bird of my heart.
How hard it is to accept
A single prey caught in two snares!

I have come here to discourse on Love:
Myself, a soldier, and a Mulla
Yet how can I respond to them?
One of us is well-done, while two are half-baked.

LADY SAKINA BEGUM SHIRAZ

Lord, You know that one who thirsts for Your love can
never be sated.

SHA'WANA

. . . O Siva
when shall I
crush you on my pitcher breasts

O lord white as jasmine
when do I join you
stripped of body's shame
and heart's modesty?

MAHĀDĒVIYAKKA

THE UNITIVE EXPERIENCE

*She has participated for an instant in the Divine Life;
knows all, and knows nought. She has learned the world's
secret, not by knowing, but by being: the only way of really
knowing anything.*

EVELYN UNDERHILL

*The day of my spiritual awakening was the day I saw—
and knew I saw—all things in God and God in all things.*

MECHTHILD OF MAGDEBURG

She moves in him unmoved, loses only herself.

MEERA

I cannot dance, O Lord,
Unless You lead me,
If You wish me to leap joyfully,
Let me see You dance and sing—

Then I will leap into Love—
And from Love into Knowledge,
And from Knowledge into the Harvest,
That sweetest Fruit beyond human sense.

There I will stay with You, whirling.

MECHTHILD OF MAGDEBURG

O God, O Creator, though You inflict me with torment,
it is nothing in comparison with what I lose from being
far from You. Though with heaven's bounty You bless me,
it is still less than the rapture with which Your love has
favored my heart.

ROQIYA

O God of too much giving, whence is this
inebriation that possesses me,
that the staid road now wanders all amiss,
and that the wind walks much too giddily,
clutching a bush for balance, or a tree?
How then can dignity and pride endure
with such inordinate mirth upon the land,

when steps and speech are somewhat insecure
and the light heart is wholly out of hand?

If there be indecorum in my songs,
fasten the blame where rightly it belongs:
on Him who offered me too many cups
of His most potent goodness—not on me,
a peasant who, because a King was host,
drank out of courtesy.

JESSICA POWERS (*But Not with Wine*)

The eyes of my soul were opened, and I beheld the
plenitude of God wherein I did comprehend the whole
world, both here and beyond the sea, and the abyss and
ocean and all things. In all these things I beheld naught
save the divine power, in a manner assuredly
undescribable; so that through excess of marvelling the
soul cried with a loud voice saying "This whole world is
full of God!"

Wherefore I now comprehended how small a thing
is the whole world, that is to say both here and beyond
the seas, the abyss, the ocean, and all things; and that
the Power of God exceeds and fills all.

ANGELA OF FOLIGNO

My soul has just been rapt to a state in which I
tasted unspeakable joy. I knew all I longed to know,
possessed all I longed to possess. I saw all Good. In this
state the soul cannot believe that this Good will ever
depart from her, or that she will depart from it, or that
she will again be separated from it. But she delights
herself in that Sovereign Good. My soul sees nothing

whatever that can be told of the lips or the heart, she
sees nothing and she sees All. . . .

ANGELA OF FOLIGNO

It was that God walked with me in the garden as He did
before the Fall. Whether I sat, whether I walked, He was
there—radiant, burningly pure, holy beyond holy.

When I breathed, I breathed Him; when I asked a
question He both asked and answered it.

My heart was unshuttered to Him and He came and
went at will; my head had no limit or boundary of skull,
but the Spirit of God played on me as though my mind
were a harp which reached the zenith.

Every prayer was fulfilled, every possible desire for
the whole world consummated; for His Kingdom had
come and I had beheld it with my very eyes. Never again
the need to meditate for He was here, to be STOOD in,
SAT in, as a child might play on the edges of a great
sunny river. And, indeed, I found myself only a child,
playing in Him, laughing in Him at the way He was
visiting His world. When I stood within Him, He gave
and was everything. The years to come, which He
showed me as easily as a father shows his child a curious
shell beside the great river, held in them no surprise; only
wonder and joy.

KATHARINE TREVELYAN

. . . Lie down in the Fire
See and taste the Flowing
Godhead through your being;
Feel the Holy Spirit

Moving and compelling
You within the Flowing
Fire and Light of God.

MECHTHILD OF MAGDEBURG

PAIN

*For the more the soul is given from above, the more she
desires, and the more that is revealed to her, the more she is
seized to draw near to the light of truth, of purity, of sanctity
and of love's delight. And thus she is driven and goaded on
more and more and knows no peace or satisfaction; for the
very thing that tortures her and gives her the greatest
suffering, makes her whole and what wounds her most deeply,
is the source of her greatest relief.*

BEATRICE OF NAZARETH

*Whoever loves God, will gain intimacy with Him. Whoever
becomes joyous will become desirous. Whoever becomes
desirous will become bewildered in love. Whoever becomes
bewildered in love will become bold. Whoever becomes bold
will reach Him. Whoever reaches Him will enter into Union.
Whoever enters into Union will become a knower. Whoever
becomes a knower will be drawn near. Whoever draws near
will not fall asleep, and the rays of heartache engulf such a
person.*

HAYYUNA

Be pleased now, my King, I beseech You, to ordain that since I write this, I am, by Your goodness and mercy, not yet recovered from this holy heavenly madness—a favour which You granted me through no merits of my own—either those with whom I shall have to do may also become mad through Your love or I myself may have no part in anything to do with the world or may be taken from it. This servant of Yours, my God, can no longer endure such trials as come when she finds herself without You; for, if she is to live, she desires no repose in this life nor would she have You give her any. This soul would fain see itself free: eating is killing it; sleep brings it anguish. It finds itself in this life spending its time upon comforts, yet nothing can comfort it but You: it seems to be living against nature, for it no longer desires to live to itself, but only to You.

O my true Lord and Glory, what a cross—light and yet most heavy—have You prepared for those who attain to this state! Light, because it is sweet; heavy, because there come times when there is no patience that can endure it: never would the soul desire to be free from it save to find itself with You. When it remembers that as yet it has rendered You no service and that by living it can still serve You, it would gladly take up a much heavier cross and never die until the end of the world. It sets no store by its own repose if by forfeiting this it can do You a small service. It knows not what to desire, but it well knows that it desires nothing else but You.

ST. TERESA OF ÁVILA

O soaring eagle! darling lamb!
O glowing spark! Set me on fire!
How long must I endure this thirst?
One hour is already too long,

A day is a thousand years
When You are absent!
Should this continue for eight days
I would rather go down to Hell—
(Where indeed I already am!)
Than that God should hide Himself
From the loving soul;
For that were anguish greater than human death,
Pain beyond all pain.
The nightingale must ever sing
Because its nature is love;
Whoso would take that from it
Would bring it death.
     Ah! Mighty Lord! Look on my need!
Then the Holy Spirit spoke to the soul—
"Come, noble maid! Prepare yourself
     Your Lover comes!"
Startled but inwardly rejoicing
She said: "Welcome, faithful messenger,
Would that it were ever so!
I am so evil and so faithless
That I can find no peace of mind
Apart from my Love.
The moment it seems that I cool
But a little from love of Him,
Then am I in deep distress
And can do nothing but seek for Him lamenting."
     Then the messenger spoke:
"You must purify yourself,
Sprinkle the dust with water,
Scatter flowers in your room."
     And the exiled soul replied:
"When I purify, I blush,
When I sprinkle, I weep,
When I pray, then must I hope,
When I gather flowers, I love.

When my Lord comes
I am beside myself
For there comes with Him such sweet melody
That all carnal desire dies within me:
And His sweet music puts far from me
All sorrow of heart.
     The mighty voice of the Godhead
Has spoken to me in powerful words
Which I have received
With the dull hearing of my misery—
A light of utmost splendour
Glows on the eyes of my soul.
Therein have I seen the inexpressible ordering
Of all things, and recognized God's unspeakable glory—
That incomprehensible wonder—
The tender caress between God and the soul,
The sufficiency in the Highest,
Discipline in understanding,
Realization with withdrawal,
According to the power of the senses,
The unmingled joy of union,
The living love of Eternity
As it now is and evermore shall be.

MECHTHILD OF MAGDEBURG

SOLITUDE

*Anything less than an immediate encounter with the divine
yields inadequate knowledge.*

MARY E. GILES

My God, all has quieted, and every outer motion has
reached tranquillity. Every lover has secreted himself
with his sweetheart. Now with You I am at last secluded.
O Beloved, let my solitude with You tonight serve to save
me from Hellfire hereafter.

RĀBE'AH OF BASRA

THE SPIRITUAL MARRIAGE

*... she is joined to the One Husband Whom sin never
touched, without any lust of the flesh, but flowering
perpetually with Him in the joy of the regal marriage.*

HILDEGARD OF BINGEN

*The spiritual marriage may also be compared to water falling
from the sky into a river or fountain, where the waters are
united, and it would no longer be possible to divide them, or
to separate the water of the river from that which has fallen
from the heavens.*

ST. TERESA OF ÁVILA

*No separation exists between the Beloved and the lover.
I do not belong to myself. I am His possession.*

RĀBE'AH OF BASRA

Within my heart I established you
As a Friend with whom I could converse;
My body I offered to one

Who wished to be next to me.
I view this body as suitable
For sitting next to, but my heart's lover
Alone befriends my heart.

RĀBE'AH OF SYRIA

I gave all my heart to the Lord of Love,
And my life is so completely transformed
That my Beloved One has become mine
And without a doubt I am his at last.

When that tender hunter from paradise
Released his piercing arrow at me,
My wounded soul fell in his loving arms;
And my life is so completely transformed
That my Beloved One has become mine
And without a doubt I am his at last.

He pierced my heart with his arrow of love
And made me one with the Lord who made me,
This is the only love I have to prove,
And my life is so completely transformed
That my Beloved One has become mine
And without a doubt I am his at last.

ST. TERESA OF ÁVILA

O Lord! how little do we Christians know You! What
will that day be in which You come as our Judge, since
now, when You come as a Friend to Your spouse, the
sight of You strikes us with such awe?

ST. TERESA OF ÁVILA

PART FOUR

CONTEMPLATION

*P*assive prayer is prayer of voluntary inaction, and is that of contemplation. To contemplate in prayer requires us to watchfully wait, to meditate, to sometimes feel we are in a stagnant state of going nowhere fast, or to simply "be" in the divine presence and in the divine heart. The need to be still, and to look into the even stiller waters of our own souls, is a necessity in this stage of prayer. By doing what we may perceive to be nothing, we invariably discover that much is happening that is guiding us to a deeper spiritual place.

Most of us are not able—or are not called—to live a completely contemplative life like that of many of the mystics represented in the last chapter. But many of us give too little time or no attention to our soul's very real need for contemplation, although often we are forced into it by sickness or fatigue. As human beings we are naturally contemplative at our core, yet we are good at "doing," and not so good at "being." And because of this, much of the "doing" lacks the consciousness, intent, and dedication that is necessary for leading a balanced spiritual life.

Margaret Brennan, a professor of theology, wrote this about contemplative prayer: ". . . in meditation and silence the inner eye is awakened to the recognition of injustice and suffering and, above all, to the compassion of Jesus that enables us to see, love, understand, and forgive as he does, and to give our lives over that others may live as well. Furthermore, I sense that all of us have known those whose fire for social justice has burned out, or is only smoldering coals because an inner fire could no longer ignite their efforts." The ultimate balanced spiritual life is that of contemplation *combined with* action, of being and doing together. But it is necessary for those who have given no time yet to silence and stillness in their lives to learn what just "being" is like. This requires some withdrawal from one's daily activities and the demands of others, into the inner sanctuary of our beings.

The first aspect of the divine call is to prepare, and the preparation always has to take place within. We go within "at the beginning of a new road," wrote Evelyn Underhill. Miracles occur from just sitting still. I have found, from my own experience, that from going nowhere physically and everywhere internally, my life fell into true happiness, joy, fulfillment, and peace.

Still, contemplation and action (which is deeply explored in part five) eventually complement each other, drawing from the energies of the yin and yang. Contemplation is yin and action is yang. Patricia Joudry and Maurie D. Pressman, authors of *Twin Souls*, explained this as follows:

> Yang is the initiating impulse, which divides and delineates; yin is the responsive impulse, which nurtures and reunites. Without yang nothing would come into being; without yin all that comes into being would die. Yang is mental activity in its forceful aspect, yin the imaginative and poetic exalting the merely mental to the beautiful. Yang goes ahead with things, yin contains things within herself. Yang does, yin is. Yang in masculine givingness bestows the gifts; yin in feminine being receives, preserves, enhances, and

redistributes them. Yang constructs, yin instructs; yang implements, yin complements; yang is strength, yin endurance; yang is knowledge, yin the mystery that reveals itself and becomes knowledge. Yang is the self-developer, inspired by yin, the self-dedicator, for her development and his dedication. Yang is will and yin is wisdom, and one without the other is neither, and together they are joy. Yang is as the day, turning into night, and yin the night preceding the day; the one is the force that drives the waves of the ocean forward, the other the force that draws them back so that they may go forward again.*

Contemplation and action, like yin and yang, cannot do without the other. But first, Taoist Zhou Xuanjing instructs:

*"The secret of the receptive
must be sought in stillness;
Within stillness there remains
The potential for action."*

*Patricia Joudry and Maurie D. Pressman, *Twin Souls, Eternal Feminine, Eternal Masculine* (Toronto: Somerville House Publishing, 1993), page 27.

21

THE LUMINOUS PEARL

In one golden room
Lives a pair of beauties:
Whoever acts at whimsy
Is not sincere at heart,
If you can produce
A sun within the moon,
The black dragon spews forth
The luminous pearl.

FAN YUNQIAO

*I*n Taoist writings, like the piece above, all language, words, and symbols mean something much deeper
than anyone who is not a practicing Taoist could ever de-
cipher. However, I have chosen "The Luminous Pearl" as
the name for this chapter on contemplation because it is
an image of pure simplicity and beauty—even taken at
face value! The pearl, the jewel of our souls, is the genu-

ine goodness that can come from transformation of Self through contemplative exercises. It is like a dewdrop of grace—God-sent, white, pure, strong. Its luminosity allows it to glow, to radiate, to be suffused with light and intelligible—clear, straightforward, direct, definite, explicit, connected, and conscious.

We need to contemplate in order to still our minds; to begin to understand the lessons of inaction; to pray, meditate, focus, and study our souls. Contemplation feeds our souls, and focuses our intention. The soul begins to learn about her own bliss, understands the feelings "of an exalted kind" (Underhill), and develops the ability to see things from God's point of view—the infinite priority. Through contemplative practices we develop our intuition, our inner wisdom, where God or Truth instructs. And without a developed intuition, we cannot make true and conscious decisions about our actions.

This chapter is divided into four short sections on the contemplative practice. The first is "Solitude and Silence." Anne Morrow Lindbergh wrote, "We need solitude in order to find again the true essence of ourselves." She spoke of women's need for "inner stillness" and of the need for a woman to be "the still axis within the revolving wheel of relationships, obligations, and activities." Then there is "Listening Prayer," which is purely contemplative prayer. Meditations contributed here speak of the need to hear women's wisdom from the past, and to listen in the mountains. Mountains in Taoism represent our most important connection with our own bodies, joining heaven and earth. Similarly, Cherokee Dhyani Ywahoo once wrote, "Listen to the breath and know it is also the mountain's breath."

Next there is "Meditation," the most common of all contemplative exercises. It comes in many forms—from stillness, to breathing exercises and visualization, to practicing "no-mind" (whereby the mind becomes still and the heart opens) and movement meditation, like tai chi and chi kung. Yoga, too, provides numerous exercises towards wholeness, stillness, strength, and purification. "Purification" is the last section of this chapter. Sun Bu'er wrote of the need for "brambles to be cut away." Many women who have written of the soul like a plant or flower in God's garden emphasize the necessity of purification in the growth of a soul. As in pruning in a garden, old and unwanted growth is cut away to allow the sun to shine on us, the rain to water us, and the space to be made for new growth to blossom.

If you are called to contemplative prayer, which is not some esoteric adventure for the very few but by God's grace a normal flowering of baptismal life, you have to live in day-to-day fidelity to mysteries you do not fully understand, like Mary.

MARIA BOULDING

The contemplative experience is a centering and a centered seeing, a seeing that proceeds from the heart as well as the mind and perceives the person in his relatedness to all things, including himself. Through the contemplative eye humankind is known in its harmonious relationship to the divine and to the world. In this relational seeing a knowledge is found that can more truly be called love, for it is a knowledge that cannot be gained independently of the experience of the depths of love. It is a knowledge of the vital principle of relatedness—love—that binds all things, the principle that is the internal dynamic of the Godhead itself.

MARY E. GILES

Place your mind before the mirror of eternity!
Place your soul in the brilliance of glory!
Place your heart in the figure of the divine substance!
And transform your entire being into the image
of the Godhead Itself through contemplation.

ST. CLARE OF ASSISI

SOLITUDE AND SILENCE

*Women need solitude in order to find again the true
essence of themselves: that firm strand which will be the
indispensable center of a whole web of human relationships.
She must find that inner stillness which Charles Morgan
describes as "the stilling of the soul within the activities of the
mind and body so that it might be still as the axis of a
revolving wheel is still."*

*This beautiful image is to my mind the one that women
could hold before their eyes. This is an end toward which we
could strive—to be the still axis within the revolving wheel of
relationships, obligations, and activities. Solitude alone is not
the answer to this, it is only a step toward it, a mechanical
aid, like the "room of one's own" demanded for women,
before they could make their place in the world. The problem
is not entirely in finding the room of one's own, the time
alone, difficult and necessary as this is. The problem is more
how to still the soul in the midst of its activities. In fact, the
problem is how to feed the soul.*

ANNE MORROW LINDBERGH

*. . . another kind of prayer—this is a kind of recollection
which, I believe, is supernatural. There is no occasion to retire*

nor to shut the eyes, nor does it depend on anything exterior;
involuntarily the eyes suddenly close and solitude is found.
Without any labour of one's own, the temple of which I spoke
is reared for the soul in which to pray: the sense and exterior
surroundings appear to lose their hold, while the spirit
gradually regains its lost sovereignty. Some say the soul enters
into itself; others, that it rises above itself.

ST. TERESA OF ÁVILA

Silence is not the absence of sounds, but something
infinitely more real than sounds and the centre of a harmony
more perfect than anything which a combination of sounds
can produce. Furthermore, there are degrees of silence. There
is a silence in the beauty of the universe which is like a noise
when compared with the silence of God.

SIMONE WEIL

There is a solitude of space
A solitude of sea
A solitude of death, but these
Society shall be
Compared with that profounder site
That polar privacy
A soul admitted to itself—
Finite infinity.

EMILY DICKINSON

MEDITATION

*The quiet mind one gets through meditation is indeed of short
duration, for as soon as you come out from meditation you
come out at the same time from the quietness of mind. The
true lasting quietness in the vital and the physical as well as in
the mind comes from a complete consecration to the Divine;
for when you can no more call anything, not even yourself,
yours, when everything, including your body, sensations,
feelings and thoughts, belongs to the Divine, the Divine takes
the entire responsibility of all and you have nothing more to
worry about.*

THE MOTHER

Bliss comes not from book knowledge
Bliss comes not from debate
Blissful the wise, Sahjo *says,*
Who in solitude meditate.

SAHJO BAI

To nurture essence,
First quiet the mind.
Why bother seeking skill
With thread and needle anymore?
When you lead the iron ox
To go along with you,
Then you reveal the depth
Of boundless wisdom's deeds.

FAN YUNQIAO

Let the meditation of my heart and the words of my
mouth be always acceptable in Your sight, O Lord, my
Strength and my Redeemer.

FRANCES RIDLEY HAVERGAL

PURIFICATION

Wonderful to come out living
From the fiery furnace-blast,
But yet more, that after testing
I shall be fine gold at last;
Time of cleansing! Time of Winnowing!
Yet 'tis calm, without dismay;
He who shall be my refuge
Holds the winnowing-fan today.

ANN GRIFFITHS

It is not by fasting but improving the will that one obtains the
Truth.

THE MOTHER

To be reborn among the gods
I fasted and fasted
every two weeks,
day eight, fourteen, fifteen
and a special day.

Now with a shaved head
and Buddhist robes

I eat one meal a day.
I don't long to be a god.
There is no fear in my heart.

MITTA

Cut brambles long enough,
Sprout after sprout,
And the lotus will bloom
Of its own accord:
Already waiting in the clearing,
The single image of light.
The day you see this,
That day you will become it.

SUN BU-ER

PART FIVE

THE FRAGRANT
FLOWERING
OF THE SOUL

"*A*ction is what manifests that which you perceive in the meditation," wrote Dhyani Ywahoo. This is the reason I have called this last part "The Fragrant Flowering of the Soul," a title taken from St. Catherine of Siena's interpretation of what the prayer of action is. The seed once hidden in Mother Earth (that of contemplation; see the introduction to part four) eventually sprouts and grows into something glorious. We have a responsibility to the flowers that have seeded: the women who acted before, who reformed, pioneered, and contributed to the changing world. "The lives we lead, the songs we sing, will be our woman's story" (Chris Carol).

Many of the women included in this book prayed ceaselessly for strength, guidance, and divine intervention. Here Antoinette Doolittle suggests the very real necessity to pray to our heavenly mother. Angela of Foligno advised, "How one acts is the sign and measure of love. And the test of pure, true, and upright love is whether one loves and acts in accordance with love and action of the loved one."

Pray the prayer of action, which is the fragrant flowering of the soul.

ST. CATHERINE OF SIENA

❀ 367

Real love is empathic—an act of service. We must manifest the love of God in action as well as in thought and word.

RIANE ESLER

As long as we have all male Gods in heaven, we shall have all male rulers on the earth. But when the heavenly mother is revealed, and is sought unto as free and confidingly as the Heavenly Father, then will woman find her proper sphere of action.

ANTOINETTE DOOLITTLE

23

LEADING A
SPIRITUAL LIFE

*W*e are called to become "what we are in the depths of our being" (The Mother), and to manifest this in our actions and the way we live. Without expecting too much of ourselves, we must "lead a holy life here below" (Mechthild of Magdeburg). The rewards to us, and the gifts to the world, by our actions are too numerous to mention, but the real joy is being able to put into practice our beliefs.

Once we have prayed and are conscious of the Divine's working in our lives, all we can possibly do then is our consistent best in every moment.

Don't speak. Act.
Don't announce. Realise.

To know is good,
to live is better,
to be, that is perfect.

It is good to read a Divine Teaching,
It is better to learn it.
The best is to live it.

THE MOTHER

For we make a heaven on earth
When we lead a holy life here below.

MECHTHILD OF MAGDEBURG

In general I recommend a balance between worldly life and
spiritual life. One must love the world and its people, not feel
a repulsion for them. There is nothing wrong with the
world—the Divine is everywhere. It is just that usually we are
not good enough to truly see the world.

MOTHER MEERA

O may I join the choir invisible
Of those immortal dead who live again
In minds made better by their presence: live
In pulses stirred to generosity,
In deeds of daring rectitude, in scorn
For miserable aims that end with self,
In thoughts sublime that pierce the night like stars,
And with their mild persistence urge man's search
To vaster issues.

So to live in Heaven;
To make undying music in the world!

MARIAN EVANS (GEORGE ELIOT)

THE CALL

. . . what does to be called mean? A call must have been sent from someone, to someone, for something in a distinct manner.

EDITH STEIN (St. Teresa Benedicta of the Cross)

. . . it is very simple, we have only to become what we are in the depths of our being.

THE MOTHER

You need companions to travel
To the Isle of Immortals—
It is hard to climb
The azure cliffs alone.
If you take dead stillness for refinement,
The weak water brimming
Will lack a convenient boat.

SUN BU-ER

I am bending my knee
In the eye of the Father who created me,
In the eye of the Son who purchased me,
In the eye of the Spirit who cleansed me,
    In friendship and affection.
Through Thine own Anointed One, O God,
Bestow upon us fullness in our need,
    Love towards God,

The affection of God,
The smile of God,
The wisdom of God,
The grace of God,
The fear of God,
And the will of God
To do in the world of the Three,
As angels and saints
Do in heaven;
Each shade and light,
Each day and night,
Each time in kindness,
Give Thou as Thy Spirit

ANN MACDONALD

Omniscient Master of mysteries,
Let evil run rife, allow your enemies
To do the world's work. Unto friends
Grant everlasting life beyond.
—As for me, I'm always beyond both.

In this life or the life hereafter
If I be destitute or deprived,
If but one moment alone You befriend me—
my distress is less.
Your bounty overwhelms me,
Grand is such destitution!

Were I once to seek other than You
Or be attentive to either realm,
I'd be a faithless infidel.
To one who for His sake lives,
Everything else lives for him.

Beneath his bridge surge the seven seas.

All that is, that was or will be
Can be simulated except the Almighty
For all one seeks in life, a likeness does exist
Only He is ever unequalled to everything else.

RĀBE'AH OF BASRA

DOING YOUR BEST

To do at each moment the best we can and leave the result to the Divine's decision, is the surest way to peace, happiness, strength, progress, and final perfection.

THE MOTHER

Do simple things well.

MARY WARD

And if we do not cease in our striving, then we will know God.

MECHTHILD OF MAGDEBURG

I am truly happy only when I am about Your business.

CATHERINE DE HUECK DOHERTY

May it be Your pleasure, my God, that the time may come in which I shall be able to pay at least a few mites of all I owe You; ordain it, Lord, according to Your pleasure, that this Your handmaiden may in some way serve You. There have been other women who have done heroic deeds for love of You. I myself am fit only to talk, and therefore, my God, it is not Your good pleasure to test me by actions. All my will to serve You peters out in words and desires, and even here I have no freedom, for it is always possible that I may fail altogether.

Strengthen and prepare my soul first of all, Good of all good, my Jesus, and then ordain means whereby I may do something for You, for no one could bear to receive as much as I have done and pay nothing in return. Cost what it may, Lord, permit me not to come into Your presence with such empty hands, since a man's reward must be in accordance with his works. Here is my life; here is my honour and my will. I have given it all to You; I am Yours; dispose of me according to Your desire. Well do I know, my Lord, of how little I am capable. But now that I have approached You, now that I have mounted this watch-tower whence truths can be seen, I shall be able to do all things provided You do not withdraw from me.

ST. TERESA OF ÁVILA

When I entered a rock, you too entered the rock;
When I entered a mountain, you too entered the
   mountain;
Hurray for life! You came following me,
Lord, who is as white as jasmine,
     what else shall I do?

MAHĀDĒVIYAKKA

24

THE FLOWERS AND
THE FRUITS

*T*he fragrance of the flower of conscious love in action spreads "for the benefit of many" from its own interior root. St. Teresa of Ávila said that it is a "fragrance that lasts, not passing quickly, but having great effect." St. Teresa, who perfected the idea of the soul's journey according to the life of a garden, adds that "the fragrance of these flowers and works produced and flowing from the tree of such fervent love lasts much longer." I believe her to mean that the tree is of God's love, and we are all attached to it in some way and have our roles to produce the gifts from it.

Hildegard of Bingen herself used similar analogies, but with a twist in meaning. She wrote that the sap in a tree is like the spiritual energy in our bodies: "By the sap, the tree grows green and produces flowers and then fruit." The fruit provides nourishment to others, but Hildegard added that in human terms, by providing flowers and fruits, and continuing to learn and grow in our "good deeds," we become greater than trees in that our actions "are preserved in true faith for the rewards of eternal blessedness, after that person's end."

This idea is very similar to that of karma, which means "action." The Bhagavad Gita instructs that the highest type of karma is actions performed by a person who is detached from the end result. If we strive to act in charity and true partnership with the Divine's intent, then we are doing our best in the "here and now" in prayerful activity, with no expectation or thirst for pre-conceived outcomes. Hadewijch of Brabant said that we need to work "with no other goal than that Love should take her rightful place among us," and Angela of Foligno wrote, "I do not intend to serve or love for any reward, but I intend to serve and to love because of the incomprehensible goodness of God."

Below are prayers of women who have made a difference, who have contributed much to reset the course of the world towards love in action. Their whole lives were devoted to the relief of poverty. And poverty is a state that women have known, and still know well. But poverty is not purely about lacking financial means. The concept can also be applied to not having a balanced life, without comfort in mind and in body—in other words, being helpless, unwanted, silenced, imprisoned, or sick. Poverty can also be the way to peace and freedom—the richest gift of all. Evelyn Underhill explained, "The true rule of poverty consists in giving up those things which enchain the spirit, divide its interests, and deflect it on its road to God—whether these things be riches, habits, religious observances, friends, interests, distastes, or desires."

Voluntary poverty, and the practice of it, is a necessity if we wish to lead a holy, loving life.

Catherine de Hueck Doherty (1896–1985) worked in Canada for racial justice before arriving in New York in the winter of 1938 to found Friendship House in Harlem.

Elizabeth Fry (1780–1845) began visiting women

and children in appalling prison conditions; she set up schools to educate them, provided hope, and reformed prisons in Britain as well as in other countries. She also founded schools for training nurses, and homes for "wayward women." In a moving letter, a woman called Harriet (one of the women from Newgate prison, which Elizabeth described as "hell upon earth") wrote, "Believe me, my dear Madam, I bless the day that brought me inside Newgate walls, for there it was that the rays of Divine Truth shone into my dark mind. And may the Holy Spirit shine more and more upon my understanding that I may be enabled so to walk as one whose heart is set to seek a city, whose builder and whose maker is God."

Dorothy Day (1897–1980) founded the Catholic magazine for social justice for workers, *The Catholic Worker*, which became a forum for those who had no voice. She also formed, with Peter Maurin, the Catholic worker movement, with its Houses of Mercy around the U.S. for the homeless and the poor, and she contributed to the spirit of nonviolence within the Catholic Church. In the course of her life, she was jailed seven times—first when she was twenty years of age, and last in 1972, when she was seventy-five.

Simone Weil (1909–1943) was a brilliant French philosopher who chose to live with workers, to understand their way of life. She worked at the Renault car factory and in vineyards, and she also spent time with the Spanish Republican Army to experience the horror of war. For her it was the dignity of the worker that was the basis for spirituality at work, and she fought personally against oppression, especially for the French poor. In her struggle for peace, she chose to live as the poor in a homeless simplicity, eating only that which they had to eat.

The lives of these women are the definition of Goodness and Truth, and emblematic of love in action.

. . . in the active—and seemingly exterior—the work of the soul is working interiorly. And when the active works rise from this interior root, they become lovely and very fragrant flowers. For they proceed from this tree of God's love and are done for Him alone, without any self-interest. The fragrance from these flowers spreads to the benefit of many. It is a fragrance that lasts, not passing quickly, but having great effect.

ST. TERESA OF ÁVILA

It seems to me that one of the greatest consolations a person can have on earth must be to see other souls helped through his own efforts. Then, it seems to me, one eats the delicious fruit of these flowers. Happy are those to whom the Lord grants these favors.

ST. TERESA OF ÁVILA

. . . the soul rejoices in a sweet deed as the body delights in sweet food. And the soul flows through the body like sap through a tree. What does this mean? By the sap, the tree grows green and produces flowers and then fruit.

. . . the soul is a fruitful power, which makes the entire person live by moving with it; and just as someone puts on a cloth woven from threads and wears it, the soul, putting on all these works—whether good or ill—as a garment, is covered with the deeds that it performed with the person, just as it is covered by the body in which it lives. And the good deeds, when the soul leaves the body, will appear like clothes shining in purest gold, because they are decorated with every adornment; but wicked deeds will stink on it, like a garment polluted with all filth.

So the soul acts in the person like the air, which sends its strength to the earth to make it fruitful and produce its bounty, and which dries it out with winter's cold; however, this force preserves heat within to fructify the earth, since through the strength of the soul, childhood, adolescence, youth and old age perform and perfect the fruits of good deeds, which decrepit age, as it were, dries up through its debility. But they are preserved in true faith for the rewards of eternal blessedness, after that person's end.

HILDEGARD OF BINGEN

Each and every action carries in itself its fruit and its consequences.

THE MOTHER

GOOD WORK

. . . as the earth brings forth all fruits, so in Woman the fruit of all good works is perfected.

HILDEGARD OF BINGEN

Thus we must stand with renewed vigour and with hands which are ever ready for virtuous work, and with a will that is ready for all those virtues in which Love is honoured, with no other goal than that Love should take her rightful place among us and in all creatures, according to our debt to her.

HADEWIJCH OF BRABANT

And there is another manner of loving, which is when the soul seeks to serve our Lord for nothing in return, for love alone, without demanding to know the reason why and without any reward of grace or glory; just as the lady serves her lord for the sake of her love without any thought of reward, for whom simply to serve him is enough and that he should allow her to serve him. In the same way she desires to serve love with love beyond measure and beyond all human reason with all her deeds of fidelity.

And when this comes upon her, then she is so consumed with desire, so ready to perform any service, so cheerful in toil, so gentle in tribulation, so light-hearted in sadness, and she desires with all her being to serve him. And so it is her delight when she finds something she can do or endure in the service of love and in its honour.

BEATRICE OF NAZARETH

Where there is a need there is also an obligation.

SIMONE WEIL

How true, my Lord, that it is not because of You that those who love You fail to do great works but because of our own cowardice and pusillanimity. . . . Who is more fond than You of giving, or of serving even at a cost to Yourself, when there is someone open to receive?

ST. TERESA OF ÁVILA

"Without me, you can do nothing" (John 15.5)

Beloved, how true this is! Only in You can things be accomplished. Help me to go on trusting and abandoning myself to Your providence. I love You! I want to be all Yours and work for Your poor. And since it is Your work, why should I worry? Alone I am nothing.

In You, all things are possible for me, for You are God! Prostrate, I adore You and leave my work, myself, and my life in Your hands. Teach me that even overcoming myself is possible in You. Having realized this, let me begin with faith and courage. You know my poverty. But in You I can do all things. So, dear Lord, help me to carry on and bless me!

CATHERINE DE HUECK DOHERTY

We sing of new beginnings every day,
Each in our time to praise in deeds and dreams
The wonder of life, God's work in all our ways.
We gather in the scattered, radiant beams.
Moses did not see the promised land
Expanding new horizons round the bend;
His task to lead a slave-accustomed band
To march toward freedom, searchers without end.
Can I do my share, each day we ask,
Mindful of the past, building for tomorrow.
Not Moses, nor Sarah, nor any borrowed mask;
To be ourselves today, this road we furrow.
Ours not to end the work, nor even start;
Ours to give each day a willing heart.

NORMA U. LEVITT

The fruit of silence is prayer.
The fruit of prayer is faith.
The fruit of faith is love.
The fruit of love is service.
The fruit of service is peace.

MOTHER TERESA

25

THE FIRE OF
PROGRESS

*W*e enter the new millennium with shifts and changes in the air. For want of a better term, the Second Coming, believed by Christians to be Christ coming again, and which can best be interpreted by Christians and non-Christians alike as the Great and Holy Spirit revealed inside us and among us, blowing radical conversion throughout our world.

In Hinduism, the oldest religion in the world, the spirit of Shakti, which means "power," is feminine, and so this wind could be perceived as a feminine wind, where the world will slowly change to the ways of the feminine, as it transforms the old patriarchy. As Shakti is partnered with Shiva (see the Introduction for more details), destruction is part of transformation; so we will witness much destruction, much fire, as we progress towards harmony of the feminine and masculine energies.

Susan Eaton's opening statement calls for a feminine way of operating—of cooperating instead of being competitive, of being concerned for the whole over individual rights. Sheila Cassidy speaks of bearing within us "Your Spirit of life." With love as "the effective weapon" (Jessica Powers), we pray "O God let me make some mark on this world" (Judith M. Hertz).

The women quoted in this final chapter come from a diversity of faiths. They offer their wisdom about women's mission—of affecting the collective by our own individual actions, "to bring true humanity in oneself and in others to development" (Edith Stein). Native American Brooke Medicine Eagle is advised by Rainbow Woman "to be receptive, surrender and serve"; Jewish/Catholic Edith Stein advised women "to institute grace by counselling and helping."

In the last section, which I have called "The Single Song," women teachers instruct us on the music of this song. Its composition is formed by the notes of women who have gone before us for hundreds of years: "Your voice becomes her voice . . . your dance . . . her dance . . . your labor . . . her labor" (Starhawk). Through remembering, through joining with their struggles and their faith through prayer, we transform their hardships, we rejoice in their perseverance and the gain they gave the world. Starhawk reminds us that women's experience is like the experience of birth: in the creation of joy comes pain and labor; after the shedding of water and blood, the mystery of new life begins.

In the nineteenth century, Elizabeth Fry prayed for equality among Christians. Now our prayer becomes one for equality among not only Christians but men and women of all nationalities and faith. For we all share the same spirit in our depths. Fry asked that, "Your Spirit . . . may cover the earth, even as the waters cover the sea." Pagan white witch Starhawk now prays for the great feminine virtue of inclusivity to bind us and guide us. And finally, American artist Judy Chicago visualizes this new world, where "everywhere / will be called Eden once again."

Let us keep flaming in our heart the fire of progress.

THE MOTHER

THE GREATER GOOD

What if, [instead], the economic system were adjusted to fit my values? Cooperation would replace competition. Concern for the well-being of the whole human family would supersede individual rights. Protection of the weakest would take precedence over survival of the fittest. Everyone (including me) would benefit.

SUSAN L. EATON

When the dominator model no longer obstructs our search, we can begin the real spiritual journey. The task of clearing the obstacles is to get us to the point when we can explore our relationship to the divine. The more we move toward a partnership model of society, the more we can search for our higher potential. Humans have the capacity for creativity, for love, for justice, for searching for wisdom and beauty. All these are paths to the divine.

RIANE ESLER

. . . [while] we, ourselves, may never live to see "Utopia," we cannot leave it to others to work toward bettering the lot of people wherever they may be.

MARIANNE ADLER AARON

Having no gift of strategy or arms,
no secret weapon and no walled defense,
I shall become a citizen of love,
that little nation with the blood-stained sod
where even the slain have power, the only country
that sends forth an ambassador to God.

Renouncing self and crying out to evil
to end its wars, I seek a land that lies
all unprotected like a sleeping child;
nor is my journey reckless and unwise,
Who doubts that love has an effective weapon
may meet with a surprise.

JESSICA POWERS (*The Little Nation*)

O God our deliverer,
you cast down the mighty,
and lift up those of no account;
as Elisabeth and Mary embraced
with songs of liberation,
so may we also be pregnant with your Spirit,
and affirm one another in hope for the world,
through Jesus Christ.

ST. HILDA COMMUNITY

Almighty God and Father of us all,
Have mercy upon this troubled world of ours.
We are a pilgrim people,
Men of clay,

Captives of our own greed and frailty.
And yet,
We are the work of your hands.
You have made us in your own image
And we bear within us
Your Spirit of life,
The seeds of immortality.
Give us, we pray,
A stronger faith
So that we may walk joyously into the unknown,
An unshakeable hope
So that we may comfort the despairing,
And a love
As vast as all the oceans
So that we may hold all mankind
In our hearts.
All powerful God,
Look in your love upon us, your pilgrim people,
As we struggle towards you.
Be our food for the journey,
Our wine for rejoicing,
Our light in the darkness,
And our welcome at the journey's end.

SHEILA CASSIDY

Oh! may all end in good and blessing.

ELIZABETH FRY

We ponder the past
We think about the future:
Where have we been?
Where are we now?
What is the connection?

What heritage did I receive from my parents?
What will I bequeath to my children (and
   grandchildren)?
What gifts have I received from my brothers, my sisters,
   my friends?
What can I give to others?
Where does my people, my community fit in my life?

If I can make someone's life better
I will not regret the past.
If I can help someone grow
I will not fear the future.

Oh God, let me make some mark on this world,
Let me create some image,
Let me leave some memory of myself.
If only even for an instant—
Let someone think or say:
The world is better because I passed this way.

JUDITH M. HERTZ

WOMEN'S MISSION

*It's more natural for us to be receptive and nurturing. That's
what being a woman in this body is about. But even the
women in our society don't do that very well. None of us has
ever been taught how to do that. We know how to do
something; we know how to make something, how to do, how
to try. But we need to allow, to be receptive, to surrender, to
serve. These are things we don't know very well.*

BROOKE MEDICINE EAGLE

. . . a high vocation is designated in feminine
singularity—that is, to bring true humanity in oneself and in
others to development, but hazardous germs also lie in
feminine singularity which endanger the essential value in its
development and, thereby, the realization of mission. The
dangers can only be conquered through rigorous discipline in
the school of work and through the liberating power of divine
grace. Our mission is to become flexible instruments in God's
hand and to effect His work to which He leads us. If we fulfill
our mission, we do what is best for ourselves, for our
immediate environment, and together with it, what is best for
the entire nation.

EDITH STEIN (St. Teresa Benedicta of the Cross)

Three Steps towards the Supreme Identification:
   Give all you have, this is the beginning.
   Give all you do, this is the way.
   Give all you are, this is the fulfillment.

THE MOTHER

Woman whose work is words
What will you do when words are gone?

   Grow in silence like the trees
   find strength in solitude
   listen to wind, water, and living things
   hear what God speaks in silence.

Woman who lives by words
What will you do when words are strange?

Listen for a change
learn what people mean in other ways
smile, gesture—weep even—
live with questions and powerlessness.

Woman who cares for words
What will you do when words overwhelm?

Laugh at jargon, be angry
when talk and papers oppress people—
care more for them, remember
the first and last Word that makes us one.

JAN SUTCH PICKARD

Dear God,

We thank you for the years gone by, and we
    thank you for the years ahead.
This woman has lived, dear Lord.
She has seen the cycles of life and death.
She has rejoiced at morning and mourned its passing.
Thus she has now gained sacred knowledge:
The power to heal through the depth of her compassion;
The power to teach through the depth of her
    understanding;
The power to bring forth a new and better world
    through the depth of her vision.

May all now see in her, and may she see within herself,
    the elder, the wise one, the one who holds the candle
    of illumination for all the world to see.
May she be honored and revered.
May her heart be as a womb to new life.

May her children's children see the power of the ages as
   it is written in her eyes.
She has arrived, dear Lord.
May she be blessed.
She has come so far.
May she now know peace.
She has worked so hard.
May she now find rest.
And may a cycle now begin for her, more powerful than
   any other, most glorious of all.
For she is now the fullness of human, of woman, of God's
   servant and child.
Bless her always.
May she shine.

MARIANNE WILLIAMSON

THE SINGLE SONG

*I believe in the peaceful Second Coming as the solution
to the world—not the exclusive Coming in which people will
be destroyed, but the inclusive Coming in which God in the
heart of everyone will gently rise and we shall all be changed.*

BARBARA MARX HUBBARD

*. . . as I consider the transformations in my life and
work, I also think about the enduring quality of spiritual
practice exemplified in the Stone Guardians in the Mojave
Desert and in Ireland (and other places I've not been). There
they stand, facing into the Winds, seeming to Call all that
lives and grows, rooted in the Earth, drawing strength from
Sun and Air, manifesting their own strength of purpose, their*

changes often imperceptible within the lifetime of other beings
who share their habitat. Sentinels to all who live within their
landscape.

Like these Stone Guardians, we have ancient resources,
rivers of ancestral wisdom, to whom we can call and from
whom we find nourishment.

And we have a covenant, chosen or unchosen, with
future generations to leave Sentinels, footprints of blessing.
May we live and walk in a blessing way.

CAROL PROUDFOOT-EDGAR

And so the time comes when all the people of the earth
    can bring their gifts to the fire
    and look into each other's faces
    unafraid

Breathe deep
Feel the sacred well that is your own breath, and
    look at that circle.
See us come from every direction
    from the four quarters of the earth
See the lines that stretch to the horizon
    the procession, the gifts borne
    see us feed the fire
Feel the earth's life renewed
And the circle is complete again
    the medicine wheel is formed anew
    and the knowledge within each one of us
    made whole
Feel the great turning, feel the change
    the new life runs through your blood like fire
    and all of nature rises with it
    greening, burgeoning, bursting into flower
At that mighty rising

do the vines rise up, do the grains rise up
and the desert turns green
the wasteland blooms like a garden
Hear the earth sing
of her own loveliness
her hillock lands, her valleys
her furrows well-watered
her untamed wild places
She arises in you
as you in her
Your voice becomes her voice
Sing!
Your dance is her dance
of the circling stars
and the ever-renewing flame
As your labor has become her labor

Out of the bone, ash
Out of the ash, pain
Out of the pain, the swelling
Out of the swelling, the opening
Out of the opening, the labor
Out of the labor, the birth
Out of the birth, the turning wheel
the turning tide
This is the story we like to tell ourselves
In the night
When the labor is too hard, and goes on too long
When the fire seems nothing but dying embers winking
out
We say we remember
a time when we were free
We say
that we are free, still, and always
And the pain we feel
is that of labor

And the cries we hear
    are those of birth
And so you come to the fire
    where the old ones sit
You are young
    just on the edge of ripening
They are ancient
    their faces lined
    with spiderwebs of wrinkle
Their faces brown, bronze, cream, black
    their eyes are wells of memory
They say
    Listen child
    For this is your night of passage
    And it is time to learn
    Your history
    Tonight you will run free, out into the wild
    Fearing only the spirit of your own power
    And no one in this world would harm you or lay a
    hand on you
But there was a time
    When children were not safe.

STARHAWK

So be it, most merciful Lord God, that the day may
hasten forward, when the knowledge of Yourself and
Your Christ, through the power of Your Spirit, may cover
the earth, even as the waters cover the sea!

ELIZABETH FRY

Nameless One   of many names
Eternal   and ever-changing One
Who is found nowhere   but appears everywhere
Beyond   and within all.
Timeless   circle of the seasons,
Unknowable mystery   known by all.
Lord of the dance,   Mother of all life,
Be radiant within us,   Engulf us with your love,
See with our eyes, Hear with our ears, Breathe with
our nostrils, Touch with our hands, Kiss with our lips,
Open our hearts!
That we may live free at last
Joyful in the single song
Of all that is, was, or ever shall be!

STARHAWK

And then all that has divided us will merge
And then compassion will be wedded to power
And then softness will come to a world
that is harsh and unkind
And then both men and women will be gentle
And then both women and men will be strong
And then no person
will be subject to another's will
And then all will be rich and free and varied
And then the greed of some
will give way to the needs of many
And then all will share equally
in the earth's abundance
And then all will care
for the sick and the weak and the old
And then all will nourish the young
And then all will cherish life's creatures

And then all will live
in harmony with each other and the earth.
And then everywhere
will be called Eden once again.

JUDY CHICAGO

The road is long, but at the end is joy, is peace.

CATHERINE DE HUECK DOHERTY

The murmur of the prayers are to me like stepping stones, the
mysteries like wings.
All things spoken on the beads are now accomplished
and today
I walk on their slender, incredible strength.

CATHERINE DE HUECK DOHERTY

CONTRIBUTOR BIOGRAPHIES AND INDEX

The letters beside the name indicate the contributor's religious affiliation:

A   Agnostic
B   Buddhist
C   Christian
CE Celtic
H   Hindu
HU Humanist
J   Jewish
M   Muslim
NS Natural Spirituality
P   Pagan
SH Shamanic
T   Taoist
U   Unknown

J   **Aaron, Marianne Adler** (b. 1931) German-born American, she had a father who was a cantor and composer; thus religion and music have played an important role in her life. She is a freelance artist and calligrapher. *[386]*

B   **Abhirupaz Nanda** (6th century B.C.E.) Originally from the northern part of India, she was permitted by her parents to choose her husband; on the day she did, he died. This was perceived to be a sign that she was to live the life of a nun, but she resisted this, for she wanted marriage. It was the Buddha himself who helped her see the way, and she became a Buddhist nun practicing a particular meditation of bodily purification. *[211]*

M **Ajradah 'Amiyah** (12th century) Sufi mystic who spent most of her days and nights in constant prayer, fasting, and vigilance. *[68]*

C **Alacoque, St. Margaret-Mary** (1647–1690) Born in France, she was sent to school with the Poor Clares when her father died. She became a sister at the Visitation convent at Paray-le-Monial. She received many visions, the most prominent being that of Christ as the Sacred Heart. Although rebuked, she persevered in teaching devotion to the Sacred Heart of Jesus. *[129]*

U **Alcott, Louisa May** (1832–1888) American author who, after some years as a schoolteacher and a Civil War army nurse, began to support her family through magazine writing. She attained fame with her novels for children including *Little Women, Little Men,* and *Jo's Boys.* She was a staunch supporter of women's suffrage and the rights of African Americans. *[177–178]*

H **Andal** (9th century) Daughter of one of the great Indian sages in the bhakta (devotional) tradition. Her name means "she who rules." A religious poet and songwriter, she lived, according to legend, for only sixteen years. *[259]*

C **Angela of Foligno** (1248–1309) A wealthy Italian who underwent a deep spiritual conversion at the time her husband, mother, and many members of her household died. She gave away all she owned, moved to a hovel, and took up a life of penance and prayer as a Franciscan tertiary. Her holiness and her erudite writings (mostly dictated to her confessor), published as a memoir and book of spiritual instructions for her followers, gained her the title of Teacher of Theologians and placed her in the center of the classic mystical tradition. *[134, 146, 183, 237, 343–344]*

B **Aui, Sahle** (11th/12th century) A leading disciple of the great Tibetan teacher, songwriter, and poet Milarepa (1040–1123), Aui is described in Milarepa's *Hundred Thousand Songs* as pretty and sixteen years of age. She offered him gold and persuaded him to accept her as a disciple. *[189–190]*

U **Aung San Suu Kyi** (b. 1945) The daughter of Burma's hero, Aung San, she became the leader of the National League for Democracy and won election for the party. She was placed under house arrest by the military junta, and in 1991 was awarded the Nobel Peace Prize for promoting democracy in her country. She was released four years later. *[205–206]*

C **Austen, Jane** (1775–1817) English novelist who was the daughter of a clergyman. She wrote six novels, including *Pride and Prejudice*, *Sense and Sensibility*, and *Emma*, that were about the English country society of her time. A few of her prayers were discovered and published after her death. *[283–284]*

H **Bai, Sahjo** (1683–1765) An Indian disciple of Sant Charandas, Sahjo Bai described her life as one of service to her guru. In her writings, she details with pride the hard work she undertook, such as grinding grain, carrying water, and digging. Her verses are collected in the *Sahaj Prakash*, the major text of the Charandasi sect. *[361]*

U **Batchelder, Ann** (1882–1955) Early American campaigner for women's suffrage, she later became a newspaper reporter. She was the food editor of *The Ladies Home Journal*, and published a number of cookery books. *[209]*

C **Battler, Helen** (b. 1968) An English-born Canadian, she was a founding member of an Ontario repertory theater company, for which she was an actor, teacher, and stage manager. She later lived and worked in the L'Arche Daybreak community, caring for disabled adolescents. She is pursuing a degree in theology at Regis College, as well as giving spiritual direction and workshops in body prayer and creative spirituality. *[64]*

C **Beatrice of Nazareth** (c.1200–1268) Born in the Belgian Brabant, she spent most of her life in convents. She was educated by the Cistercians and became prioress of a convent founded by her father at her request. She wrote numerous works, yet only a copy of her *Seven Degrees of Love* has survived. Her prominent theme was the soul's ascent to God. *[216–217, 331, 345, 381]*

C **Bernadette, St.** (1844–1879) Born in France and christened Marie Bernarde Soubirous, she was known to her family as Bernadette. At the age of fourteen she experienced numerous visions of Mary, the mother of Jesus Christ, at a grotto near Lourdes. "The Lady" instructed her to have a chapel built to which pilgrims could come and wash in a spring that miraculously appeared at the young girl's feet. To avoid the crowds visiting the miraculous grove (where many healings of the sick still take place), Bernadette, who was sickly, moved into a convent and later became a sister of the order of Notre-Dame de Nevers. She died young and was canonized in 1933. *[137]*

C **Catherine of Genoa, St.** (1447–1510) Of Italian nobility, she showed a spiritual calling from an early age. She tried to enter an Augustinian convent at the age of thirteen but was turned away because of her youth. Marriage with a socialite husband was arranged for her at age sixteen. After he lost his fortune and she underwent a deep revelation of God's divine love, they both changed their lives to live and work among the poor and sick. Catherine established an infirmary during the plague of 1493, and her healing and ministry became well known. Although she never officially joined a religious order, she attracted many disciples and followers. Her main literary works are *Treatise on Purgatory* and *Dialogue (of the Body and Soul and God)*. She is renowned for being a constructive mystic as well as an intellectual and a practical philanthropist. [128, 210, 239–240, 331–332]

C **Catherine of Siena, St.** (1347–1380) Born in Italy, Catherine received many visions as a child. She secluded herself in her family home to pray and be in solitude, defying her family's wish for her marriage. After a few years she emerged as a leading light for peace and reform. She worked among the sick and poor, and became a Dominican tertiary. After she learned to read at seventeen and began a series of letters and teachings to her group of followers, her renown as a woman of deep spiritual wisdom spread. She was called upon to become a peace negotiator among warring states and cities. She also became an adviser to Pope Gregory XI; he was living in Avignon, France, and Catherine persuaded him to return the papacy to Rome. Her mystical abilities and ecstatic experiences are recorded in her *Dialogue*, and her prayers are considered to be works of theological genius. She is patron saint of Italy and a Doctor of the Roman Catholic Church. [51, 75, 77–78, 93–95, 134, 136–137, 152, 167–169, 177, 223–225]

C **Chantal, St. Jane Frances de** (1572–1641) A Frenchwoman who chose the religious life after overcoming a depression that resulted from her husband's death. She befriended St. Francis de Sales, who guided her spiritual growth. Together they founded the Congregation of the Visitation of Holy Mary for women who wished to live a religious life without the austerity of religious orders. She committed her life to working with the sick and the poor, and left many writings and letters. [96, 240, 304]

J **Chicago, Judy** (b. 1939) American artist, author, feminist, and educator. She has a reputation for contributing to the cause of feminism and art, founding the feminist art program in the California Institute of the Arts and the famous Womanhouse. In 1979 she created her most renowned work, *The Dinner Party Project*, which focused on women's history. *The Birth Project* (birth images in needlework), *Powerplay* (on the issues of power and powerlessness), and the *Holocaust Project: From Darkness into Light* followed. In addition to prodigious artmaking, she has written seven books, including *Through the Flower: My Struggle as a Woman Artist* and *Beyond the Flower: The Autobiography of a Feminist Artist*. [396–397]

C   **Ching, Julia** (b. 1934) Born in Shanghai, she spent many years in the Ursuline order before she left religious life to pursue her studies. She has taught in Australia, and at Columbia and Yale Universities in the United States, and is the author of many books, including one on Christianity and Buddhism with renowned theologian Hans Küng. She is currently professor of religious studies at the University of Toronto. [102]

C   **Chittister, Joan D.** (contemporary) Born in North America, she is a Roman Catholic who entered the community of the Benedictine Sisters of Erie, Pennsylvania. An international lecturer and the author of many books and articles on spirituality, monasticism, and women's issues, she is currently the executive director of Benetvision: A Resource and Research Center for Contemporary Spirituality. Her books include *Heart of Flesh: A Feminist Spirituality for Women and Men*; *Light in the Darkness*; and *The Struggle to Believe: Spirituality for the New Millennium*. [203–205]

C   **Clare of Assisi, St.** (1194–1253) The first woman Franciscan, she left her wealthy family at age eighteen and vowed to follow the life of poverty that St. Francis and his early friars had established. Within the cloister walls of San Damiano, she lived a life of exemplary purity, faith, and sacrifice. She founded the Poor Clares order, which established a tradition of cloistered life for women. After Francis died, she was one of the few early Franciscans to uphold his way of life of perfect poverty. She is believed to have saved Assisi from destruction through prayer and holding up the Eucharist in front of invaders. [119, 359]

C   **Clare, Jessie** (b. 1935) Born in England, she trained for Christian ministry in Bristol and was ordained into the ministry of the Congregational Church (now called the United Reformed Church). She currently ministers in a united Methodist/United Reformed church in North Devon. [259–261]

U   **Coleridge, Mary Elizabeth** (1861–1907) English poet and novelist whose first novel, *The Seven Sleepers of Ephesus*, won national acclaim. Her last book of poems, *Gathered Leaves*, was published posthumously. [127]

C   **Colonna, Vittoria** (1492–1547) Born into Roman nobility, she was betrothed as a child to a Neapolitan prince, whom she married in her teens. She gained renown as a writer and befriended many leading poets, churchmen, and painters of the Renaissance. Michelangelo and she were close, spiritual friends, and they exchanged many letters and poems. After her husband died in military battle, she lived the rest of her life in convents, although she never took formal vows. *[152–153, 303]*

C **Compston, Kate** (contemporary) Ordained in the United Reformed Church in England, she writes, edits, and leads retreats. She is also a psychodynamic counselor. *[151–152]*

C **Corti, Adrienne** (b. 1947) Italian-born Canadian, she is a Catholic, who is an author of catechetical resources as well as a teacher of languages and religious educator. Presently she is a spiritual guide and director at the Shepherd's Field Retreat Centre in Clarksburg, Ontario. *[100]*

U **Crawford, Pauline (Afolashade)** (b. 1957) A Jamaican teacher and actress who works with the Sistren Theatre Collective, a group of working-class women that concentrates on issues affecting women. *[271]*

T **Cui Shaoxuan** There is nothing known or written about this Immortal Sister in the Taoist tradition except that she was the youngest daughter of a government official in northern China. *[309]*

C **Day, Dorothy** (1897–1980) An American whose first experience of helping the homeless was after the tragic 1906 San Francisco earthquake. A journalist, who wrote steadily on issues of social justice, she converted to Catholicism and founded *The Catholic Worker*, a newspaper committed to covering the issues of the day, economic depression, class struggles, the nuclear threat, and the civil rights movement. She helped found the Community of Homes mostly for the urban poor. She lived with the poor, following closely the examples of Christ's life, and was jailed seven times for civil disobedience over issues of social injustice and nuclear weapons. She is arguably the most influential person in the history of American Catholicism. *[97, 154, 180, 250, 258, 268, 275]*

HU **Deming, Barbara** (1917–1984) American who was inspired after reading Gandhi to become active in civil rights and the antiwar movements during the 1960s. She published six books on the subjects of women, feminism, peace, and nonviolence. She described herself as a radical pacifist lesbian feminist. *[262]*

U **Dickinson, Emily** (1830–1886) American poet who was lively and outgoing until her mid-twenties, when she became a recluse, (some speculate that her seclusion was due to unhappiness in love). She spent the bulk of her life within the confines of her family's home and garden. She refused to embrace organized religion of any kind. Most of her approximately 1,700 poems were discovered after her death and published posthumously. She is considered the preeminent nineteenth-century American poet. *[81–82, 303, 314–315, 360]*

C **Dillard, Annie** (b. 1945) American writer, who began composing poetry in her teens. She left her fundamentalist Presbyterian Church background, becoming, after college, what she calls "spiritually promiscuous"; eventually she converted to Catholicism. After suffering pneumonia in 1971, she moved to the country to be cloistered from the world. Her writings of this time were published in the Pulitzer Prize–winning book *Pilgrim at Tinker Creek*. Author of eight other books, she is currently professor of English and writer in residence at Wesleyan University. *[72]*

C **Doherty, Catherine de Hueck** (1896–1985) Born in Russia, she fled with her husband during the Revolution in 1916. Captured by the Bolsheviks and locked in a room in Finland to starve, she vowed that if she survived she would dedicate her life to justice. Upon arriving in Canada, she founded Madonna House, a lay apostolate committed to living in poverty and serving the poor. She also founded Friendship House in Harlem, one of the first interracial apostolates in the 1930s. She viewed her vocation as being "to restore all things to Christ." She was a mystic and woman of prayer who left behind many writings. Her diaries which illustrate her longings and love of God, have recently been published. *[125, 155, 158, 160, 178, 212, 222, 228, 238, 269–270, 298, 300, 317, 373, 382, 397]*

U **Doolittle, Antoinette** (approx. 19th century) No biographical information found. *[368]*

C **Eaton, Susan L.** (b. 1952) Born in Canada, she is a professional adult educator and freelance writer. She worked for the Canadian Catholic Organization for Development and Peace, and is the principal author of an adult religious education course at St. Francis Xavier University. *[386]*

C **Ebert, Mary Ann** (b. 1938) Born in England, she became a Christian in her teens through the influence of her Methodist aunt. She is now a lay preacher in a London multiracial, multifaith community. She is also active in the Christian peace movement, and has traveled widely to promote pacifism. *[45]*

C **Elaw, Zilpha** (1790–?) An African-American born into a free family, she embraced Methodism in her teens, when she began to have religious visions. It was during her attendance at a Presbyterian camp meeting that she was "divinely commissioned" to preach. She published *Memoirs*, which detail these rural camp meetings. After her husband's death she opened a school for black children. She attained considerable success as an evangelist, and preached not only in free but in slaveholding states. *[87, 269]*

C **Élisabeth de France** (1764–1794) Sister of the ill-fated Louis XVI, she was, during her short life, praised for her charity work. During the French Revolution, she tried to escape but was caught and imprisoned in Paris, and finally was guillotined. *[309]*

C **Elizabeth of the Trinity** (1880–1906) Born in France as Elizabeth Catez, she lost her father when still a child. Her mother was devoted to the Carmelite saint Teresa of Ávila, but resisted the Carmelite vocation emerging her daughter. In her early twenties Elizabeth entered the Carmelite convent at Dijon. Her devotional life, recorded in many of her writings, was mystical and dedicated to the Trinity. She contributed greatly to the understanding of the Trinity—Father, Son, and Holy Spirit. *[213, 222–223]*

C **Elizabeth I, Queen of England and Ireland** (1533–1603) The only child of Henry VIII and Anne Boleyn, she succeeded her half-sister Mary Tudor to the throne in 1558 and reigned for forty-five years. She had a remarkable grasp of languages and classical scholarship, and studied theology in the Erasmian tradition. She tried to find a middle way to establish a broadly based church to satisfy all her subjects, both Catholic and Protestant. She was accused of disloyalty by Rome, and the Pope issued a bull that absolved her subjects of allegiance to her and thus turned all practicing Catholics into potential traitors. This caused a rebellion in the north, where her Catholic cousin, Mary, Queen of Scots, attempted to secure the throne. Despite all this, Elizabeth showed great fortitude and attempted to rule with fairness. Her long reign finally strengthened Protestantism not only at home but abroad, where it was seen as synonymous with patriotism. *[132–133]*

C **Elizabeth, Countess of Craven** (1750–1828) All that is known of her is that she was a writer and dramatist. *[310]*

C **Elliot, Elisabeth** (contemporary) Born of missionary parents in Belgium, she grew up in America, then in 1952 moved to Ecuador, where she met and married her first husband, a missionary who was killed by Auca Indians four years later. Since her return to the United States in 1963, she has been writing and speaking. Her daily broadcast, "Gateway to Joy," is heard on more than 250 radio stations, and her books include *Passion and Purity; A Path Through Suffering; Keep a Quiet Heart;* and *Quest for Love.* [95–96]

HU   **Esler, Riane** (contemporary) An internationally known American scholar, futurist, and activist. She is the author of many articles and books, including the bestseller *The Chalice and the Blade.* She is presently codirector of the Center of Partnership Studies in Pacific Grove, California. [368, 386]

J   **Esther, Queen** (Hebrew Bible source) Esther, a Hebrew orphan, was chosen by King Ahasuerus of Persia to replace Queen Vashti, whose disobedience cost her the crown. As queen, Esther was instrumental in saving the Jewish nation from its enemies by persuading the king to proclaim publicly and in writing that the Jewish people could openly observe their customs without fear and should be protected by all the people. The Jews' deliverance is commemorated in Purim, a holiday and feast that is still celebrated. [207]

A   **Evans, Marian** (1819–1880) A leading British novelist who wrote under the pen name of George Eliot. She renounced the narrow religious views with which she had been brought up, after making the acquaintance of freethinker Charles Bray and his brother-in-law Charles Hennell, author of a rationalistic study of Christianity. She began translating Christian writings, but it wasn't until she was forty that her true literary genius was established. Her novels include *Adam Bede, The Mill on the Floss, Silas Marner,* and *Middlemarch.* [370]

C   **Fairlie, Paula** (b. 1940) A German by birth, she studied in London and later in Florence, specializing in the Renaissance. She converted to Catholicism in 1965 and lived in Italy as a nun. She currently lives in England. [62–63]

J   **Falk, Marcia** (contemporary) An American poet and translator whose many books include *The Book of Blessings: New Jewish Prayers for Daily Life, the Sabbath, and the New Moon Festival* and *The Song of Songs: A New Translation and Interpretation.* [116, 214]

T   **Fan Yunqiao** (3rd century) Married to a Taoist adept who was also a wise governor, she studied Taoism with her husband and was reported to have had great magical powers beyond his. It was said that they left the world together at the same time and ascended to heaven. [356, 361]

U   **Farjeon, Eleanor** (1881–1965) English children's writer. Although she received no formal education, she was always encouraged to write stories and poems. Her first publication—*Nursery Rhymes of London*

Town—was in 1916, and in all she wrote thirty books of children's verse, many of them linked poems. Her other writings included plays for children and twelve adult novels. She was awarded the Carnegie Medal and the Hans Christian Andersen International Medal for *The Little Bookroom*, a collection of stories. *[103]*

M **Farrukhzad, Furugh** (1935–1967) Born in Tehran, she gained a reputation in Iran for establishing a feminine voice in Persian poetry. *[225–227]*

J **Feingold, Dena A.** (b. 1955) American rabbi who was ordained in 1982 at the Hebrew Union College Jewish Institute of Religion after receiving her master of arts in Hebrew letters. She has served as the rabbi of Beth Hillel Temple in Kenosha, Wisconsin. *[87]*

J **Feld, Merle** (b. 1947) Raised in a nonreligious Jewish American family, she began traditional Jewish observances after college. She married a rabbi and helped found Havurat Shalom, a group of Jews who meet regularly for worship and study together, in Boston. She has contributed to the growth of *havurot* throughout the United States and has served on the board of directors of the National Havurah Committee. She describes her poetry as a process of inner prayer. *[242]*

C **Foote, Julia A. J.** (1823–1900) American-born daughter of former slaves who purchased their freedom and were strong Christian believers. She began studying the Bible at a young age, and underwent a conversion at fifteen, when she experienced what she called "the sweet peace" of sanctification. At eighteen she began to proclaim within the African Methodist Episcopal Zion Church about sanctification through household ministry. She encountered resistance to her preaching from the men around her, including her husband. After moving to Philadelphia she hired halls to hold religious meetings, and began traveling around the Eastern states to preach. She became the first woman ordained deacon in the A.M.E. Zion church, and before her death was ordained an elder in the church—the second woman to hold such an office. *[85, 275]*

J **Friedman, Randee Rosenberg** (b. 1951) She is president of Sounds Write Productions, a California-based Jewish music production, publishing, and distribution company. As a writer, she has published contemporary midrashim, an ethical will, and numerous poems reflecting her spiritual journey. *[55–56]*

C **Fry, Elizabeth** (1780–1845) English Quaker who became an influential minister of her faith, an educator, and a reformer of prisons while raising her eleven children. She became an adviser to many European rulers, especially about the conditions of imprisoned women and the dreadful conditions of prison life. *[86–87, 151, 155, 199, 252, 268, 270, 299, 319, 388, 395]*

c **Furlong, Monica** (b. 1930) An English convert to Christianity and a former journalist, she is now an established poet, novelist, and spiritual writer. *[131]*

c **Galloway, Kathy** (contemporary) Born in Scotland, she trained in divinity and pastoral studies and was ordained a minister of the Church of Scotland in 1977. As a theologian and writer (she has written twelve books of poems, prayers, reflections, and liturgical commentary), she is a member of the Iona Community and editor of its magazine, *Coracle*. Her interests are ecumenical and focus on the spirituality of people who are marginalized or excluded. *[52–53, 120–121, 231–232]*

u **Gellie, Christine** (contemporary, French) No biographical information found. *[277]*

b **Genso, Ryōnen** (1646–1711) A Japanese Zen nun, she began her life serving in the Japanese court. She then married and had many children, and was recognized for her high education and her creativity. Her poems, paintings, and calligraphy were widely admired. After ten years of marriage she became a nun and followed her Zen master. In her later years, she became abbot of her own monastery and gained renown for her good deeds and for her care of the community and children. *[309]*

c **Gertrude the Great, St.** (1256–1302) Born in Saxony, she was placed in the care of nuns at Helfta, and became a nun herself. She lived at the Cistercian convent, which was a center of mystical activity. At the age of twenty-four Gertrude received many visions; these and her spiritual directions and instructions are described in five books. St. Gertrude is recognized as possessing a poetic command of the language of mysticism. *[90–91, 224]*

u **Giles, Mary E.** (contemporary) Professor of humanities and religious studies at California State University, she is the founding editor of *Studia Mystica*, a quarterly journal of mysticism and the arts. She has translated Spanish spiritual classics, and teaches seminars and gives retreats on prayer and spirituality. *[348, 358]*

j **Gilmore, Linda** (contemporary) An American Reform Jew, she has a masters degree in elementary education and teaches elementary school. *[102]*

B **Gotami, Mahapajapati.** (6th century B.C.E.) Recognized as the Mother of Buddhism, as she founded the first order of Buddhist nuns. Born in India, she adopted her nephew, the Buddha, as her own son when his mother Maya died shortly after giving birth. She also converted to his teachings and had hundreds of followers, and at the end of her life—at the age of 120—she embraced her own realized spiritual perfection. *[84]*

HU **Grahn, Judy** (b. 1940). American who follows a panhuman spirituality based in (inherited) spirits, and her own metaformic theory that consciousness derives from worldwide menstrual ritual. Her writings and her theories are internationally known and widely used. An originator of lesbian-feminism, she teaches in the women's spirituality program at New College of California, in San Francisco. *[321–323]*

C **Greiffenberg, Catharina Regina von** (1633–1694) Born into Austrian Protestant nobility, she wrote many letters about the struggle between Protestant and Catholic beliefs. Her spiritual sonnets are considered to be the greatest work by a woman writer of the German High Baroque. *[130]*

C **Grey, Lady Jane** (1537–1554) Born in England into a royal family—her mother was the daughter of Princess Mary of England—she became manipulated by the politics of the time and was made Queen of England after the death of Edward VI. She reluctantly took the throne for only nine days and was subsequently imprisoned for high treason and then beheaded. *[206]*

C **Griffiths, Ann** (1776–1805) The eldest daughter of a Welsh farmer, she transformed her life after hearing a sermon and joined the Methodist Church at the age of 21. She married and died during childbirth. Her hymns were numerous and published posthumously. *[362]*

C **Guérin, Eugénie de** (1805–1848) A French diarist who helped her brother, the poet Maurice de Guérin, return to the Christian church through ceaseless prayer. Her *Journal* was published posthumously and became a literary success. *[211–212]*

C **Gullick, Etta** (1922–1986) English lecturer in spirituality at St. Stephen's College, Oxford. An Anglican, she cowrote many books with Michael Hollings about prayer, as well as producing several collections of prayers. *[255]*

C **Guyon du Chesnoy, Mme.** (1648–1717) Born in France, she had mystical tendencies as a girl and longed to join a cloistered community, but was rejected. She went into French society and later married—which, she said, put an end to her gaiety. In her suffering she moved inward and became a student of mysticism and of the inner life. Her devotional writings reflect the common interest of the time in contemplative prayer, the prayer of Quiet. *[334]*

M **Habiba 'Adawiyah** (11th/12th century) A member of one of the clans of the great Sufi tradition. The only thing known of her is that she would often ascend to her rooftop clothed in her chador to pray and sing all night. *[74]*

C **Hackett, Jean** (b. 1948) Born in England, she studied theology and is married to an Anglican clergyman. She is an organist and teaches music part-time. She is on the British Committee of the Women's World Day of Prayer. *[171–172]*

C **Hadewijch of Brabant** (1210–c.1290) She came from an area around Brussels, and she introduced her noble background and experience of courtly love into her spiritual writings. She was scholarly, and knew French and Latin. She is thought to have run a community of Beguines (laywomen who lived a communal religious life), which she was forced to leave because of her metaphysical writings about love. She wrote letters, spiritual direction, and poetry. *[216, 380]*

B and SH **Halifax, Joan** (b. 1944) A Buddhist teacher, shaman, lecturer, editor, and ecologist, she has been in the forefront of contemporary spiritual exploration. A trained medical anthropologist, she specializes in psychiatry and religion, and worked for Joseph Campbell in studying world mythology. She has done fieldwork around the world, and is the author of many scholarly articles and coauthor, with Stanislav Grof, of *The Human Encounter with Death*. *[228]*

C **Hare, Maria** (1807–1870) An Englishwoman who was married to an Anglican clergyman, she was renowned for her written prayers, which gained wide acceptance throughout England. *[125]*

C **Havergal, Frances Ridley** (1836–1879) Born in England to an Episcopal clergyman who was a composer of music and hymns, she was a talented singer and pianist. She sang only sacred music, with the intent of winning souls for God. She taught at Sunday school, and wrote letters, devotional poetry and prose, and many hymns. *[86, 125–126, 299, 362]*

M **Ḥayāti, Bibi** (d. 1853) She was born in the Kerman province of Persia (now Iraq) to a devout Sufi family. She was taught by her brother and through his wisdom was led to her Sufi master, Nur' Ali Shah. She became not only his disciple but his wife. She is known for her *Divan* of devotional poems and for her mystical love for the divine. *[220–221, 331–334]*

M **Ḥayyuna** (8th/9th century) A Sufi who was a contemporary and friend of Rābe'ah of Syria. Her words and wisdom were renowned. *[69, 211, 345]*

C **Herbert, Mary, Countess of Pembroke** (1561–1621) English patroness of a number of poets of the time, including Ben Jonson. She wrote her own poems and collaborated with her brother, Sir Philip Sidney, in translating the Psalms into an English metrical version. *[169]*

J **Hertz, Judith M.** (b. 1935) An American, she is past president of the Women of Reform Judaism, a cochair on the Commission on Interreligious Affairs, the chairperson for the Interreligous Advisory Committee at Auburn Seminary, and vice president of the World Conference on Religion and Peace. *[388–389]*

U **Higginson, Ella** (1860–1941) Popular American lyricist. Many composers set her words to music, and many singers of the twentieth century, including Caruso, performed them. *[109]*

C **Hildegard of Bingen** (1098–1179) One of the most prominent Western women mystics, she became a Benedictine novice at the age of seven, a nun at fourteen, and an abbess at thirty-eight. She later founded a convent at Rupertsberg. She was a healer, a teacher, and an adviser to the clergy, the Pope, and the nobility. During her life she wrote extensively on a wide range of subjects, including natural science, medicine, ethics, cosmology, and mathematics, as well as books and treatises on the divine life. Her special emphasis was on relation with the divine light, and she wrote and illustrated her visions. Her most famous work is *Scivias*, which means "Know the Ways of the Lord." She contributed to—and perhaps established—the first feminine imagery of the Divine by using such descriptions as "cosmic egg." Her lyrics and sacred music have gained wide recognition in recent years. *[88–89, 92–93, 101, 147, 167, 187, 194–197, 246, 248, 330, 349, 379–380]*

J **Hillesum, Etty** (1914–1943) Born into a privileged family of Dutch Jews, she lived in Amsterdam, and during the years of Nazi occupation there kept journals, which are referred to as the mature versions of Anne Frank's diary. The tone of the journals changed over the course of her short life as her own path changed, shifting from accounts of her life and loves to a voice of despair, compassion, and deep faith as the reality of the Holocaust set in. She died at Auschwitz. *[74–75, 135]*

J **Hollander, Vicki** (b. 1952) American rabbi who serves as spiritual leader to Eitz Or, a Jewish renewal group in Seattle. A trained marriage and family therapist, she also specializes in spiritual renewal and ritual, and writes poetic liturgical works. *[87]*

U **Holtby, Winifred** (1898–1935) Englishwoman who was a member of the Women's Auxiliary Army Corps during World War I. She became a novelist and traveled throughout Europe, lecturing for the League of Nations Union. She died after completing her eighth book, *South Riding.* [269]

C **Houselander, Caryll** (1901–1954) Born in England, she was baptized a Catholic after her mother's conversion. After the separation of her parents, she abandoned her faith and attended art school, exploring different religions. She made a career of writing and illustrating for lesser-known religious magazines, but after World War II found her real voice: she spoke directly to those scarred by the ravages of war in her book *The War Is the Passion,* and taught that personal suffering can be transformed and united in the ongoing work of Redemption. She wrote many other books, becoming one of the most widely read contemporary Catholic writers of her time. [129, 139–140, 153–154, 179–180, 184–185, 230–231, 257–258, 320]

C **Hovnanian, Louise Wheatley Cook** (contemporary) A Christian Science teacher, she is the author of a novel and a regular contributor to both prose and poetry in Christian Science publications. [284–285]

HU **Hubbard, Barbara Marx** (contemporary) A noted American author, futurist, social architect, and public speaker, she is dedicated to communicating humanity's potential for a positive future. In 1984 her name was placed in nomination for the vice presidency of the United States at the Democratic National Convention. She developed Evolutionary Circles, a group process for inner work and spiritual growth focusing on basic ideas of conscious evolution and cocreation. She is a founding member of the World Future Society, and cofounder of the Foundation of Conscious Evolution. [392]

C **Isaacs-Mascoll, June** (b. 1938) Born in St. Vincent and the Grenadines, she was a committed Anglican when she emigrated to Canada. She returned to live in Barbados, her husband's native country, and wrote unpublished poetry for years. Only at the birth of her twin granddaughters did she publish her first book, *Prayers for Little People.* She has since written other books of prayers, poetry, and song lyrics. [279]

C **Jackson, Rebecca Cox** (1795–1891) American founder of the first black Shaker community in Philadelphia, she was one of the evangelical preachers who roused African American women to a self-empowering religious faith and a sense of universal justice. A gifted visionary and eldress in the Shaker tradition, she recorded much of her visions and teachings in her diaries. [63–64]

B **Jenti** (6th century B.C.E.) Born in India, she was a member of the Licchavis tribe. As a Buddhist nun, she was known to attain the seven qualities of enlightenment. *[214]*

U **Jewsbury, Maria Jane** (1800–1833) English poet and essayist. Of her many books, one of the better known was *Letters to the Young*, a compilation of religious meditations. *[70–71]*

NS **Joudry, Patricia** (b. 1921) Canadian writer of many novels and plays and an autobiography, and coauthor, with Dr. Maurie Pressman, of *Twin Souls*. Her plays include *The Song of Louise in the Morning* and *Teach Me How to Cry*. Her spiritual orientation is toward Universal Truth, and her guide and mentor is Srí Aurobindo. *[73–74]*

J **Judith** (Hebrew Bible source) Her name means "the Jewess," and she was referred to as "the glory of Jerusalem" and "the great pride of Israel," having saved the nation from invasion and destruction by the Assyrians. She had been widowed and living a solitary life in sackcloth when she dressed in finery and approached Holofernes, the Assyrian king's military general. As he lay drunk in his tent at the foot of the mountains of Bethulia, she beheaded him, and thereby saved her nation from imminent ruin. *[82–83]*

C **Julian of Norwich** (c.1342–c.1416) Born in England, she received many visions from meditating upon the Passion of Christ; she recorded these in her book, *The Revelations of Divine Love*, or *Showings*. She later lived as a solitary Benedictine nun and recluse in a cell attached to the Church of St. Julian in Norwich. She was the first female English mystical writer to refer to God and Christ as Mother, and to promote feminine language and imagery in describing the Divine. *[62, 149, 157, 159, 160, 166, 219, 237, 293]*

C **Juliana of Nicodemia** (approx. 2nd century) Born and raised in the capital of Rome's Eastern Empire, she was denounced by her pagan parents for her Christian beliefs. Inprisoned for her beliefs when she was only twenty, she found support in prayer. She died in prison, five years later. *[318]*

J **Kaplan, Reine** (contemporary) An American who spent her early years in a traditional Orthodox Jewish family. She became a Reform Jew in her adult life, and has since written installation services and convention and pulpit presentations. She is working on an art book for children. *[97]*

J **Katz, Goldie J.** (b. 1946) Born in the United States, she was a president of Rodef Shalom Congregation Sisterhood. Currently she is a language, art, and French teacher, and a volunteer for Jewish and community organizations. *[203]*

C **Kaye-Smith, Sheila** (1887–1956) English novelist who became a literary hit of the 1920s with a series of works that included *The End of the House of Alard*. She married an Anglican priest who, with her, later converted to Roman Catholicism. She presented her religious beliefs as well as the essence of rural life in her novels. She was buried in a chapel dedicated to St. Thérèse of Lisieux, which she had built beside her house. *[247–248, 272–273]*

C **Keevil, E. Gwendoline** (b. 1911) A resident of England, she has written over 260 hymns. She is a great-granddaughter of the Methodist Manse, and has been a speaker, singer, and writer all her life, in what she describes as "a quiet way." *[261–262]*

U **Kersten, Maria** (contemporary) No biographical information found. *[118]*

U **Khouri, Hanna.** No biographical information found. *[98]*

B **Kisagotami** (6th century B.C.E.) She came from a poor family, and her uncle was the father of the Buddha. She lost her mind when her son died, and she roamed the countryside seeking someone to heal her "sick" child. It was the Buddha who helped her see the truth, and she buried her child and became a Buddhist nun of great austerity. *[244–245]*

U **Kitson, Margaret.** No biographical information found. *[73, 91]*

J **Korn, Rachel** (1898–1982) A native of Poland, she began writing poems and stories in Polish. After World War II she fled to Russia, then emigrated to Canada. From 1919 on she wrote all her work in Yiddish, and many selections and translations of her work have appeared in anthologies. She received many prestigious literary awards, including the Award for Yiddish Poetry from the Jewish Book Council in the United States. *[138–139]*

B **Lapdron, Machig** (11th century) A Tibetan Buddhist, she is recognized primarily as the creator of the Cöd ritual, a tantric practice in which the celebrant, under the guidance of a guru, mentally cuts up his or her own body and offers it to the deities. This practice, which helps eradicate the ego, continues today among high adepts. *[83]*

U **Larcom, Lucy** (1824–1893) An American educator, she gained fame as a poet and anthologizer. *[285]*

J **Leah, Sarah Rebecca Rachel** (19th century) She was the wife of the luminary rabbi Shabbetai, who was the head of the rabbinical court of Krasny in Russia, and daughter of the famous rabbi Yokel Segal Horowitz. *[116, 167]*

U **Levertov, Denise** (b. 1923) An English-born American, she is a leading poet of our time, particularly on issues involving political activism and social conscience. Her writing also reflects her sense of the mystical and the oneness of all creation. *[43–44]*

J **Levitt, Norma U.** (contemporary) She is a prominent leader of Jewish, ecumenical, and international organizations, including the Synagogue Council of America, the Jewish Braille Institute and the Jewish Congress, the Women of Reform Judaism, the Federation of Temple Sisterhoods. Apart from her dynamic and significant role in international interreligious dialogue, she is a distinguished poet and author. *[382]*

U **Lewin, Ann** (contemporary) No biographical information found. *[336]*

C **Lewis, K. C.** (contemporary) All that could be learned of her is that she is a native of Barbados. *[323]*

U **Lindbergh, Anne Morrow** (b. 1906) American writer famous for her marriage to aviator Charles Lindbergh and the tragic death of her first child. Her 1955 classic, *Gift from the Sea*, spoke to women about simplifying their busy lives and spending more time in inner quiet. *[177, 276, 359]*

U **Lyon, Mary.** No biographical information found. *[267]*

C **MacConmidhe, Giollabhrighde** (late 13th century) No biographical information found except that she was childless. *[271–272]*

C **Macdonald, Ann** (19th century) Born in Scotland, she was a daughter of a crofter. *[208, 371–372]*

C **Madeleva, Sister Mary** (1887–1964) Born Mary Evaline Wolff in America, she was still a student when the magazine *Atlantic Monthly* published her first poem. She went on to write two books of poetry, three books of essays, speeches, and an autobiography. In 1908 she entered the Sisters of the Holy Cross order and took the name Madeleva. As president of her alma mater, Saint Mary's College, in Notre Dame, Indiana, she established a School of Sacred Theology, which was especially designed for laypeople who wanted to study theology. *[247]*

H **Mahādēviyakka** (12th century) Born in Northern India, she became a devotee of Lord Shiva as her supreme god, whom she called "lord white as jasmine" in her writings. In the true mystic style he became her husband, although she was forced to marry a local king. She left the king due to his lack of faith, and joined a movement called Virashaivism, which recognised the dignity of women and their human equality. Her poetry and devotion reflect the physical sensuousness of her relationship with the Divine. *[43, 52, 68, 221, 341, 375]*

M   **Manqusa** (11th/12th century?) Little is known of her except that she was a Sufi and daughter of Zayd Ebn Abol-Fawares, and that her son died. *[320–21]*

U   **Mansfield, Katherine** (1888–1923) Born Kathleen Mansfield Beauchamp in New Zealand, she studied to be a musician. She settled in England, where she began writing short stories. She had little publishing success until she met and married her second husband, critic and essayist John Middleton Murry, who edited literary magazines. After writing about her childhood in New Zealand (*The Aloe*), she received acclaim as the most remarkable short story writer of her generation in England. She died at thirty-four of consumption, but left more than one hundred short stories, her most famous collection being *The Garden Party, and Other Stories*. *[189]*

C   **Margherita, Teresa** (1747–1790) Little is known of her except that she was an Italian Carmelite nun whose exemplary life caused her to be known as "the flower of the Carmel with the purity of a lily." *[130–131]*

C   **Marie of the Incarnation, Blessed** (1599–1672) The first missionary woman sent to the New World, as well as the founder of the Catholic school system in French Canada. Born Marie Guyart in France, she was married and then widowed three years later with a small son. She felt called to the religious life and, leaving her son in the care of her sister, joined the Ursulines. In 1639 she sailed with two other Ursuline sisters to Canada; they settled in Quebec, then called New France, and opened a school for the native people there. They suffered much sickness and poverty. She wrote full accounts of her spiritual life, was known as a great mystic, and composed catechisms in Huron and Algonquin and a French-Algonquin dictionary. Her writings were preserved and collected by her son, who became a Benedictine monk. *[336]*

C   **Martin, Lyn** (1897–?) A native of Barbados, she began writing religious poetry at the age of ten, and would spend hours contemplating flowers in her garden. *[118, 297–298]*

H   **Mata Amritanandamayi** (contemporary) Recognized as one of India's greatest living saints, she is a yogini from southwest India who espouses devotion to the Holy Motherhood of God. While a child she spent much time in devotional singing, dancing, and praying. At the World Parliament of Religions in 1993 she was named one of the three presidents of the Hindu tradition. Under her guidance her followers have initiated training programs for the poor, shelters for battered women, and free hospitals, hospices, and orphanages. Many are healed just by sitting in her divine presence. *[135]*

C **McDonald, Connie Nungulla** (b. 1933) Born in Australia of Aboriginal descent, she was brought up by Anglican missionaries. After working as a teaching assistant she moved to Sydney, where she trained as an Anglican Church Army sister. She traveled and worked all over Australia. Now retired, she volunteers her time with Aboriginal people and speaks to school and church groups. Her book with Jill Finnane, *When You Grow Up,* was published to wide acclaim. *[99]*

C **Mechthild of Magdeburg** (1212–1297) Born into a wealthy German family, she had her first mystical experience at the age of twelve, when she saw "all things in God, and God in all things." In her early twenties she joined the Beguines (laywomen leading a communal spiritual life of poverty and service), and became quite ill for a while. Little is known of her time as a Beguine, and after forty years she entered the Cistercian convent at Helfta, already in her senior years, where she was a contemporary of St. Gertrude the Great. She is recognized as a leading mystic, especially for her major work, *The Flowing Light of the Godhead. [44–45, 67, 76, 217–218, 224, 251–252, 310–311, 337–339, 341, 342, 344–348, 370, 373]*

SH **Medicine Eagle, Brooke (contemporary)** The great-great-grandniece of a holy man, she was raised on the Crow Reservation in Montana. In her twenties, she undertook ritual training with a Northern Cheyenne medicine woman called The Woman Who Knows Everything. She is a poet and chanter of sacred songs, a dancer of traditional forms, and a healer. *[389]*

H **Meera** or **Meerabai** (1498–1565) Considered to be one of the greatest *bhakta* poets in Hindi. Her passion and devotion to Lord Krishna was expressed in devotional songs of mysticism. She was reputedly a Rajput princess from Rajasthan, who married royalty but was mistreated by her in-laws after the death of her husband. She became a wandering devotee to Krishna, whom she always perceived to be her true husband. *[59–60, 69–70, 127, 189, 218, 307, 342]*

H **Meera, Mother** (b. 1960) Born in southern India, she showed herself spiritually advanced by the age of three, as she was in a constant state of samadhi (enlightenment). She lived for a while at Sri Aurobindo's ashram at Pondicherry, where her exceptional presence gained her much attention. She now lives in Germany, and thousands of devotees from around the world visit her for her blessings and teachings. She is considered one of the incarnations of the Divine Mother. *[65, 124, 131, 188, 370]*

U **Millay, Edna St. Vincent** (1892–1950) Born in Maine, she was a student when her first poem was published in 1912. She later was awarded the Pulitzer Prize for *The Harp Weaver and Other Poems*. She published plays and other collections of poems, and in her forties was considered to be the most popular American woman poet of her day. *[103]*

B **Mitta** (6th century B.C.E.) A Sakyan woman from what is now northern India, she was first a Buddhist laywoman and then a nun, a vocation in which she found the peace she had sought all her life. *[362–363]*

M **Mohammad, Omm** (13th century) A devout Sufi, she was the aunt of the well-known Sufi master Muhyi'd-Din 'Abdo'l Qadire Gilani. She was implored to intercede when there had been a year's drought in the land and no other prayers had been answered. No sooner had she prayed then it rained. *[175]*

J **Molodowsky, Kadya** (1894–1975) Born in Lithuania, she began publishing poetry in her twenties. With her husband, she moved to Warsaw, where she taught in Yiddish schools and practiced journalism. She later published many books of poems and prose prayers in Yiddish instead of the more traditional Hebrew. These prose poems were about the sacredness of everyday life, and many of her supplicatory prayers addressed the biblical mothers of Israel. *[157–158, 190–191]*

C **Morley, Janet** (b. 1951) A member of the Church of England, she works for an ecumenically based overseas development charity called Christian Aid. She has published two books, *All Desires Known* and *Bread of Tomorrow*. *[114, 160–163, 237–238, 250–251]*

M **Mota'abedah, Lobabah** (12th/14th century) A resident of Jerusalem, she was a Sufi woman renowned for declaring that she was ashamed that God saw her engaged in aught besides God. *[68]*

H **The Mother** (1878–1973) Born in France as Mira Richard, she was educated privately and was a talented pianist. She received many spiritual experiences in her young adulthood and studied occultism. At thirty-six she visited Sri Aurobindo in India and recognized him as her spiritual teacher. After she joined his community, it grew rapidly, and Aurobindo entrusted her as the spiritual head of the ashram. Under her fifty-year guidance, it became one of the leading ashrams in the world. She also established an international center for education at the ashram, and for the last ten years of her life lived in confinement in her room, from whence she continued to teach and guide. The Mother is considered to have been one of the leading spiritual teachers of the yogic way to the Divine. *[43, 48, 94, 149, 157, 166, 177, 187, 195, 199, 205, 211, 219, 224, 237, 266, 292, 300, 361, 362, 370, 371, 373, 380, 386, 390]*

SH **Mountain Dreamer, Oriah** (b. 1954) A Canadian, she is a writer and teacher who has studied with Native elders who gave her her medicine name. Author of *Confessions of a Spiritual Thrillseeker* and *Dreams of Desire*, she has most recently written *The Invitation*. She is currently studying philosophy and leading retreats. *[58–59]*

J **Naomi** (Hebrew Bible source) Naomi's story is told in the Book of Ruth. She was a woman who moved to the plains of Moab to escape famine, and losing her husband and two sons to death, returned to Judah with one daughter-in-law, Ruth, who refused to leave her. Ruth later remarried and Naomi cared for her son. *[299]*

C **Neu, Diann L.** (b. 1948) Born in Indiana, she is cofounder and codirector of WATER, the Women's Alliance for Theology, Ethics, and Ritual in Silver Spring, Maryland. A Catholic feminist theologian, she practices as a psychotherapist who specializes in creating women-church liturgies. *[113, 116–117, 119, 214]*

J **Neuda, Fanny** (mid 19th century) Born in Germany, she was the author of *Hours of Devotion*, a collection of more than fifty prayers and private meditations for Jewish women, for use at home or in public services. Her work was very popular among German Jewish women of the time and up to World War II. *[97–98, 273–274]*

C **Nightingale, Florence** (1820–1910) An Englishwoman, she alarmed her family when she announced that God had called her to God's service and she began her life of devotion in caring for the sick and nursing members of the infantry. Her bravery during the Crimean War is legendary, and her influence, especially for women, is still exemplary. *[253]*

B **Obum, Nangsa** (11th century) Born in Tibet, and a devotee of Buddhist meditation and dharma practice, she married a prince and had a son, who was taken from her at birth and given to a wet-nurse. She died of a broken heart. She came back to life as a *delog* (a person who returns to life after death), and returned to be with her parents, but soon disappeared into the mountains, leaving her thigh print and footprints in the rocks. *[241]*

J **Pappenheim, Bertha** (late 19th/early 20th century) Born in Germany, she gained prominence as a social worker and founder of Care for Women, a Jewish women's aid society that attempted to help women who sought refuge in Germany from Eastern Europe. She was also cofounder and leader of Germany's Jewish feminist movement, established in 1904 to gain economic, political, and social rights for German Jewish women. As a writer and translator, she championed the fight against white slavery—where women and girls were sold for prostitution—and she became a promoter of women's right to vote. *[261, 267]*

B **Patacara, Pancasata** (6th century B.C.E.) Sometimes confused with the great Buddhist teacher Patacara, she would have been a follower of Patacara, and, like her, a woman who had lost her children. *[243–245]*

C **Pickard, Jan Sutch** (contemporary) Born in England, she spent some time teaching in Nigeria and working for the Christian Council of Nigeria. Now she lives near Manchester, and works as an editor for the Methodist Church Overseas Division and the magazine *Connect*. A member of the Iona Community, she has written many poems and prayers; her most recent book is on Biblical meditations. *[390–391]*

NS **Piercy, Marge** (b. 1936) An American poet and novelist, she is the author of twelve volumes of poetry and twelve novels. She is a feminist writer who confesses a faith in ecology. All her poetry reflect the themes of women's spirituality. Her works include *The Moon Is Always Female*, *Circles on the Water*, and *City of Darkness, City of Light*. *[105–108]*

U **Pigott, Jean Sophia** No biographical information found. *[219–220]*

U **Pitter, Ruth** (1897–1992) Born in England, she began writing poetry at an early age and found most of her inspiration in the beauty of nature. She published at least eleven collections of poetry, and won the Hawthornden Prize in 1936 for *A Trophy of Arms*. She was awarded the Queen's Gold Medal for Poetry in 1955, and the C.B.E. in 1979. *[54]*

C **Porete, Marguerite** (d. 1310) A Beguine from Hainaut in Belgium. In her book *The Mirror of Simple Souls*, she explained that the voice of Love within each of us is wiser than the voice of Reason. Because of her free spirit and understanding of the soul's mystical journey through a growing personal relationship with the Divine, she was condemned for heresy by the Inquisition. She spent eighteen months in prison refusing to answer her inquisitor's questions, and was burned at the stake in Paris in 1310. *[163–164, 224, 227–228, 294–295, 299–300]*

C **Powers, Jessica** (1905–1988) An American poet who was a member of the Catholic Poetry Society of America in New York. In 1939 she published her first book of poetry, *The Lantern Burns*. Entering the Carmelite convent in Wisconsin, she was elected prioress in 1955, and helped build a new convent in a more pastoral setting. She published many books while prioress, and by the end of her life, had written more than four hundred poems. *[49, 61, 76, 81, 88, 90, 101, 124, 183, 207–208, 250, 254–255, 323–324, 342–343, 387]*

C **Procter, Adelaide Ann** (1825–1864) English poet who converted to Roman Catholicism and took much interest in social questions affecting women. She wrote the well-known song *The Lost Chord*, as well as many hymns. *[212–213]*

SH **Proudfoot-Edgar, Carol** (b. 1945) A Californian of Native American and Irish descent, she is both a student and a teacher of the shamanic path. Formerly a counseling psychologist, she now devotes herself full time—through ceremony and retreats—to recovering our souls, both for the health of all living beings and for future generations. *[108, 392–393]*

M **Rābe'ah Al-'adawiya (of Basra)** (716–801) Born to a poor family in Basra, Persia, which is now in Iraq. When her parents died in a famine, she and her sisters took to the streets; Rābe'ah was captured and sold as a slave. She began praying and fasting, and after her master saw a light that lit the whole house over her as she prayed, he freed her. She chose the life of a celibate ascetic, and established a retreat house on the outskirts of Basra. Many came to her for guidance, and wrote accounts of her life as well as of her poems and prayers. She is recognized as one of the highest Sufi saints and mystics, unparalleled among all the masters. *[68–69, 81, 157, 308, 331, 349, 372–373]*

M **Rābe'ah (of Syria)** (d. c.850) Often confused with Rābe'ah of Basra, she was a saintly woman who was given in marriage to an important Sufi master who was referred to as "The Fortunate"; he took three other wives after her. She was pious, devout, and very charitable. Her grave is located on the Mount of Olives in Jerusalem. *[349–350]*

HU **Reilly, Patricia Lynn** (b. 1951) An American who is a master of divinity, and is the founder of Open Window Creations. She conducts women's spirituality and creativity retreats, as well as women's issues training for men. She is the codirector of the Circle of Life Women's Center in Berkeley, California, which provides support services for women and their families in times of crisis, challenge, celebration, and creativity. She's the author of *A God Who Looks Like Me: Discovering a Woman-Affirming Spirituality. [45–46, 88, 158, 279]*

M **Reyhāna** (8th century) A devout Sufi who lived in Basra. *[335]*

C **Rich, Elaine Sommers** (contemporary) An American adviser to international students at Bluffton College in Ohio. She has been a contributor to the *Mennonite Weekly Review,* among other journals, and has written and edited many devotional books for women. As a teacher, she has lived and worked in many countries. *[72–73]*

C **Riley, Katie** (d. 1980s) Born in England, she was a Quaker of the Clifford Street Meeting at York and a teacher of the deaf. After her death her prayer, quoted in this book, was found inside her Bible. *[256–257]*

M **Roqiya** (13th century?) A gnostic, a Sufi, and a grand lover of God from Mosul, in what is now Iraq. She taught sincerity in devotion and the importance of abandoning the world so that our "hearts would take wing in the world of angels" where, she said, we would greatly profit. *[342]*

J **Rosefield, Virginia Moise** (b. 1909) American woman who is a direct descendant of Abraham Moise, one of the founders of the Reformed Society of Israelites, which was the precursor to Reform Judaism in America. She is active in Women of Reform Judaism, and with her husband was awarded the Order of the Palmetto from the state of South Carolina in recognition of their lifelong volunteer service. *[150, 234–235]*

C **Rossetti, Christina** (1830–1894) Born in London into an artistic family she had an Italian poet as a father and a brother who was the famous Pre-Raphaelite painter and poet, Dante Gabriel Rossetti. Raised as an Anglican, she was devout and a serious poet from an early age, and published more than one thousand poems, mostly devotional in nature, as well as six volumes of essays. She refused marriage twice due to the lack of shared religious views. She is considered to be one of the greatest English-language poets of her day. *[94, 111, 130, 137, 155, 157, 175, 190, 191, 202, 281, 315–316]*

J **Salaman, Nina Davis** (1877–1925) An English poet and translator of Hebrew literature, as well as a committed Zionist. Her many friends were members of the Jewish literary elite, and she published a poetry collection called *Voices of the River*. *[181]*

SH **Sanchez, Carol Lee** (contemporary) A teacher of American Indian and women's studies courses at California universities, she also has conducted workshops on tribal communities annually in Europe since 1983. She lives in Santa Barbara, where she runs a gallery of contemporary Indian art. *[120]*

B **Sangha** (6th century B.C.E.) A contemporary of the Buddha, she was a member of the *vaisya* caste and a keeper of cows. She had a son and was probably a farmer's wife. *[302]*

P **Sappho** (610–580 B.C.E.) Born on the Greek island of Lesbos, she was married and had a daughter. She is the earliest woman poet in the lineage of Western literature. Her poems were mostly love poems written to the feminine. Nine books of her poems exist, and a hundred fragments; most of her work was lost in the fire that destroyed the great library of Alexandria. *[59]*

M **Ṣarimiyah, Bardah-Ye** (10th century?) A devout Sufi woman from Basra who possessed a gnostic inclination. In response to the question about how she passed her day, she answered, "Upon this earth of lonely exile, we are mere guests, waiting in expectation for a response from our Host." *[308]*

U **Sarton, May** (1912–1995) Belgian-born American woman of letters, and the last surviving member of the Bloomsbury Group—she published a substantial body of novels and poetry in over fifty volumes. Her memoir of living alone in a Vermont village, *Plant Dreaming Deep*, brought her recognition, and this was followed by her *Journal of a Solitude*. Later in her life she wrote many self-scrutinies under titles including *At Seventy, After the Stroke, Endgame, Encore*, and then her last book, published posthumously, *At Eighty-Two*. *[308]*

U **Sayers, Peig** (1873–1958) Born in the parish of Dunquin in County Kerry, Ireland, she married and spent most of her life on a neighboring isle. She lost several children to death, and most of the surviving ones emigrated to the United States. She was known to have lived a hard life. *[169]*

M **Schimmel, Anne Marie** (b. 1922) Born in Germany, she obtained a doctorate in Islamic studies from Berlin University at the age of nineteen. She has taught at many universities around the world, and is professor of Indo-Muslim culture at Harvard. She has published many important works in English and German, and has won several awards. Among her books are *Pain and Grace, Mystical Dimensions of Islam*, and *The Triumphal Sun: A Study of the Works of Jalaloddin Rumi*. *[62]*

C **Schmitt, Mary Kathleen Speegle** (contemporary) A native of Texas, she was the first woman deacon ordained in the diocese of Quebec, and the first woman priest ordained in the diocese of Edmonton, Alberta. She is the rector of Christ the King Anglican Church in Burnaby, British Columbia. *[56–58, 159, 188–189, 195, 228–230, 263–264, 270]*

C **Seton, St. Elizabeth Ann** (1774–1821) A native of New York City, she was born into a wealthy family of colonists. At a young age she showed deep concern for the poor and sick, and was known for her charity and ministering to them. After the death of her husband, she converted to Catholicism and founded a school for girls in Baltimore. She later founded the Sisters of Charity. During this time, she laid the foundation of the American parochial school system, and she trained teachers and prepared textbooks, translated from French, and wrote many spiritual reflections. She spent the latter part of her life working with the poor and established several orphanages. In 1975 she was the first American-born saint to be canonized. *[75, 86, 125, 154, 171, 178–179, 199, 222, 241–242, 267, 277, 293, 317, 320, 321]*

M **Sha'wana** (10th century?) A Persian Sufi who lived in Oballah on the Tigris. Having a good voice, she used to preach and chant beautifully. She instructed her son and her followers in the ways of God. *[240, 341]*

M **Shiraz, Lady Sakina Begum** (early 19th century) The daughter of a family from Shiraz descended from a prophet, she was considered an outstanding gnostic scholar. [340]

U **Sinetar, Marsha** (contemporary) An educator, organizational psychologist, and mediator, she heads a human resource development firm in California. She authored *Ordinary People as Monks and Mystics*. [52]

C **Smith, Hannah Whitall** (1832–1911) An American evangelist who was a founder of the Woman's Christian Temperance Union, a supporter of women's suffrage, and a student of the emerging religious movement in the late nineteenth century. She wrote the evangelical devotional classic *The Christian's Secret to a Happy Life*, and collected more than two thousand items documenting the religious ferment of the time. [302]

C **Snowden, Rita** (1907–?) Born in New Zealand, she trained as a deaconess of the New Zealand Methodist Church. While bedridden she wrote her first book, *Through Open Windows*. After her convalescence, she spoke and presented in Methodist meetings around the world. She became a broadcaster and wrote more than forty books for adults and children, among them *A Woman's Book of Prayers*. [119, 133, 273]

C **Soulsby, Lucy H. M.** (1857–1927) An Englishwoman, she was headmistress of a high school for girls in Oxford, and contributed greatly to the advancement of secondary education for young women. [117]

P **Starhawk** (b. 1951) An American of Jewish background, whose birth name is Miriam Simos, she is a feminist and a wicca (a witch), who sees the earth and the rituals upon it as representative of the Goddess. She also writes and teaches and her books include *The Spiral Dance*, *Dreaming the Dark*, and *Truth or Dare*. [393–396]

C **Steele, Anne** (1717–1778) One of England's most distinguished writers of Baptist hymns. She had a series of tragedies, in her life, including the accidental drowning of her fiancé a few hours before their wedding. [184]

C **Stein, Edith, St. Teresa Benedicta of the Cross** (1891–1942) A German Jew who converted to Catholicism and became a Carmelite nun (Sr. Teresa Benedicta of the Cross) after spending years as a successful philosopher and feminist thinker and lecturer. She was martyred at Auschwitz. Her example, way of life, and writings gained her an international reputation for holiness after her death, and led to her beatification in 1987 and canonization in 1998. [46–48, 268, 302, 371, 390] c **Stewart, Maria W.** (1803–?) An American brought up in a clergyman's family, she received little education until she attended Sabbath schools in her twenties. After she was widowed she began preaching and writing about freedom for slaves and of God's protection for all African Americans. *[171, 286]*

J **Stone-Halpern, C. Ariel** (contemporary) A rabbi in the Reform Movement of Judaism, she was the first Reform rabbi to live and work in the former Soviet Union. Ordained in 1991 in Atlanta, she has published scholarly and pragmatic works on the subjects of Jewish classical texts, marriage, and Jewish law, and has written a feminist Haggadah (script for the Passover seder). She is currently associate rabbi of Congregation Beth Israel in Portland, Oregon. *[115]*

c **Stuart, Mary** (1542–1587) Proclaimed Mary, Queen of Scots when she was only six days old, she was raised in France as a Roman Catholic and married Francis II. Widowed early, she returned to Scotland to reign, but her unpopularity made her abdicate and seek refuge in England, where Queen Elizabeth I, to protect her own claim to the throne, imprisoned her and eventually had her beheaded. *[233, 318]*

T **Sun Bu-er** (1124–?) The most famous Taoist sage, whose name means "peerless," she took up Taoist practice in her early fifties, learned the secrets of talismen and mystics, and taught in the guise of making divination statements. She had a circle of initiate followers, and became well known for her set of fourteen verses on secret doctrine. *[332, 363, 371]*

c **St. Hilda Community** A British-based community whose women members construct liturgies around the celebration of God as Mother. Open to men and women, St. Hildas consciously work at drawing sources from the Hebrew bible and the medieval Christian mystical teachings, as well as from goddess and Celtic material. *[49–50, 83, 121, 259, 387]*

J **Temple Israel Sisterhood** is based in Minneapolis, Minnesota, and is an affiliate of Women of Reform Judaism, the Federation of Temple Sisterhoods. For many years it has joined together in worship and celebration at weekend retreats called *kol isha* (Hebrew for "the voices of women.") The prayer in this book was written jointly by members for Sabbath services at *kol isha*. *[95]*

c **Teresa of Ávila, St.** (1515–1582) Born Teresa de Cepeda y Ahumada in Ávila, Spain, to a noble family with Jewish roots, she entered a Carmelite convent and became a nun after the death of her mother. Shortly thereafter she became seriously ill and bedridden. During this time, she discovered a deep spiritual life within her and experienced many visions, and when she recovered she embraced a new spiritual discipline with vigor and intention. She reformed the Carmelite Reform (Discalced) order by returning to a rule of poverty and living cloistered in contemplative prayer. Her spiritual masterpieces include her autobiography, as well as *The Way of Perfection* and *The Interior Castle*, works that outlined her mystical teachings. A close friend and colleague of St. John of the Cross, she is known as the Mother of Carmelites. *[55, 76–77, 91, 121, 129, 135–136, 147, 158–159, 188, 191–194, 206, 225, 227, 253–254, 281, 286, 295–296, 304, 307, 311–314, 320, 334–336, 340, 346, 349, 350, 359–360, 374, 379, 381]*

C **Teresa, Mother** (1910–1997) Born in Skopje, Albania, she entered the Sisters of Loreto order in Ireland and later served in India. She was a schoolteacher for many years before receiving the call to leave the Sisters of Loreto and work among the "poorest of the poor" in the streets of Calcutta. For over forty years she built up her Missionaries of Charity order from a few sisters to a full international community of sisters, brothers, priests, lay workers, and volunteers. Devoted to serving the dying, the sick, and the orphaned all over the world, she received the Nobel Peace Prize in 1979. *[171, 185, 227, 233, 255–256, 269, 281–282, 383]*

U **Thayer, Mary Dixon** (early 20th century) American secular and religious writer who won several important awards, including the Browning Medal in 1925. *[131]*

C **Thérèse of Lisieux, St.** (1873–1897) Born Marie-Françoise-Thérèse Martin, she followed her sisters into religious life, entering the Carmelite convent in Lisieux at the age of fifteen. During her short life, she practiced what she called her "little way" of doing the ordinary things of daily life with extraordinary love, and being like a child in God's care. Her autobiography, *The Story of a Soul*, was published posthumously, and gained her a reputation as an extraordinary woman of wisdom. She is best known and honored as the Little Flower of Jesus. She was canonized in 1925. *[127–128, 133–134, 221–222, 318–319]*

U **Trevelyan, Katharine** (b. 1909) Englishwoman who published her "autobiography of a natural mystic," called *Fool in Love*, in 1962. *[344]*

U **Tsvetaeva, Marina** (1892–1941) Born in Moscow, she published her first book of poetry at sixteen years of age. She married and had two children; the younger child died of malnutrition during World War I. Her husband served as an officer in the counterrevolutionary White Russian army, and fled to Europe following the Bolshevik victory. After many years with no knowledge of his fate, she joined him and they settled in Paris. When they returned to Russia, her husband was executed during the Stalinist terror and she, poor and with little hope of income, hanged herself. *[117, 317]*

C **Underhill, Evelyn** (1875–1941) Born in England, she was educated at King's College for Women in London and spent much of her time as a lecturer and writer. She contributed so much to the understanding of mysticism—her best known book being called *Mysticism*—that she helped to make it a respected subject of modern theology. She also wrote novels and verse, but her finest works are those on the subjects of spiritual devotion and the growth of the interior life. *[136, 179, 232, 330, 341]*

SH **Uvavnuk** (19th century) As an Eskimo woman, she was transformed into a shaman. After her death it was reported that her village had a year of great abundance in whales, walruses, seals, and caribou. *[109]*

B **Vajira** (6th century B.C.E.) Nothing is known of her background or life, but the dialogue of hers that appears in this anthology was written in the *Therigatha*—the earliest canon of poems in feminine Buddhist literature—and is conducted with Mara, who is known as the "evil one," the Buddhist devil who represents death or the principle of destruction. *[240–241]*

C **Vardey, Lucinda** (contemporary) See About the Editor, page 449. *[88]*

B **Vimala** (6th century B.C.E.) Originally a prostitute, she tried to seduce a Buddhist monk whose rejection of her advances highlighted the baseness of her ways. Renouncing sensuality and sexual pleasure, she became a Buddhist lay disciple and then an ordained nun. *[305]*

C/CE **Waal, Esther de** (contemporary) An English Anglican writer, lecturer, retreat director, and pilgrimage guide, she has written numerous books on Celtic spirituality and on the Rule of St. Benedict. *[126]*

HU **Walker, Barbara G.** (contemporary) An American writer on women's sprituality and feminist themes, she designs knitting patterns and is an artist-designer. In 1993 she was declared Humanist Heroine of the Year by the American Humanist Association, and in 1995 she received the Women Making Herstory Award. *[263]*

C **Ward, Mary** (1585–1645) Born in England, she spent time in a Poor Clares convent in Flankers, and then began an apostolate of teaching young girls based on the Jesuit model. Although criticized by church authorities, she was relentless in her call for equality and said, "There is no such difference between men and women that women may not do great things." Called to Rome by Pope Urban VIII and charged with being a heretic and schismatic, she was finally allowed to return to England where the institute she had established was restored. She died in isolation in Yorkshire after the English Civil War. [296–297, 373]

C **Weddell, Suzanne (Sue) E.** (contemporary) A graduate of Bucknell University she began her career with the Foreign Missions Conference of North America. Her work embraced India, the Near East, Women's work, and Christian literature. She wrote many books and contributed to the devotional services of the World Day of Prayer. President of the Missionary Education Movement (Friendship Press), she chaired the committee on Christian literature for women and children in mission fields. [148]

C **Weil, Simone** (1909–1943) A French Jew, she later embraced informally the Christian way. A brilliant philosopher and teacher, she worked in the Renault car factory and in the vineyards of France in her effort to understand the plight of workers. She also spent time on the Catalonian front during the Spanish Civil War. While working with the French resistance in England during World War II, she prepared a long study of the reciprocal duties of the individual and the state (published later as *The Need for Roots*). As an essayist and a spiritual correspondent, she was interested in other religions, especially Catholicism, her learned faith. [157, 182, 254, 266–267, 304, 318, 360, 381]

C **Wesley, Susanna** (1669–1742) A member of the Church of England, she married a man who was sent to debtors' prison. She brought up her nineteen children alone, educating them at home and providing for them with limited means. Her letters and writings to her surviving children inspired her sons John and Charles Wesley to found Methodism. In fact, she is considered its founder, a model of women's Christian ministry. She also wrote three religious textbooks. She believed in meditation and solitary daily prayer, and practiced this for two hours a day even while bringing up her children. [65–66, 91–92, 147, 160, 183–184]

C **Wheatcroft, Anita** (contemporary) Born and educated in New York, she has always been interested in God and our relationship with the Divine through prayer. She has written many articles, stories, and devotional works for parents and children. [274–275]

U **Willetts, Phoebe** (contemporary) No biographical information found. [86]

C **Williamson, Marianne** (contemporary) An American spiritual and metaphysical lecturer, she is also involved in extensive charitable work, serving people with life-challenging illnesses. An internationally acclaimed author, she wrote the well-known *Return to Love, A Woman's Worth*, and *Illuminata*, a book of prayers. *[134, 252–253, 278, 298, 391–392]*

U **Wilson, Lois** (contemporary) No biographical information found. *[111]*

C **Winkley, Lala** (b. 1941) Born in Iran, she was reared by an Assyrian Christian woman, and was subsequently educated in the United Kingdom. She has taught in mixed inner city schools and to those with learning difficulties. She is a feminist, community activist, and teacher who specializes in movement as prayer. As a Catholic she lobbies and organizes protests around the exclusion of women from ordained ministry, as well as exposes the denial of human rights within the Roman Catholic Church. *[131–132]*

NS **Wood, Nancy** (b. 1936) American author of more than twenty-five books, she is best known for her award-winning books of poetry about the Taos Indians. She lives in Santa Fe, near the wilderness she writes about, and her beliefs are rooted in the natural world of her Native American subjects. *[128–129]*

C **Woodman, Marion** (contemporary) A Canadian author best known for her books on emerging feminine imagery and the psyche (*The Pregnant Virgin, Dancing in the Flames*). She began her career as a high school teacher of English and drama, and later pursued her love of metaphor as a Jungian analyst. She is a lecturer and gives many workshops internationally, and recently coauthored *The Maiden King* with Robert Bly. *[108, 239]*

B **Wu, Empress** (627–705) Wu Zetian held power in China for half a century, first as consort to her imperial husband, Kaozong of the Tang dynasty, and then after his death, when she ruled in her own right. She was known to have spent a brief time as a young woman in a Buddhist nunnery, and she remained a great patron of Buddhism. *[60]*

J **Wylen, Cheryl** (contemporary) An American, she is currently the librarian of the YMA-YWHA of North Jersey, and copresident of the regional Association of Jewish Librarians. Married to a rabbi, she is also affiliated with Women of Reform Judaism, the Federation of Temple Sisterhoods, and with Hadassah, Jewish Women International, and the American Red Cross. *[147]*

Feld, Merle: "Healing After a Miscarriage" by Merle Feld. Previously published in *Response: A Contemporary Jewish Review*, 14 (Spring 1985). Reprinted with permission of the publisher.

Friedman Rosenberg, Randee: From *Covenant of the Heart: Prayers, Poems and Meditations from the Women of Reform Judaism*. Copyright © 1993 National Federation of Temple Sisterhoods. Reprinted by permission of Women of Reform Judaism, The Federation of Temple Sisterhoods, 633 Third Avenue, New York, NY 10017.

Galloway, Kathy: From the book *Celebrating Women*, edited by Hannah Ward, Jennifer Wild, and Janet Morley. Copyright © by Kathy Galloway. Reprinted by permission of Morehouse Publishing, Harrisburg, PA, and SPCK (1995) Holy Trinity Church, Marylebone Road, London NW1 4DU, England.

Gellie, Christine: The prayer "A Mother's Prayer." Translated from the French by Mary-Theresa McCarthy. Reprinted by permission of the translator.

Gilmore, Linda: From *Covenant of the Heart: Prayers, Poems and Meditations from the Women of Reform Judaism*. Copyright © 1993 National Federation of Temple Sisterhoods. Reprinted by permission of Women of Reform Judaism, The Federation of Temple Sisterhoods, 633 Third Avenue, New York, NY 10017.

Gotami, Mahapajapati: From *The First Buddhist Women: Translations and Commentary on the* Therigatha by Susan Murcott. Copyright © 1991 by Susan Murcott. Reprinted with permission of Parallax Press, Berkeley, CA.

Grahn, Judy: Excerpt from "a funeral/plainsong from a younger woman to an older woman" from *The She Who Poems*, copyright © 1972 by Judy Grahn (first published by Diana Press).

Greiffenberg, Catharina Regina von: "On the Sweet Comfort Brought by Grace" by Catharina Regina von Greiffenberg from *Women in Praise of the Sacred* by Jane Hirshfield, editor. Copyright © 1994 by Jane Hirshfield. Reprinted by permission of HarperCollins Publishers, Inc., New York, and Michael Katz.

Gullick, Etta: Reprinted by permission of McCrimmon Publishing Co. Ltd., Southend-on-Sea, Essex, U.K.

Habiba 'Adawiyah: From the book, *Sufi Women*. Copyright © 1990 by Dr. Javad Nurbakhsh. Translated by Leonard Lewisohn. Reprinted by permission of Khaniqahi-Nimatullahi Publications, London.

Hackett, Jean: The prayer "My Neighbours." Copyright © Jean Hackett. Reprinted by kind permission of author.

ABOUT THE EDITOR

LUCINDA VARDEY is a Catholic whose spiritual interest is in bridging the teachings of the East and the West. Born in England, she divides her time between Toronto, Canada, where she lives with her husband, writer John Dalla Costa, and Tuscany, Italy, where she runs summer retreats. She is the author of *Belonging: A Book for the Questioning Catholic Today*; editor of *God in All Worlds: An Anthology of Contemporary Spiritual Writing*; and she compiled Mother Teresa's *A Simple Path*. In addition to writing, she teaches yoga, prayer, meditation, and sacred ritual.

mystics - visionesses
nuns - those Maybe wout
visions
contemplatives - recluses, impoverished
recluses - social workers

→ mystics - visions

impoverished life → Caring for the poor
St. Clare of Assisi 1194-1253
St. Catherine of Genoa 1447-15

writers
politicians

→ writing + politics

Hildegard of Bingen
1098-1179

St. Catherine of Siena

politicians   1347-1380
writers   - deliberately impoverished
             - mystic
             - inside/outside vow-taking
* Intro of options for 9 - social workers
* 9's ways of being faithful - recluses
* Two Italian Catherines

(1347-1380) - St. Catherine of Siena - mystic
33yrs.old   writer
                                       politician
(1447-)
/1510) - St. Catherine of Genoa - married
63yrs.old   healer to sick/poor   leader
                         minister   mediator
*What is their legacy/ies? rejector of status quo
   or so what?   philanthropist
                           "constructive mystic"